ABELARD IN FOUR DIMENSIONS

MEDIEVAL
INSTITUTE
UNIVERSITY OF NOTRE DAME

The Conway Lectures in Medieval Studies
2009

The Medieval Institute gratefully acknowledges the generosity of Robert M. Conway and his support for the lecture series and the publications resulting from it.

PREVIOUS TITLES IN THIS SERIES:

Paul Strohm
Politique: Languages of Statecraft between Chaucer and Shakespeare (2005)

Ulrich Horst, O.P.
The Dominicans and the Pope: Papal Teaching Authority in the Medieval and Early Modern Thomist Tradition (2006)

Rosamond McKitterick
Perceptions of the Past in the Early Middle Ages (2006)

Jonathan Riley-Smith
Templars and Hospitallers as Professed Religious in the Holy Land (2010)

A. C. Spearing
Medieval Autographies: The "I" of the Text (2012)

Barbara Newman
Medieval Crossover: Reading the Secular against the Sacred (2013)

ABELARD

IN

FOUR DIMENSIONS

A Twelfth-Century Philosopher
in His Context and Ours

JOHN MARENBON

University of Notre Dame Press
Notre Dame, Indiana

Manufactured in the United States of America

Library of Congress Cataloging-in-Publication Data

Marenbon, John.
Abelard in four dimensions : a twelfth-century philosopher in his context
and ours / John Marenbon.
    pages cm. — (The Conway lectures in medieval studies)
Includes bibliographical references and index.
ISBN 978-0-268-03530-3 (pbk. : alk. paper) — ISBN 0-268-03530-X
(pbk. : alk. paper)
1. Abelard, Peter, 1079–1142.   I. Title.
B765.A24M365   2013
189'.4—dc23

                                                    2013022742

To
SHEILA
and
MAXIMUS

CONTENTS

ACKNOWLEDGEMENTS

This book originated in the three Conway Lectures I gave at the Medieval Institute at the University of Notre Dame in 2009. My first debt of gratitude is to the Medieval Institute and its director, Remie Constable, not only for the invitation, but also for the wonderful nine days I spent there, fully provided with both a house and a bicycle, regally entertained, and intellectually feasted too, with the galaxy of outstanding medievalists and bright graduate students gathered together at Notre Dame. The then managing director of the Notre Dame University Press suggested that I take my time and make a proper book of my material, and I am grateful to her successor for the patience he has shown whilst I have been following, perhaps too literally, this advice. I have given versions of chapters of the following book as lectures or papers in many parts of the world, from Jinan University, Shanghai and Peking University, Beijing, to the Universities of Western Ontario and of Toronto and at L'Université du Québec à Montréal in Montreal, to (nearer home) Warwick, Leeds and the wonderfully titled 'Serious Metaphysics Seminar' here in Cambridge. Each occasion has enabled me to correct mistakes and re-think my positions, and so I am immensely grateful to all who arranged and took part in these occasions. Andrew Arlig produced a careful and intelligent response at a Toronto conference to what is now (much helped by his criticisms) chapter 5. I am particularly grateful to Chris Martin, who has read various parts of the book and talked to me in detail about many of the subjects I cover, and to him and Peter King for sharing with me their preliminary findings as editors of the *Glossae secundum vocales* and *Logica nostrorum petitioni sociorum*. And I am no less grateful to Caterina Tarlazzi, who read through the whole manuscript with scrupulous attention, both spotting minor errors and making valuable substantive criticisms and comments. My gratitude is also due to the two anonymous readers appointed by the publishers and to Stephen Little, acquisitions editor of University of Notre Dame Press, who has guided me through the unexpectedly complex procedure between the manuscript's submission and its being handed over to the production department, and to the production and editorial department there. I appreciate especially their having chosen so skilled, intelligent, attentive and tactful a copy editor as Elisabeth Magnus, for whose work I am enormously grateful. To Trinity College I owe an almost incalculable debt, for giving me ideal conditions in which to work. The dedication expresses a different, even less calculable, gratitude.

Cambridge, December 2012

INTRODUCTION

For historians of philosophy, time should have four dimensions. Three of them relate just to the philosophers who are being studied. The first dimension is their present. Whether, as here, the subject is someone who lived nine hundred years ago, or whether it is a more recent thinker, this present is not our present, and understanding it requires special historical knowledge and skills. The second dimension is their past. Philosophers look back to teachers, predecessors and the sources from which they have learned to think. The third dimension is their future: the ways in which their ideas and words have been understood or mis-understood, neglected, studied, adapted and distorted, up to the present day. The fourth dimension lies in the relation between the past thinkers and philosophy today, between their times and our present.

In the three Conway Lectures in 2009, on which this book—though much altered and greatly expanded—is based, I devoted a lec-ture to each of the three dimensions: Abelard's present, his past and his future. The fourth dimension did not form the subject of a particular lecture, because it ran through all the lectures. Its presence, I argued, is the methodological feature which distinguishes historians of medieval philosophy from other medievalists, making them both philosophers and historians. But is it as straightforward to combine the first, second and third dimensions with the fourth as the plan of my lectures sup-posed? The lectures themselves, in their detail, suggested not; they showed, rather, that at every point there are tensions between more historical and more philosophical concerns. This book therefore adds two new chapters, which look specifically at this fourth dimension in a manner appreciative and yet also critical. Chapter 5 examines the various comparisons which have been made between Abelard, on the one hand, and Frege and other more recent logicians and philosophers of language, such as Putnam and Kripke, on the other. Chapter 6 looks at Abelard's metaphysics in the light of contemporary trope theory and some other recent interpretations.

The earlier chapters begin by looking at Abelard's present and go on to consider his past and future. The first chapter looks at the difficulties, especially in the case of his logic, in reconstructing Abelard's views from the textual material that survives, and examines the extent to which the records that survive allow changes and developments to be traced in his thinking. The second chapter concentrates on a particular example of Abelard working in the context of his own present. It examines his argument that God can do only what he does, how his contemporaries reacted to it and how Abelard, perhaps in reaction to them, modified and extended it. The third chapter turns to Abelard's past by considering his relation to his most distinguished recent predecessor, Anselm of Canterbury. The fourth chapter, on Abelard's future, returns to his argument that God can do only what he does, showing how, from Peter the Lombard to the end of the Middle Ages and even up to Leibniz, this position was discussed, often dismissively, but sometimes with careful attention to its substance.

My approach, therefore, juxtaposes historical and philosophical considerations. It might be argued, however, that another type of consideration should also be taken into account. Many of the discussions examined, especially in chapters 2, 3 and 4, come in works about Christian doctrine, including the versions of what Abelard himself called 'theologia'. Should they not be treated as theology, rather than philosophy? But it is not clear what such a treatment would involve. By 'theologia'—a word considered at the time as a neologism—Abelard simply meant talking about God, and any discussion, however philosophical, of arguments about, for instance, God's will and its freedom cannot but acknowledge that their subject matter is God and that many of their conclusions would not at all apply to human will and freedom.

There does not, then, seem be room for complaint here. Perhaps, though, the demand for a theological perspective is a call for less scrutiny of the arguments and more attention to how biblical and patristic authorities are used. Such a shift of focus, however, would go against Abelard's own spirit and practice. He quoted the Bible and the church fathers frequently, but he was acutely aware that citations from both could be found apparently to support and to oppose almost any contentious view. He respected the inviolable authority of scripture—but only of scripture as subject to interpretation. And in his logical works he gave to Aristotle the same degree of respect, or perhaps more, since he usually strove to interpret Aristotle in accord with what seemed to be his real intentions. Moreover, although he had no wish to be the heretic some of his contemporaries thought him, Abelard was willing to follow a line of reasoning to its logical conclusion, even if that put him at odds with the whole tradition of Christian thought (nowhere is this better illustrated than in his argument about God's lack of freedom to do other than he does, examined in chapters 2 and 4). In the decades immediately after Abelard, writers on theology such as Gilbert of Poitiers followed the hints given by Boethius in his theological works and developed a conception of how, at a certain stage in thinking about God, the ordinary rules of human discourse break down, though they can be applied in a special, oblique way. Abelard made no such distinction, and his interpreters today are most able to grasp the train of his thinking by subjecting it, whether it is about logic or God and attributes, to the sort of rigorous philosophical analysis which he never hesitated to use on his own and other people's thinking in every domain.

Abelard in Four Dimensions can be read from various different perspectives and addresses itself to at least three different sorts of readers. Although it is not a general book on Abelard and his thought (I have written one already), it is written so as to be comprehensible to readers who are approaching him for the first time. Chapter 1 begins with a brief account of his life and writings which, along with the detailed list of editions of Abelard's works in the bibliography, provides an introductory framework. The body of the book discusses some of

Abelard's most striking and characteristic ideas, through a wide range of his thought: his sophisticated semantics (chapter 5), his theories about the metaphysical structure of concrete things and about identity and difference (chapter 6), the place of intention in his moral psychology (chapter 3) and his conception of God and divine omnipotence (chapters 2 and 4).

For specialists in Abelard and his times, there is both new material and fresh interpretation. The examination in chapter 1 of the manuscript sources for Abelard's logic brings together for the first time work which I and others have been doing on the character and genres of twelfth-century logic and takes a fresh look at what can be known about the chronology and authenticity of the logical works usually attributed to him. Although Abelard's basic position on God's inability to do other than he does is well known, the details of the argument and how Abelard developed them have not before been studied closely, nor have the reactions to it by his contemporaries (chapter 2)—and even less the reception of the argument in later centuries (chapter 4). A number of scholars have looked recently at what Abelard's debts to Anselm may have been, but the account offered in chapter 3 is different in many ways from theirs, in particular by providing a detailed comparison of how each writer considers the necessity of God's actions, especially his incarnation. Chapters 6 and 7 take issue with some of the most active recent interpreters of Abelard, including Norman Kretzmann, Klaus Jacobi, Alain de Libera, Chris Martin, Peter King—and myself. I have taken the opportunity to correct misinterpretations I made in my book *The Philosophy of Peter Abelard,* now fifteen years old, and in subsequent articles, though also to re-assert, with more careful supporting arguments, readings and positions I believe to be justified.

Finally, as a methodological investigation, this book should have some lessons to teach and, more important, problems to raise and approaches to suggest for all who try to study the philosophy of the past, especially that of periods which, like Abelard's twelfth century, are distant from our own day both chronologically and in their conditions of life. It is with this wider audience in mind that I can answer a criticism which might be made about what I have chosen to discuss in the following pages. Each of the four dimensions might have been filled with a different choice of topics; that, however, is perhaps not a fault but a sign that the four dimensions, more than just a way of organizing one book about Abelard, could serve far more widely as a tool for thinking and writing about the history of philosophy.

Part I

ABELARD'S PRESENT

INTRODUCTION TO PART I

To study a philosopher's present means doing many things. They include, for example, looking at the social and the intellectual assumptions of the time, the literary forms then current for philosophical writing; in the case of a twelfth-century thinker, such Abelard, they would also involve exploring the links between his work and both the school curriculum and religious developments of his time. The following two chapters, however, concentrate, not on Abelard's context, but on his present in a more immediate and intimate sense: on Abelard as a philosopher living through time and, like any human being, developing and changing his ideas.

Chapter 1 sets out to establish a solid basis for looking at Abelard chronologically. To do so, it must treat the evidence for chronology in the opposite way to that usually favoured by exponents of a developmental reading. Typically, they arrive at an idea of the main lines of a thinker's development, and they use it, often along with subtle evidence based on minute comparisons of different passages, to arrive at a comprehensive, precise chronology of writings, on the basis of which the account of the thinker's changing thought can be further refined. Here, rather, the aim has been to use all reasonable scepticism so as to arrive at an imprecise and incomplete ordering of works, uninfluenced by any prior view about Abelard's direction of development. The chapter also explores a related question: the relationship between the manuscript material that survives and the philosopher's own teaching and writing, which is often much less direct than today's ideas of authorship assume.

Chapter 2 illustrates the study of Abelard as a developing writer by looking at his argument that God cannot do otherwise than he does in his earlier and later formulations of it, and in relation to other twelfth-century thinkers' responses to it. Developmental study is sometimes seen as an alternative, or even an antithesis, to properly philosophical analysis. This chapter aims to show how the two methods can complement each other, presenting the argument from the beginning step by step, and ending with a critical examination of Abelard's reasoning, which leads to a perhaps unexpected conclusion about his general views on God's providence and human freedom. This first dimension, which looks at a philosopher's own time, should not, then, be seen as opposed to the fourth, which links the philosopher in question to today's philosophical concerns. Rather, it is, as it were, at right angles to it. The best work in the history of philosophy plots a graph using these two axes.

CHAPTER ONE

ABELARD'S DEVELOPING THOUGHT

A philosopher's own present is always a *period* of time—a philosophical career which may span many decades. Few thinkers, even the steadiest and most consistent ones, retain entirely the same ideas and interests throughout their lives, and many change their views radically. Is it, then, one of the tasks of historians of philosophy to trace how their chosen thinkers developed philosophically from their earliest to their latest works? Recent work on Abelard implies both positive and negative answers to this question. From 1980 onwards, Constant Mews has tried to establish a detailed chronology of Abelard's works and to show how Abelard's thinking changed over the years;[1] my own book *The Philosophy of Peter Abelard* (1997) relies at various points on positing a development in Abelard's views and takes a view about the general way in which his interests developed. By contrast, the leading specialists whose background is a purely philosophical one have had little to say about Abelardian chronology or the development of his ideas.[2] A student approaching this author through either of two gateways much used in the anglophone philosophical community—the *Cambridge*

Companion and the article in the *Stanford Encyclopedia* dedicated to him—would receive, for the most part, the impression of a single, unchanging body of thought.[3]

Although the 'development sceptics'—those who avoid any attempt to trace a chronological development in Abelard's thinking—do not usually put their case explicitly, two sorts of reasons seem to lie behind their attitude. It is no coincidence that their background is usually strongly philosophical. There is a general tendency for such scholars, especially the anglophone ones, to concentrate on the relevance of their chosen author's ideas to contemporary debates and to consider, at least implicitly, that looking at an author's development is a sidetrack, a task for the biographer or intellectual historian but not for them. To this doubt about the desirability of developmental study, they add one about whether it is even possible in Abelard's case. In order to trace a development, a firm chronology is needed, but for ancient and medieval authors there are often no clear indications of the date or even the order of the texts. Interpretations of Aristotle illustrate the problem clearly. Since Jaeger in the 1920s, scholars have produced hypotheses about the chronology of Aristotle's works and, very often, discussed his thought in terms of its development. Many still do, but others find the whole enterprise dubious. They point out that, for the most part, the ordering of the works is based on assumptions about which positions are the more mature, or on an overall view about the direction of his thinking (that, for example, he moved from an early dependence on Plato to a more empirical approach), which are not based on any solid evidence. Moreover, the very nature of the Aristotelian works that have survived, it can be argued, makes it impossible to put them into a chronological order: they are working drafts, subject to various authorial revisions perhaps over the course of many years.[4] It may well seem that an author like Abelard raises the same sort of problems. Indeed, the leading development sceptic among Abelard specialists, Peter King, claims that he does: 'The dates of composition and even the number of Abelard's writings remain largely obscure and a matter of controversy among scholars. One reason for this is that Abelard constantly revised and rewrote, so that several distinct versions of a given work might be in circulation; another reason is that several of his writings might represent "teaching notes" constantly evolving in courses and seminars. Hence it is not clear that "date of composition" is a well-defined notion when applied to the body of Abelard's work that we now possess.'[5]

My previous book on Abelard, as already mentioned, is developmentalist in its method. Given the development sceptics' arguments, is it not time to give up such an approach? The present chapter is an attempt to provide a reasoned answer to this question. Investigators of the truth must steer a course between the two extremes of complete credulity, which allows them to form an abundance of beliefs, many of which will, however, be false, and excessive doubt, which ensures the truth of their beliefs only by greatly limiting their number. How to steer this course depends on the particular area of investigation. The development sceptics, it will be urged, doubt too much and so must go without a number of important, well-grounded beliefs, but they are right to urge caution. A moderate, tentative developmentalism can be used for studying Abelard, but there are more areas of uncertainty than most scholars (myself included) have recognized.

The theoretical argument against developmentalism mentioned above—that it is an unphilosophical approach—applies to scholars who are so keen to see how writers change their ideas that they do not take sufficient care to understand any of them properly in the first place. It has no weight against those who see tracing a development as one aspect of one dimension—their author's present—among the four they are studying. And the practical problems of establishing a chronology for Abelard's works are less universally intractable than King, for instance, suggests. The main events of Abelard's life and some of their dates can be known with near certainty, and there is evidence which allows a number of his texts to be placed within this chronological framework. King argues that, because of his tendency to revise, Abelard's works may not in principle be datable. Here, however, it is important to distinguish between his non-logical and his logical writings. Among his non-logical writings, only two were substantially revised: the *Theologia* and *Sic et non*. But the *Theologia* exists in three clearly ordered versions, which in fact provide some excellent material that illustrates well his developing ideas.[6] The exact history of how *Sic et non* was expanded is less clear; it is not, however, a work by Abelard at all, but rather an ordered dossier of authoritative texts for him to use.[7] True, Abelard introduced revisions into almost all his other texts (and within the three recensions of the *Theologia*), but these are almost all small verbal changes or minor additions.[8] By contrast, twelfth-century logical texts, in general, present all the difficulties King mentions and more—in many cases they seem to be the products, not only of several substantive revisions, but of a number of writers. For this reason, Abelard's logical texts certainly need to be treated with great caution when it comes to both attribution and dating. Admittedly, there are reasons to think that, to an extent, Abelard's work is an exception to the rule about how the logic of his period has been preserved and that, especially given its links with his theological writings, a chronological ordering may be possible. There are also, unfortunately, a number of factors which, at least in the present state of research, make such an arrangement rough, incomplete and, in some respects, less than fully reliable.

The chapter begins therefore with a chronology of events in Abelard's life for which there is strong evidence. The chronology provides a framework for ordering and, in some cases, dating Abelard's non-logical works. The larger part of it, however, is about the logical works, which present much more difficult problems of both dating and authenticity. The manuscript material will be surveyed and considered against the norms for twelfth-century logical texts, before the chapter examines the relationship of the texts transmitted under Abelard's name to Abelard himself and, finally, what can be established about their chronology.

PETER ABELARD: A LIFE IN BRIEF

For all but the last ten years of his life, the major source for the events of Abelard's life is a letter he wrote early in the 1130s, the *His-*

toria calamitatum.[9] Supposedly addressed to an unnamed friend, whom Abelard sets out to console by showing that, however bad his misfortunes, his own have been worse, it seems clearly intended by Abelard, who was a well-known, indeed somewhat notorious figure, to present to his contemporaries the events of his life and his present attitude to them. Since Abelard wants to appear in the best light, at once a properly repentant sinner and a man much wronged, it is only to be expected that he will often distort the account of his own views and intentions and perhaps also omit facts he finds unimportant or awkward. Yet there would be no point in his telling lies about external events themselves, such as when and where he taught, since these facts would have been widely known. But what if the *Historia calamitatum* was not written by Abelard himself at all?

The *Historia* apparently sparked off one of the most famous epistolary exchanges of all time—the letters between Abelard and his former lover and wife, Heloise, now an abbess, who had seen a copy of it. Doubts about the authenticity of this correspondence go back more than two centuries. But, first, most specialists on Abelard today consider that these doubts have been adequately answered.[10] Second, it was only the more extreme proponents of inauthenticity who questioned the attribution of the *Historia.* The more moderate and less implausible position held the whole correspondence, including the *Historia,* to have been composed by Abelard, denying Heloise any role in the composition. In any case, even those who saw the *Historia* as a forgery accepted that it was based on authentic biographical material. There seems, then, no good reason to distrust the broad account of events—as opposed to their interpretation—given in the *Historia,* especially since many of the main incidents are confirmed by other testimony.

From boyhood until the dramatic events that can be dated to 1117, Abelard, the *Historia* tells us, led a life centred on logic (*dialectica*), first as an eager and brilliant student, then as a teacher, of it.[11] Abelard was born in around 1079 at Le Pallet in Brittany and was given an initial education by his father, Berengar, a knight (*HC* 18–19).[12] His ability made him shun a career as a knight and give up the inheritance he was due as the oldest son so as to pursue logic

(*HC* 19–28). Abelard says that he travelled in the area to wherever the subject flourished and engaged in disputations (*HC* 28–30). He does not mention that, as a beginner ('the least of his pupils'), he was taught at Loches and at Tours by Roscelin, a logician and a controversial theologian, with whom his relations later became very hostile.[13] Abelard then recounts a series of events, based on his rapid rise to celebrity as a logician and the enmity he inspired. He was drawn to Paris by the fame of William of Champeaux as a teacher of logic, and at first he was a favoured student but then aroused his hostility and that of his leading pupils because, Abelard says, he argued against him and sometimes proved his superior in disputation (*HC* 31–41). Abelard therefore decided to set up his own school, first at Melun (about forty miles from Paris) and then at Corbeil (twenty miles nearer) (*HC* 45–65). By his own account, Abelard was already by this time a famous teacher, whose reputation eclipsed that of William's other pupils and even William's own. Shortly after he set up the school in Corbeil (*non multo . . . interiecto tempore*), Abelard became ill through overwork and returned home to Brittany for a few years—where, he says, eager students of logic still came to him (*HC* 65–69).

When he returned to Paris, William of Champeaux had 'converted himself to the order of Canons Regular'—that is to say, he was following a semi-monastic life, based on the Rule of St Augustine— but was still teaching publicly in a convent in Paris. Abelard attended his lectures on rhetoric, where he attacked and forced William to abandon his theory of universals (*HC* 70–100). Abelard gained many students as a result of this success and William's successor at Notre Dame handed over his position to him. But William swiftly acted to remove Abelard, by making accusations against the master who had made way for him and replacing him with another. Abelard set up his school at Melun again, but 'not long afterwards' William, sensitive to accusations that his conversion was incomplete, moved for a time far away from Paris, and Abelard began to teach on the Montagne Sainte-Geneviève, at that time just outside the boundary of Paris (*HC* 101–32). William then returned to Paris and started teaching there again in the same monastery as before, robbing the master he had installed at Notre Dame of his remaining pupils (*HC* 132–54). After another trip back to Brittany, by which time William had already become bishop of Châlons, Abelard went to Laon to study Christian doctrine with Anselm, the famous teacher there. But he was not impressed by Anselm's lectures on the Bible and began to give his own, on the notoriously difficult book of Eze-kiel, until Anselm forbad them (*HC* 158–240). Abelard then re-turned, where finally 'for some years' (*annis aliquibus*) he was mas-ter at Notre Dame. It was during this time that he became the lover of Heloise, secretly married her and was castrated on the orders of her uncle and guardian, Fulbert, who thought Abelard was going to renege on his marriage by making Heloise become a nun.

According to most specialists, Abelard's arrival in Paris can be dated to around the turn of the century, his first schools at Melun and Corbeil to 1102–4 and his return to Paris and attack on William's theory of universals to 1108. His studies at Laon are placed in 1113 and the castration in 1117.[14] For these last two dates there is indeed solid evidence. William was consecrated as bishop of Châlons in 1113, and the context of the comment in the *Historia* suggests that it was shortly afterwards that Abelard went to Laon. And, with regard to the castration, it is known that those who carried it out were pun-ished by blinding and castration; it seems very likely that Fulbert too would have been punished, and his name is indeed absent from those of the canons of Notre Dame in a charter of 1117 (it would re-appear by 1119).[15] Links between Abelard's career and William of Champeaux's conversion promise to provide more chronological precision, but there is some uncertainty over these dates. William had definitely given up his position as archdeacon of Paris by the summer of 1112.[16] A very detailed examination of the various sources has led Charles de Miramon to suggest that William's process of conversion extended over a number of years, beginning in about 1109, and that it would have been in this year or thereabouts that Abelard's successful challenge to his position on universals took place.[17] Constant Mews sees the process of conversion as much more rapid and argues that Abelard's return to Paris to challenge William should be dated to after Easter 1111.[18] On this basis, Mews revises the usual datings for Abelard's early career, suggesting that he studied under William from about 1100 to 1104, before setting up his own schools at Melun and Corbeil, and then spending roughly the years 1108 to 1111 in Brittany.[19] This chronology has the advantage of allowing Abelard to have spent a few years as William's pupil, as his attitude to William in the *Dialectica* suggest he may well have done;[20] but Miramon's reconstruction of William's conversion is more convincing.[21] An alternative possibility would be to date Abelard's arrival in Paris a little earlier, around 1098, his teaching at Melun and Corbeil beginning four or five years later and going on to 1106 at the latest, with the return to Paris and the defeat of William over universals taking place in 1109 (Miramon's suggestion) or (better) 1110.

Following his castration, Abelard became a monk of Saint Denis (*HC* 628). Living in a house owned by the monastery, he continued to teach logic but also began to lecture on the Bible (*HC* 668–79). He then (*HC* 690–701) wrote a treatise (known now as the *Theologia Summi Boni*) in which he presented testimony to the Trinity not just from the Old Testament but also from pagan philosophers, before engaging in an analytical discussion of difference and sameness, designed to make sense of the doctrine that there are three persons of the Trinity which are one and the same God. Abelard's rivals—he names Alberic (of Rheims) and Lotulf (of Novara), pupils of Anselm of Laon and William of Champeaux—accused it of being heretical and persuaded the papal legate to have him summoned to defend it at a council held in Soissons in March 1121. There, after what Abelard depicts as the travesty of a fair trial, the treatise was condemned (*HC* 714–906). After a very brief period of quasi-imprisonment in the monastery of St Medard, Abelard returned to St Denis (*HC* 934–36), where he quickly became involved in a quarrel about the identity of the Dionysius who had founded the monastery (*HC* 941–61). He fled from the monastery and went to live in a monastic dependency at St Ayoul of Provins, where a friend was prior (*HC* 991–95). These events took place before the death of Abbot Adam of St Denis in 1122, who had refused to grant Abelard's request to lead a monastic life 'wherever he could find a suitable place' (*HC*

999–1016). His successor, Suger, also refused at first, but then, it seems not long afterwards, gave his permission, though requiring that Abelard should not put himself under obedience to any another abbot (*HC* 1020–37).

The remaining twenty years of Abelard's life, though no less dramatic and complex from a biographer's perspective, are much simpler to block out roughly, since they divide into four fairly clear periods. First, Abelard set up an oratory in Quincey in Champagne, dedicated originally to the Trinity and then to the Paraclete (*HC* 1037–42, 1116–24). Students came to him there and, mainly because he needed to earn some money, he returned to teaching (*HC* 1109–13). Then, second, he accepted the abbacy of the monastery of St Gildas de Rhuys, in a remote part of his native Brittany. After his unsuccessful attempts to reform the monastery led to attempts to murder him (*HC* 1497–1511), which drove him to live outside the monastery (*HC* 1525–26), he succeeded in having the most rebellious monks expelled, only to find that those who remained were no better and that his life was still in danger (*HC* 1534–59). The third stage of Abelard's later career was a return to teaching at Paris, on the Montagne Sainte-Geneviève. This period came to an end, if not before, then with Abelard's appearance and condemnation at the Council of Sens, after which Peter the Venerable persuaded him to live at his monastery of Cluny and, then, during his final months, in a dependency at Chalon-sur-Saône.

Some of the dates for these stages are fairly clear. The period at Quincey must have begun not long after Suger's abbacy (so in 1122 or 1123). By 15 March 1128, Abelard was certainly abbot of St Gildas, since he signs a charter using this title.[22] At the end of the *Historia calamitatum*, Abelard places himself still as abbot of St Gildas, living once again in the monastery and fearing for his life. A little earlier in the text (*HC* 1317–20) he mentions the papal confirmation of his gift of the Paraclete to Heloise and her followers, who had been expelled from Argenteuil. This papal privilege is dated to 28 November 1131,[23] and so the *Historia* cannot have been finished before then. It is therefore very probable either that Abelard was still at St Gildas at the end of 1131 or that he had only just abandoned it.

The Council of Sens took place in late May 1141,[24] and Abelard died on 21 April 1142, after a period in which his health had deteriorated. These datings leave the length of his second period as a master in Paris uncertain. It might have begun any time after or even in 1131, and it need not have ended until just before the Council of Sens, especially since it was not as if Abelard had been summoned there as a heretic: he went, rather, as he supposed, to defend himself against the false accusations of unorthodoxy made by Bernard and others.[25] A somewhat ambiguous piece of evidence is provided by John of Salisbury, who went to study in Paris in 1136 and made his way first to Abelard on the Montagne Sainte-Geneviève to study logic. John goes on to say that 'Abelard's departure seemed to him too speedy' (*praeproperus*)[26]—a comment which some scholars have taken to indicate that Abelard's period of teaching in Paris came to an end in 1136. But it may well have been just a temporary break or a transfer of his school to another location in Paris, perhaps where he concentrated on theology. Bernard of Clairvaux's letters indicate clearly that Abelard was teaching in the period directly before the Council.[27]

ABELARD'S NON-LOGICAL WORKS AND
THEIR CHRONOLOGY

With this framework of facts about Abelard's life as a basis, the next task is to see what can be established, with reasonable firmness, about the chronology of his works. Since any view about how Abelard developed is an unfounded assumption until the order of some of his works is established, this chronology needs to be based on evidence that involves no such judgement—principally, passages and features of individual works which link them to an event or period in his life. It is best to start with the non-logical works because here such an ordering, based on external evidence, is possible, although it is rough and not complete.

Abelard's condemnation at Soissons, though a disaster for him, is a godsend for his historians. It enables the completion of the work he was forced to burn there, the *Theologia Summi Boni,* to be dated to shortly before the Council—that is, to around 1120. Abelard produced two further, substantially revised recensions of the *Theologia* (he also made various minor revisions to each of the recensions).[28] The *Theologia Christiana* expands the three books of the previous version into five. It answers criticisms of his use of pagan authors to discuss the Trinity by an extended eulogy of ancient Greek and Roman culture, and especially the philosophers of antiquity. The presentation of biblical and pagan testimony to the Trinity is enlarged, the analytical discussion of the Trinity is greatly extended, and there is a short final book, which sets out to examine God's attributes of power, wisdom and love, but in fact breaks off before it has finished treating omnipotence. The *Theologia scholarium* returns to a three-book format, at once adding new material and developing arguments and shortening the text, by excising the detailed treatment of the ancient philosophers and concentrating the analytical discussion of the Trinity into book 2. No precise and certain date can be given for either recension, but there are good reasons to place the *Theologia Christiana* between 1122 and the late 1120s, and the *Theologia scholarium* between 1132 and the late 1130s. It must have taken Abelard some time—a year at the absolute minimum—from the Council of Soissons in 1121 to make all the changes and additions needed to turn the *Theologia Summi Boni* into the *Theologia Christiana*. But the fact that he is still attacking Roscelin, who was the special target of the earlier work, and definitely responding to criticisms of it, suggests that he cannot have delayed for many years.[29] Moreover, the book 2 discussion of the virtuous lives of the ancient philosophers, unique to this recension, emphasizes their ascetic, monastic and eremitical virtues, in a way which would fit perfectly were Abelard writing at the time when he and his followers were themselves leading such a life.[30] Again, it must have taken some time to make all the revisions which are found in the *Theologia scholarium,* and it would be most plausible to place it, as the historians have done, sometime during the period, in the 1130s, when Abelard returned to teaching in Paris. The opening from which this treatise has been named, in which Abelard says he is writing at the request of his students (*scholarium nostrum*), points to this setting, as does its connection with another work of Abelard's. A course of theology is preserved in three versions, known as the *Sententiae Florianenses,* the *Sententiae Parisienses* and the *Sententiae Abaelardi* (which used to be known as the *Sententiae Hermanni*). These all used to be considered works by Abelard's pupils, but they are now generally accepted as reports of Abelard's own lectures: the *Sententiae Parisienses* give the impression of largely uncorrected notes, which convey the vivacity of classroom discussion, whereas the *Sententiae Abaelardi* seem to be a careful presentation of the teaching, perhaps corrected and authorized by Abelard himself.[31] Only in his period in the 1130s as master in Paris is it likely that Abelard was doing such teaching, and the contents of these *Sententiae* are close to some of the material cited in the period immediately before the Council of Sens by Abelard's critics.[32] The *Theologia scholarium,* by contrast with the earlier recensions of the *Theologia,* announces at the very start the idiosyncratic division of sacred doctrine into faith, charity and the sacraments which is followed in the *Sententiae,* and it reads like a study in depth of the first part of the course in theology recorded in them.

Paris in the 1130s is also by far the most probable setting for Abelard's *Commentary on Romans,* in which he not only sets out in detail his striking explanation of how Christ's sacrifice redeemed mankind but also explores issues in moral psychology and ethics. Cross-references show that the commentary is certainly later than the *Theologia Christiana,* and they indicate strongly that it was written after he had begun to transform this recension into the three-book *Theologia scholarium.*[33] The commentary can be seen to have originated in teaching by Abelard, because of its close parallels with an anonymous commentary on all the Pauline epistles, which is full of explicit references to what Abelard (called the 'Philosophus') said. This commentator's report of Abelard's frequently asking the Jews about a point of biblical interpretation shows that this course took place in his Parisian teaching period, since only in Paris, of the places where Abelard taught after he left St Denis, was there a Jewish community.[34] *Scito teipsum* (or the *Ethics*) can be dated in relation to the *Theologia scholarium* and the *Commentary on Romans:* it refers explicitly to a matter as having been discussed in the third book of the *Theologia scholarium*,[35] and Abelard promises, in the *Commentary,* that he will consider certain questions in his *Ethics*.[36] From these references, it is clear that *Scito teipsum* was written after both the *Commentary* and the *Theologia scholarium,* and also that all three works come from much the same period.

Abelard's contacts with Heloise can be used to date a further set of material. As mentioned above, when Abelard's *Historia calamitatum* came into Heloise's hands, it began a famous exchange of letters between the couple. Since the *Historia* must have been written in about 1132, these letters, which include a history of female monasticism (*Ep.* 7) and Abelard's *Rule for the Paraclete* (*Ep.* 8), will date from the period immediately following. The correspondence makes it clear that Abelard had not been in intellectual contact with Heloise and her nuns in the period before it began, and so two other works which Abelard wrote at Heloise's request—a commentary on the *Hexaemeron* and a set of answers to theological questions posed by her (*Problemata Heloissae*)—can be confidently dated to the period after 1132.[37] Although there is no definite latest date for them, it is probable that they were written before the Council of Sens.[38] At the time of the Council, Abelard's immediate concern was with the accusations against him—his *Apologia contra Bernardum* and the two confessions of faith (one addressed to Heloise) can be dated to this period; afterwards, his health declined. Abelard also wrote sermons for the nuns of the Paraclete, and they must be dated to the period after 1132 and very probably before 1141. But by no means all of the homilies printed in the first edition and prefaced by Abelard's dedicatory letter to Heloise belong to this set; some are probably earlier, and some are not by Abelard.[39]

The *Collationes* (Comparisons), unusually for Abelard, uses a complex literary format to discuss philosophy and theology: in a dream vision, Abelard is asked to judge the discussions between a philosopher, who lives according to natural law, without any revealed scripture, and a Jew in the first dialogue, a Christian in the second. The work mentions by name the *Theologia Christiana* (this name is found in three of the work's five manuscripts and so

presumably is Abelard's own), which shows it must have been written after approximately 1123.[40] Abelard refers to it in the commentary
on the *Hexaemeron,* but the latest date for the composition of this
work is not established. The fact, however, that the reference is to
the *Theologia Christiana,* when the subject concerned is discussed in
greater detail in the *Theologia scholarium,* suggests strongly that the
Collationes were written before this final version of the *Theologia* was
being composed.[41] An attractive hypothesis, which cannot be proved,
is that Abelard wrote the *Collationes*—one of the very few of his
works that has no direct links with teaching—during the one period
when he had no pupils at all, when he was at St Gildas.

As well as these non-logical works which almost everyone now
attributes to Abelard, there is a set of letters preserved only through
a partial transcript in a fifteenth-century manuscript—the *Epistolae duorum amantium*—which a great Abelardian expert, Constant
Mews, has argued are from the pens of Abelard and Heloise, at the
time when they were lovers.[42] Most specialists (myself included)
have rejected Mews's arguments, but he has also received some
powerful support.[43] From the sceptical point of view adopted in this
discussion, however, these letters, which are attributed solely on
grounds of their alleged congruence in thought, circumstances and
language with those of Abelard and Heloise, should clearly be excluded, since there is at the moment very great doubt about their
authenticity.

ABELARD'S LOGIC: ITS RELATION TO ABELARD'S TEACHING AND ITS CHRONOLOGY

Some clear dates and a rough chronology of Abelard's non-logical
works can, therefore, be given. Dating or even ordering (or, indeed,
gauging the authenticity of) the logical works that have been attributed to Abelard is much harder. Here it is best to proceed step by
step, first setting out the textual material which has been used to
discover Abelard's logical thinking, then discussing, in each case,
what is the likely relationship between the texts and Abelard and

finally considering whether these works can be dated or ordered chronologically. But before that, a little background to the world of twelfth-century logic and logical manuscripts.

Logic and Logical Manuscripts in the Twelfth Century

For over a century since Abelard began teaching, logic had been based on the same curriculum of ancient and late ancient texts. Students studied Porphyry's *Isagoge* (Introduction), Aristotle's *Categories* and *On Interpretation* (all in Boethius's translations), and four textbooks written by Boethius himself: *On Categorical Syllogisms, On Hypothetical Syllogisms, On Division* and *On Topical Differentiae*.[44] These logical texts (or at least some of them) had been studied closely in earlier decades and centuries, but the sort of evidence for how they were studied changes dramatically from the period shortly before Abelard started work. In manuscripts from before about 1090, there survive only glosses on logical texts (and a few paraphrases). In manuscripts from the end of the eleventh century onwards, large numbers of commentaries on the texts of the logical curriculum are found: nearly a hundred altogether on the *Isagoge, Categories* and *On Interpretation* from before about 1200 and rather fewer on the Boethian textbooks.[45]

Boethius had written commentaries on the *Isagoge* (two), *Categories* (one) and *On Interpretation* (two). Early medieval glosses on these works consist mostly of extracts from Boethius. The late eleventh- and twelfth-century commentaries were in a sense even more indebted. Not only did many of them borrow large amounts of their material from Boethius, sometimes verbatim, sometimes changing and adapting it. but Boethius's commentaries also provided the model for one of the main elements found in the commentaries, the discursive exegesis. Discursive exegesis discusses the problems raised by each section of the text, and sometimes further problems related, even loosely, to the passage concerned. Boethius sometimes discussed the different answers to these problems proposed by various ancient interpreters, and medieval commentators often extended this discussion to include the debates between their own contemporaries. The medieval logicians added an element to their commentaries not found in Boethius: a literal exegesis, consisting in a word-by-word exposition of the text's argument, which sometimes provided an explicit account of the logical relation of each step to the preceding one. Often, literal exegesis seems to be addressed to beginning students, who need each sentence to be explained in a manner Boethius obviously considered unnecessary.[46] Most of the commentaries contain both literal and discursive exegesis ('composite' commentaries). Some ('literal') commentaries confine themselves mostly to literal exegesis, and a few ('problem commentaries') omit literal exegesis almost entirely or entirely.[47]

From this description, it will already be becoming clear that these commentaries are far from being literary works of the conventional sort, the original work of a particular author. Moreover, a number of them are layered compositions. As just indicated, the first, lowest layer often consists of passages, perhaps adapted, from Boethius's commentaries, between which a medieval logician has added some of his own thoughts about the problems and perhaps his account of and reactions to views of his time about them, as well as a literal exegesis of the text—a second layer. Then, in some cases at least, another master has added a further layer of passages giving, perhaps, more up-to-date views on debated issues. Comparison of versions in different manuscripts can establish the existence of at least these three levels in some cases, but there may well be more levels for which manuscript evidence has not survived.[48] A multi-level commentary is no one particular author's work, though in a sense the master has assumed as his own the existing material to which he makes additions, and his pupils would not be able to tell which points were his own and which he had inherited.[49] These works, then, were very unlike today's philosophy books and articles, which must be the work of a named author or group, and which are expected to identify their sources when they are not original. A better comparison is with school teaching. School teachers are not expected to be original, and no one condemns them for plagiarism if they repeat what they have learned from a monograph or a text-book, though they are likely to give it their own gloss.

This comparison is also appropriate because almost all the commentaries are closely associated with the business of teaching. Exactly what relation a given text bears to what happened in the classroom is rarely entirely clear. Some appear to be students' reports of a course (or more than one course) of lectures, with frequent references to what one or another famous master said (though these references might be second-hand). Others seem to be versions of lectures written up and polished quite probably by the master himself, perhaps on the basis of a reported version.[50] Transmission was, it seems, a mixture of oral and written.

Sometimes an individual master or a school is identified as holding a given view or reasoning in a certain way, though very often contemporaries are identified just as 'a certain person' or 'certain people'. But, so far as the commentaries as a whole are concerned, anonymity was the rule. The only exceptions are a couple of attributions to, it seems, long-dead authors, and—as will become apparent—Abelard himself.[51]

The work of twelfth-century logicians is also, less frequently, preserved in independent treatises, which, unlike the commentaries, do usually announce an author. From roughly the lifetime of Abelard, there are two shortish *Introductiones,* attributed to a master William, quite possibly William of Champeaux; a long and complete logical textbook, called *Dialectica,* by a master Garlandus; Adam of Balsham's idiosyncratic *Ars disserendi;* and Abelard's own, far longer *Dialectica.*[52] There are also some apparently independent treatises on universals (though they are closely related to *Isagoge* commentaries),[53] as well as notes or collections of notes on logic—a particularly rich source for them is MS Bib. mun. Orleans 266 (which also contains two notes attributed to Abelard (see (7) below).

The Textual Record

The following are or have been considered to be logical works by Abelard or to provide information about his logic:

1. *Literal Commentaries* (sometimes called *Literal Glosses* or *editiones* or the *Introductiones parvulorum*).[54] Commentaries on *On Interpretation* (missing very end), *De divisione, Isagoge* (end missing) and *Categories* (a fragment) found, in this order, in MS Paris BNF lat 13368. Ed.: Peter Abelard 1969. At the head of the *Isagoge* commentary is an ascription to 'Petri Abaelardi iunioris palatini summi peripatetici', and the commentaries on *On Interpretation* and *De divisione,* but not the *Categories* fragment, have similar ascriptions.[55] The first three commentaries are of the literal type, concentrating on explaining the text phrase by phrase, with not many longer discussions. The fragment on the *Categories* has more discursive passages.[56]

2. *Logica ingredientibus* (below, *LI*). Commentaries on *Isagoge, Categories, On Interpretation* and *De topicis differentiis* (this last is incomplete, containing just comments on book 1 and the very beginning of book 2 of the four-book work). The first three commentaries are all found in MS Milan Ambrosiana M63 sup., although the very final part of the commentary on *On Interpretation* here has been shown to be the work of a different author. The commentary on *On Interpretation* alone is found, with the authentic ending, in MS Berlin Staatsbibliothek 624. The commentary on *De topicis differentiis* is in a different manuscript, MS Paris BNF lat 7493, and a small part of it is also copied in MS Paris Arsenal 910 (fols. 120vb–121rb).[57] All three commentaries in the Milan manuscript have incipits and explicits attributing them to Peter Abelard, as does the Paris manuscript of the *De differentiis topicis* commentary. The texts in the Berlin manuscript and the fragment in MS Paris Arsenal 910 are anonymous. All four commentaries are of the composite type, combining literal, phrase-by-phrase exegesis with frequent and often lengthy discursive passages.

3. *Glossae secundum vocales* (below, *GSV*). Commentary on Part 1 only of *Isagoge* copied in Milan Ambrosiana M 63sup. after *LI*. There is no attribution to a particular author, but by '*vocales*' is meant those who hold that universals are (only) words (*voces*). This is a problem-type commentary: there is rather little de-

tailed exegesis, and the emphasis is on discussing problems raised by the text.

4. *Logica nostrorum petitioni sociorum* (below, *LNPS*). Commentary on *Isagoge* in MS Lunel Bib. mun. 6. The commentary is explicitly attributed to 'Petrus Baelardus'. Like *GSV*, it is of the problem type.

5. *Dialectica*. Treatise on logic in MS Paris BNF lat 14614. Although an independent treatise, this work is based on the standard seven texts of the logical curriculum, but the initial section on the matter of the *Isagoge* and the beginning of the discussion of the *Categories* is missing, as seems to be the very end of the work. Lacking its beginning and end, there are no attributions in an incipit or explicit, but Abelard refers explicitly to himself, both as 'Petrus', frequently, and on a couple of occasions as 'Abaelardus'.[58]

6. *De intellectibus*. A short treatise in MS Avranches Bib. mun. 232, which seems to be part of a longer work, on questions about semantics related to the logical curriculum. Its title attributes it to Peter Abelard.

7. *Secundum Magistrum Petrum sententie*. Two notes, copied without a break in MS Orleans Bib. mun. 266, on a paralogism and on the meanings of *totus*. The piece bears the name cited here in the manuscript.

8. Various *testimonia* to positions and arguments put forward by Abelard.[59] There are a number of logical commentaries and treatises, probably from the middle of the twelfth century, which attribute opinions or arguments to Abelard (who is usually called 'Master P.' or 'Master Peter'). Particularly valuable as sources of such information are commentaries in MSS Berlin Staatsbibliothek 624 (P25, C17, H17 and a commentary on *De syllogismis hypotheticis*), Padua Biblioteca Universitaria 2087 (C15), Paris BNF lat 15015 (H15), Paris Arsenal 910 (C16, H21, B14), and Vienna 2486 (P20), along with certain treatises and notes: the *Introductiones montane maiores* and the *Summa sophisticorum elenchorum* in Paris BNF lat 15141 and the *Introductiones montane minores*; the *Summa dialecticae artis* by William

of Lucca; a note on syllogisms in Vienna 2486, fol. 38r–v; the
Tractatus de dissimilitudine argumentorum; and a note in MS
Avranches Bib. mun. 232, following the text of *De intellectibus*
(see (6) above).[60]

The Textual Record in Relation to Abelard

Are all the works attributed to Abelard in the list above (that is, 1–7)
really his? This question can be taken in a more or a less radical way.
More radically, it asks whether the work in question might simply
be misattributed to Abelard, who was not in reality its author even
indirectly. Less radically, it asks whether the work, though largely
based on Abelard's teaching, might be just a report, perhaps including misunderstandings or passages based on some other source or
teacher and not always giving his precise wording.

There are grounds for believing that one item on the list has
been simply misattributed. The *Literal Commentaries* (1) were published (in part) and attributed to Abelard by Victor Cousin nearly two
hundred years ago, and their authenticity, apparently guaranteed by
the incipits, was never questioned until recently.[61] But Chris Martin
and Margaret Cameron have now, in separate articles, made a powerful case against the attribution to Abelard.[62] The manuscript attributions are in a different hand from that of the text scribe,[63] and the
fragment on the *Categories,* which lacks any attribution in the manuscript, does not have the striking parallels with *LI* alleged by Mario
Dal Pra, its editor.[64] But not only is the positive case for Abelard's authorship weak. There is also a whole series of topics on which the
Literal Commentaries either fail to give Abelard's characteristic views
or even take a position incompatible with them.[65] Almost all scholars have placed the *Literal Commentaries* at the beginning of Abelard's career, and so it might be argued that he had not yet arrived at
his distinctive views, but in at least some cases Martin shows that
the *Literal Commentaries* fail to side with Abelard over differences he
seems to have had with William of Champeaux early on in his career. The case is certainly not closed, but the doubt over the attribu-

tion certainly makes it unwise to use the *Literal Commentaries* in any account of Abelard's development.

The *Literal Commentaries* are the only item on list which should, arguably, be removed from it, though, as will be explained, in one other case, or perhaps even two, there is room to question, less radically, whether the texts we have represent exactly Abelard's own words. The short *Secundum Magistrum Petrum sententie* (7) are very probably Abelard's work—they are attributed to him in the manuscript and show a concern with different types of reference found, for instance, in the *On Interpretation* commentary in *LI*.[66] The other items divide into two groups, the *Dialectica* and *LI* (2 and 5), on the one hand, and *LNPS, GSV* and the *De intellectibus* (3, 4 and 6) on the other.

A comparison of the sections on the *Categories* and *On Interpretation* in the *Dialectica* and *LI* shows that Abelard is drawing on the same basic material in order to compile both works, although there are some important differences in the views he advances between the two works. For the most part, then, the discussions in the two works run in parallel, with the *Dialectica* usually containing more material on each point than *LI*. Given that Abelard's job for many years was to lecture on the logical curriculum, and that, as he himself explains, he normally did not just repeat what he had said before, it is reasonable to assume that, in each work, he was drawing from teaching material—perhaps his own notes, perhaps a transcript made by a student—and making a fuller (as in the *Dialectica*) or less full (as in *LI*) selection from it.[67] The various differences in doctrine between the two works can then be explained by changes Abelard made to his lecture courses from time to time (and also, possibly, by ideas Abelard had at the time he was writing up each of these works).

Peter King is, therefore, perhaps right to refer to '"teaching notes" constantly evolving in courses and seminars', but, although the process of composition may have thus been long drawn out, each of these two works seems to represent an attempt by Abelard himself to set out his views at the stage they had reached (though perhaps without the careful revision needed to remove all traces of his evolving thoughts).[68] Although its introduction and conclusion are missing, the *Dialectica* presents itself as a carefully structured treatise, written by Abelard himself for his brother, Dagobert, but also for 'the general utility of everyone'.[69] The prefaces preceding treatises 2 and 4, in which Abelard discusses the logical curriculum as a whole and the value of logic, and comments on his rivals' envy, reinforce this impression of a treatise at once personal and carefully contrived. *LI* is unlike most twelfth-century commentaries in two striking ways. First, as already observed, it is explicitly attributed to a (twelfth-century) author in one manuscript; second, one part of it, the commentary on *On Interpretation*, is copied in two manuscripts, which give substantially the same text, apart from the sort of variants normally encountered between two texts of the same work. There are no passages which appear to be written by a pupil recording in his own words what Abelard said. Everything is stated in the writer's own voice (a writer who, indeed, refers to himself as 'Peter').[70] Cross-references from the commentary on one text to discussions in the commentaries on the other texts led Geyer to conclude that the three he edited, on the *Isagoge*, *Categories* and *On Interpretation*, formed a single work, which would also (from the evidence of the cross-references) have contained a commentary on *De syllogismis hypotheticis*.[71] Dal Pra similarly used cross-references in and to the commentary on *De topicis differentiis* he had discovered to show that it belonged to *LI*.[72] Such cross-references do indeed suggest that, basing himself on his lectures, Abelard produced as a single work a commentary on these five, or perhaps all seven, works of the curriculum. To suppose so would be the most economical hypothesis, but it is not the only one possible, since cross-references might still work even if the texts which contain them were based on teaching materials from different times and which the author did not bring together as a unity. Still, the presence together, and in the right order for teaching, of the *Isagoge*, *Categories* and *On Interpretation* commentaries in the Milan manuscript gives a strong presumption in favour of regarding at least these as having been written up and published by Abelard at the same time.

LNPS, GSV and *De intellectibus* are all related both to one another and to *LI*. The closest interrelations are between *LNPS* and *GSV,* both of them commentaries to the *Isagoge* which share many passages either verbally or in sense. Since it was discovered by Ravaisson and finally edited by Geyer, *LNPS* has been considered straightforwardly a work of Abelard's, on the basis of both the manuscript attribution and the content.[73] The authenticity of *GSV* has been more suspect. Grabmann, who first noticed the work, thought it was by a pupil of Abelard's, and Geyer agreed, finding in it distinct signs of a compilation.[74] But its editor, Carmelo Ottaviano, thought not only that it was Abelard's but even that it might well be written in his hand—a very strange opinion indeed, in view of the confused and garbled state of much of the text even apart from Ottaviano's own misreadings and misconjectures.[75] Mews too has argued that Abelard is the author (though not the scribe). He believes that these glosses—that is, *GSV*—'seem to represent a revision made by Abelard' of *LI*, 'while they appear to have been themselves revised in' *LNPS*.[76]

The relationship between *LI, GSV* and *LNPS* is, however, rather more complicated than these scholars appreciated, as Peter King and Chris Martin, who have been working on a new edition of *LNPS* and *GSV,* have discovered. When it is ready, their work promises to solve these problems, at least so far as humanly possible.[77] Until then, the best that can be done is to set out the broad lines of the evidence and the rough conclusions that may be drawn from it:

i.   *LNPS* begins with a preface to the whole of logic, written in polished, elegant Latin, which suggests that what follows will be a carefully written-up collection of commentaries on the curriculum. *GSV* also has a general preface, parallel in some passages, but presented in far less polished form.

ii. At the beginning, both texts seem as though they will be composite commentaries, offering full explanation of the letter of the text as well as discursive discussion of the ideas—though the very long discussion of universals dwarfs the sections of literal commentary, which are fuller in *GSV* than *LNPS*. But, at the beginning of the first proper chapter of the *Isagoge*, *LNPS* declares that it will 'skip commentary on the letter of the text, which is sufficiently expounded in the *Glossulae*', and, in much of what follows, it concentrates on discussing the problems raised by the text, rather than phrase-by-phrase exposition. There is no such declaration at the same point in *GSV*, but rather a lemma.[78] Yet in fact, like *LNPS*, at this point it ceases to comment regularly on the letter of the text or to give lemmata.[79] Then, at almost the same point in commenting on the second chapter of the *Isagoge*, on species, both *GSV* and *LNPS* start to give lemmata once again and to provide a commentary on the text, rather than a treatise-like discussion of problems.[80] There are even some passages of close literal commentary, especially in *GSV*.

iii. The passages of close literal commentary in both *GSV* and *LNPS* are usually very close to those in *LI,* so that they seem to have been taken or adapted from it or a similar commentary. *GSV* has more of this material than *LNPS*.

iv. After the return to a lemma-based commentary noted in (ii), the two commentaries are nearer to *LI* than previously, but they contain some discursive sections not found there. In particular, there is a discussion in both *GSV* and *LNPS* of various sorts of difference, which is closely related to passages in the *Theologia Summi Boni* and the *Theologia Christiana*.[81] After the commentary of the text of the section on *differentia* has finished, *LNPS* has a discussion about whether *differentiae* are accidents which is related to, but very different in many ways (some of them surprising) from the corresponding passage in *LI*. *GSV* has nothing at this point but includes some remarks on the subject in a section at its very end.

v. Both *GSV* and *LNPS* tail away at the end, with chapters on *proprium*, accident and the common features of the predicables (in *LNPS*—there is nothing at all on this in *GSV*) much shorter than those in *LI*.

vi. Both *GSV* and *LNPS* refer to a commentary on the *Isagoge* which they call the '*glos(s)ule*'. At the beginning of the chapter on species, *GSV* says that the explanation of why species, rather than *differentia*, is treated immediately after genus, and why it needs to be discussed, is in the '*glosulis*';[82] in *LNPS*, it is said that the fourfold division (*quadrifaria spargitur*) of the usefulness of the *Isagoge* is 'sufficiently carefully explained in the *glossulae*';[83] and in *LNPS* there is the comment, already mentioned, at the beginning of the section on genus, that the writer will not from now on comment on the letter of the text 'which is sufficiently explained in *glossulae*.'[84] It is almost certain that these *glosule* are a commentary similar to *LI*, since the explanations about species to which *GSV* refers are indeed found at the beginning of the section there, and *LI* refers to the usefulness of the *Isagoge* by exactly the same phrase as *LNPS* and goes on to discuss it at length.[85]

vii. Both commentaries make references to 'our master' or 'the master':

a. In the discussion of universals, *GSV* reports that 'our master [*magister noster*] used to say [*dicebat . . . olim*]' that, when Boethius (in the second commentary on the *Isagoge*) put forward the argument (from Alexander of Aphrodisias) that genera and species do not exist, he was talking about things, but that when he solved the argument—that is to say, showed why it should be rejected—he 'shifted to talking about the meanings of words' (*transferre se ad vocabula*).[86] It adds that this suggestion 'is not very good' (*quod non multum valet*).This reference was taken by Grabmann and Geyer to be to Abelard himself, but by Mews to be a reference made by Abelard, as author of the commentary, to his own teacher, Roscelin.[87] The master who held this position seems to have held that genera and species are not things, since his reading of Boethius is an obvious attempt to interpret this authority as supporting such a view.[88] Abelard himself wanted to read Boethius's treatment of Alexander's argument as supporting his non-realism, but he did so in *LI* by considering that Boethius took species and genera to be (meaningful) words (*vocabula*) and that, when Boethius

argued that these words do not have a signification with regard to things, he intended the argument to be sound, but
when he developed the argument that they do not signify
with regard to thoughts (*intellectus*), he intended his reasoning to be recognized as sophistical.[89] *GSV* itself takes the
same line and says explicitly, before giving 'our master's for-
merly held opinion', that the words 'genus and species' are
meant by Boethius to refer to words (*voces*) alone both in
proposing the problem and in responding to it.[90] Various
possibilities are therefore open for the identity of *magister
noster* here: that he is Abelard's teacher and, therefore, given
the non-realism, which would not fit with William of Champeaux, Roscelin (but, when Abelard refers to Roscelin as his
teacher, he mentions explicitly the name 'Ros.'); that he is
Abelard, who once, before he composed *LI,* used to hold
this view; that he is Abelard *misunderstood* by a student, who
has confused the fact that he does—to judge from *LNPS*
and *GSV* itself—indeed interpret Porphyry's questions—
but not Boethius's argument derived from Alexander—as
being posed about things and answered about words; that
he is some other master altogether.[91] The third and fourth
alternatives are the least improbable.

b. At the beginning of the discussion of genus, *LNPS* says
that 'our master' allowed that 'possible' and 'necessary' are
universals.[92] A little later *LNPS* explains how a whole variety
of expressions which refer to things which might or do
not exist—including 'possible' and 'impossible'—are universal.[93] It seems likely that 'our master' here refers to the
teacher on whose lectures *LNPS* (or this part of it) is based—
probably Abelard.

c. In the discussion of universals, *LNPS* is explaining how
confusion has been caused by the habit of the ancient writers of shifting from talking about things to talking about
words and how, in particular, the word 'subsists', which
normally applies to things, is transferred to apply to speech
(*sermonem*) when it is attached to the words 'genus' and

'species', which are words for other words (*sermonibus*).[94] It then adds: 'Note however that the master holds the proposition "Genera and species subsist" to be false, because the sense of "Genera and species subsist" is: there are some subsistent things which are genera and species.'[95] A little later on, *LNPS* makes the same claim (here distinguished from the statement, which is accepted, that 'a genus is an existing thing', in the sense that it is a sound): 'We entirely deny that any subsistent thing is a genus, since no essence is universal, as has been shown above.'[96] The 'master' mentioned a little before seems, therefore, even more clearly in this case to be the teacher on whose lecture the text here is based—probably Abelard.

The upshot of these observations is that, most probably, neither *GSV* nor *LNPS* is an integral work by Abelard, or a single report of his teaching. The change in form in the chapter on species (cf. ii), as well as the contrast in *LNPS*, especially, between the sort of work which the opening leads the reader to expect and what it becomes after the initial long discussion of universals, suggest that both texts—or a text on which they are based—put together at least two sets of material. They were both clearly produced in (or relied on material from) Abelard's circle, as their use of *LI* or a similar commentary (cf. iii, iv, vi) and the parallels with the *Theologia Summi Boni* and *Theologia Christiana* show.[97] Constant Mews has shown that in places Abelard systematically changed the terminology of *voces* to that of *sermones* when he turned the *Theologia Summi Boni* into the *Theologia Christiana*.[98] The discussion of the different views on universals in *LNPS* (not in *GSV*), where the view of *LI* that they are *voces* is rejected in favour of identifying them with *sermones*, fits therefore with Abelard's changing views, whilst the metaphysical and semantic distinctions on which the theory rests are those developed by Abelard in his trinitarian theology.[99] The two mentions of 'the master' or 'our master' in *LNPS*, both quite early on, seem most probably to refer to Abelard, which would suggest that at least the first part of *LNPS* (up until the form of a lemmata commentary is resumed part of the way through the chapter on species), is a record of his teaching by pupils (or closely based on one), and maybe the beginning has been given a literary polish by Abelard himself. *GSV* is, from the start, a disordered and garbled text, not merely one that has been badly copied; it seems mostly to contain the same material as *LNPS*, but in a poorer state and with more material derived, directly or indirectly, from *LI*. Occasionally (as on the question of whether the phoenix is a species), the discussion is more extended in *GSV*,[100] but there are moments when it seems as if some of it might not go back to Abelard.[101] In short, it would be hazardous to attribute to Abelard any idea found only in *GSV*; it would be unduly sceptical to claim that the preface to *LNPS* and the ideas about universals (and probably what follows on genera)—nearly half the work—are not Abelard's, though they may not be entirely as set down by him; and it would be justifiedly sceptical to have concerns about the authenticity of the rest.

The *De intellectibus* is far less problematic. This piece— apparently from a larger treatise—is attributed to Abelard in its only manuscript, and it has many very close parallels with *LI* (both the commentary on the *Isagoge* and especially that on *On Interpretation*) and some with *LNPS*.[102] It does not seem, though, to be a compilation, since it gives a more thorough and nuanced treatment of the workings of the mind and its relation to language and reality than is found in any other known work of Abelard's.[103] The passages shared with it might, indeed, strengthen the case that *LNPS* is by Abelard, but they are all from the discussion of universals, which is the part of the commentary which seems in any case to be most clearly Abelardian, though perhaps as recorded by a student.

The *testimonia* to Abelard's logic still need to be investigated thoroughly.[104] They fall into two main classes: reports of his views in works apparently by his followers (for example, H15 and William of Lucca's treatise) and reports of his views elsewhere, especially in texts that seem to have been written by students of Alberic of Paris, who like to show how Alberic has argued successfully against them (for example, C15, C17, H17).

Dating Abelard's Logic

The basis for dating Abelard's logic has until now been provided by the relationship between *LNPS*, the *Theologia Summi Boni* and the *Theologia Christiana*, as first noted by Geyer.[105] In the discussion in *LNPS* of *differentia*, Abelard includes a treatment of sameness and difference of various types which goes far beyond anything in Porphyry. It is not found in *LI*, but it occurs, in a more elaborate form, in the *Theologia Summi Boni* and the *Theologia Christiana*. Moreover, in the *Theologia Summi Boni* Abelard says that if two things are the same in essence, then they can be predicated of each other, but in the *Theologia Christiana* he no longer makes this claim,[106] because it will be an important part of his explanation of the Trinity to say that, whilst the Persons of the Trinity (for instance, the Son and the Father) are the same in essence, they cannot be predicated of each other (it is not the case, for example, that the Son is the Father).[107] In *LNPS* this new position, like that of the *Theologia Christiana*, is proposed, whereas the *GSV* proposes the position of the *Theologia Summi Boni*.[108] *LNPS* must, therefore, date from after the *Theologia Summi Boni* and, Geyer believes, from much the same time as the *Theologia Christiana*—and so from circa 1125, he says; *LI* must date from before the *Theologia Summi Boni*, because there is nothing in it about the various ways of being the same or different.

If, as suggested above, *LNPS* may not be an integral work, then this neat argument is undermined. It could be that different parts of the commentary were taken from texts or teaching material dating from different times, or even that the discussion about *differentia* was based by a compiler directly on the *Theologia Christiana*. Still, it remains the case that changes Abelard made to the text of the *Theologia Summi Boni* when writing the *Theologia Christiana* show that between writing these two works he decided that universals should be described as *sermones*, not *voces*.[109] In the *LI* commentary on the *Isagoge*, universals are clearly considered to be *voces*, and so it should be dated to earlier than the *Theologia Christiana*—that is to say, probably earlier than about 1127. The section on universals in *LNPS*, where universals are described as *sermones*, should be dated to after 1120 at the earliest (and after the *LI Isagoge* commentary).

Moreover, it seems unlikely that Abelard had already developed the ideas about the various types of difference proposed in the *Theologia Summi Boni* when he wrote about *differentia* in the *LI Isagoge* commentary, since he does not mention them there. (*GSV* and *LNPS* show how obviously these ideas fit the commentary at this stage, whether or not Abelard himself decided to put them in there.) It is most likely, then, that the *LI Isagoge* commentary dates from 1120 or earlier.

If, as suggested above, *LI* is a work put together by Abelard, from his teaching as a whole, then the dating for the *Isagoge* commentary in it will be roughly that for the entire composition. If, as Constant Mews supposes, the commentaries were composed one by one, beginning with that on the *Isagoge,* then the final commentary of those which survive, that on *De topicis differentiis,* could be several years, or more, later. Another proposal, which questions the integrity of *LI*, has been made by the editors of the fine, new edition of the *LI On Interpretation* commentary. They have noted, most acutely, that, in *LI*, the discursive passages sometimes take the form of semi-independent discussions, very loosely related to the text, clearly demarcated from the rest of the commentary and sometimes with cross-references to one another.[110] They argue, more questionably, that some of these passages were inserted after the rest of the commentary—the sections of text exegesis and some of the other semi-independent discussions. The reasoning behind their argument is complicated, since it depends in part on a contestable interpretation of how Abelard uses the idea of a *dictum*—what is said by a proposition—in one particular discussion in the commentary on *On Interpretation*. It is based, however, on two main contentions. First, they observe that a commentary on *On Interpretation* by a pupil of Abelard's (H15), which follows *LI* closely in many places, sometimes copying it, sometimes criticizing its views, shows no knowledge of the idea of *dicta*. This ignorance would be explained if the author of H15 had been using a version of *LI* from before the insertion of the relevant passage. Second, they contend that the upshot of one of the discussions about *dicta* is that understandings (*intellectus*) should not be described as 'true' or 'false'. Yet in the textual commentary after this point Abelard continues to speak of understanding as 'true' or 'false'. This contrariety, they say, would be explained if the passage about *dicta* had been added (perhaps along with other discursive passages) to an otherwise completed commentary.[111] The first argument, however, even if it is otherwise accepted, gives grounds merely for thinking that Abelard's teaching developed. The pupil may have attended and taken literal notes from lectures earlier than those which provided the material written up in *LI*. The second argument would provide grounds for the theory of insertion, but it is based on an incorrect premise: Abelard's theory of the *dictum,* as expounded in the passage under discussion, does not make it wrong to speak about true and false thoughts.[112]

The *Dialectica* is, from all the indications, a work from the first part of Abelard's career, quite probably written before Abelard became a monk in 1117, and very probably before *LI* was put together, although it draws on an earlier form of the same teaching material.[113] Among the reasons to place its composition early and probably before 1117 are:

i.   Abelard uses as logical examples 'May my girl-friend kiss me' and 'Peter loves his girl'.[114] Of course, such phrases are not supposed to reflect the author's life or mind: they are not stock examples either, but are clearly designed to catch the audience's attention and amuse them. But would Abelard, having become a monk, as was widely known, after his secret marriage to his former mistress had been violently ended by his castration, be likely to include such comments or leave them in his text when he was writing up teaching material?[115]

ii. Abelard's teacher, William of Champeaux—referred to either by initial or (so it seems) just by the description 'my master'—is a looming presence in the *Dialectica*, very often as the proponent of positions opposed there, but sometimes for having views which Abelard is remembered as defending on his behalf. By contrast, in *LI* and even more in the *Theologia*, William hardly appears. It seems most likely, therefore, that Abelard composed the *Dialectica* not very long after the period when William was his master and at a stage when he had become his principal logical opponent.

iii. There is a passage in the *Dialectica* where Abelard defends the practice of logic against those who say that a Christian should not treat what is not concerned with the faith.[116] Although this has been, and still is, thought to be a reason for dating the *Dialectica* after Abelard's entry into St Denis, the opposite inference should be made. Were Abelard already a monk, his critics would have, and he would have had to answer, a much more difficult criticism: that *monks* should not concern themselves except with what concerns the faith.[117]

iv. For much of the discussion in the *Dialectica*, reference outside the small corpus of logical texts and commentaries, and Priscian's grammar, would be unnecessary, and so nothing can be concluded from the absence of wider allusions. But when Abelard treats divine prescience and human free will, he is touching on a theological subject. Here there is a striking difference between the treatment in the *Dialectica*, which does not look beyond Aristotle's text and Boethius's commentaries, and the discussion in *LI*, which cites Boethius's *Consolation*, Gregory the Great and Augustine.[118] Furthermore, the difference between the treatment of Plato's world soul in the *Dialectica* and in the *Theologia Summi Boni* is best explained by Abelard's general ignorance of Plato when he was writing the logical textbook.[119] Both these observations suggest that the *Dialectica* was composed before Abelard had access to the extensive library at St Denis, which he used very strikingly in writing the *Theologia Summi Boni*.

Among the reasons to place the *Dialectica* before *LI* are:

v.   Abelard knows at least parts of the *De sophisticis elenchis* in *LI* but not in the *Dialectica*.[120]

vi. A view about time, according to which each thing is measured by its own temporal accidents, which Abelard puts forward as his own in the *Dialectica,* is described in *LI* as the common opinion and rejected in favour of a new theory.[121]

vii. Although it is always hazardous to rely on a judgement that one treatment is more developed or mature than another, almost every comparison between the *Dialectica* and *LI* suggests that, although there is usually a fuller treatment of a given topic in the treatise, where the thinking in *LI* differs, it is in ways which it would be hard to explain except as a development or change *from* what is said in the *Dialectica:* consider, for instance, his discussions of the semantics of propositions, of topical reasoning and of the meaning of the verb 'to be'.[122]

From drawing together these points, a fairly well-evidenced chronology of Abelard's logical works can be established. The *Dialectica* is based on the logical teaching that made Abelard a celebrity in the first decade of the twelfth century, and it was very probably written up before 1117—indeed, before 1115, when Abelard's affair with Heloise, as he himself admits, distracted him from his work. *LI* is based on the same teaching, but in a more developed form. The *Isagoge* commentary in it might have been composed at any time between circa 1110 and 1120, but after the *Dialectica* and very possibly after 1117. The other surviving commentaries which apparently go together with it, on the *Categories, On Interpretation* and *De topicis differentiis,* might date from much the same time, or they may have been composed over a number of years. *LNPS* may well not be an unadulterated work by Abelard, but it clearly contains new Abelardian material, especially in the treatment of universals at its start. This new material dates from after the *Theologia Summi Boni*—that is to say after 1120—and most plausibly belong to the mid-1120s. *De intellectibus,* very probably part of a longer work by Abelard himself, seems to date from about this period.

SOME CONCLUSIONS

There are some philosophers, even from the Middle Ages, whose works can be dated very precisely and so whose changing intellectual life can be followed in detail. A biographical approach of this sort can greatly add to our philosophical understanding of their work, so long as it is combined with other perspectives, connecting their thought to its past, its future and our own times. But Abelard is not one of these writers. Too much is uncertain about the chronology of his writings for us to trace the detail of his developing ideas. Nonetheless, enough of his works are dated with a high degree of certainty, either absolutely or in relation to each other, to enable some consideration of how his thinking changed.

Two of the chapters which follow take advantage of this possibility. The next chapter will consider Abelard's argument that God cannot do other than he does, and how, having first put the argument forward in the *Theologia Christiana,* he refined it in the *Theologia scholarium,* which is certainly a later work, even if it is unsure by exactly how many years. In chapter 6, it will become clear that different works by Abelard express a difference in metaphysical views which is best accounted for by a change in his thinking, since the divergence is between the *Dialectica* and the *Isagoge* commentary of the *Logica Ingredientibus,* on the one hand, and the *Theologia Christiana* in especial on the other. Both of these uses of chronology therefore fit and illustrate the moderate, tentative developmentalism advocated in the preceding pages.

CHAPTER TWO

AN UNPOPULAR ARGUMENT (I)
Abelard and His Contemporaries

There are few problems Abelard considered so important or difficult as whether God can do otherwise than he does.[1] In his first exposition of it, in the *Theologia Christiana,* he even pauses, after having given the case for both sides, remarking (5.41) that he cannot easily see a way out of the net of arguments, and then adding a beautiful prayer to God for his aid. The answer Abelard went on to give, and develop and repeat in later works, is the negative one. God *cannot* do otherwise than he does. He recognized that this argument was unexpected and unpopular—in his late discussion of it in the *Theologia scholarium,* he says that not only does it *seem* 'to go against the sayings of holy writers and a little against reason' but it is an opinion that 'has few or no supporters' (3.46)—but he stuck to it, not surprisingly, because the position follows from his underlying view that there are absolute principles of goodness and justice, which an omnipotent and totally good God cannot but follow.

Studying this argument ('No Alternatives for God' or NAG for short) gives an insight into Abelard's present in many ways. First, it provides a clear case where the evolution of his thought can be traced, since the relative chronology of the two main expositions is secure. Second, it is an area where, even in his lifetime, some of Abelard's contemporaries can be seen reacting to his reasoning and, perhaps, making him alter or add to his discussion. Third, these presentations by others of Abelard's argument suggest strongly that the surviving texts we have do not contain all the ideas of his which his contemporaries knew directly or by report.[2] The unpopularity of NAG would also lead to its being one of the few distinctively Abelardian positions to be discussed by generations of scholastic theologians. The argument's fortune will be discussed in detail in chapter 4, on Abelard's future.

NAG is one of Abelard's most fascinating pieces of reasoning and, as will emerge, much less open to charges of confusion or inadequacy than it might at first appear. Those readers who want simply to learn about the argument, without looking at its development within Abelard's present and the reactions to it in Abelard's future, should read the last three paragraphs of this introductory section and then the section in this chapter on the *Theologia scholarium* and its final section, 'Assessing Abelard's Argument'.

NAG is, moreover—in so far as anything in philosophy is ever new—Abelard's invention.[3] Of course, other thinkers had explored the question of God's power and its relation to his will and his goodness or had made statements which implied a position on the subject. But no one had seen, in the way Abelard presents so clearly from the *Theologia Christiana* onwards, that there is a problem about whether God can do other than he does, because his perfect goodness arguably constrains his ability to act. When he first compiled *Sic et non*, probably early in the 1120s, Abelard must already have been thinking about issues in this area, because in question 35 he assembles many of the texts to which he returns in his discussions in the *Theologia Christiana* and *Theologia scholarium*. The question under which he puts them, however, is 'Whether when God does not will something, he cannot do it' (*ubi deest velle Dei desit et posse*)— a formulation Abelard may have taken from a Life of St Jerome which he quotes as his first passage.[4] Only in writing the *Theologia*

Christiana does Abelard seem to have seen the wider frame of argument into which this more particular question fits.

The quotations Abelard gives in the course of discussing NAG, and in *Sic et non* 35, indicate the sources in the context of which he devised this new problem, though none of them is straightforwardly a source for his argumentation. Plato's *Timaeus,* which he had begun to study seriously when he went to St Denis, provided one important basis for the problem, with its statement that, because God is the best, he is free from all envy and so wished to make all things similar to himself 'in so far as the nature of each is capable of happiness'.[5] Plato's *Timaeus* also provides the basis for the very strong principle of sufficient reason Abelard will invoke, stating that 'everything that comes to be comes to be from some necessary cause. For there is nothing which a lawful cause and reason [*legitima causa et ratio*] does not precede.'[6]

Abelard links these quotations from Plato with two from Augustine. In one, Augustine is explaining that the Son must be equal to the Father. God could not generate anything better than himself, and to have generated something lesser would imply a failure of power or an ill will: 'If he wished to do so, and could not, he is weak. If he could, but he did not wish to do so, he is envious.'[7] In another, which immediately follows Plato's comment about everything having a legitimate cause, Augustine rules out anything happening by chance, rather than being part of divine providence.[8] (In the *Collationes* Abelard shows just how closely he links these two statements, when he says that 'something lacks a reasonable cause for why it is done when it is necessary that something planned [*dispositum*] by God would be impeded, were it to happen'.[9]) Yet it would be wrong to think of Abelard as following an Augustinian line in his approach to NAG, or even in identifying NAG as a problem. Augustine thought that God is able to do things he does not will to do—as Abelard knew well, since in *Sic et non* 35 he cites various passages from him which clearly present this view.[10] When, therefore, in the *Theologia scholarium* he states—using the exact phraseology of his question in *Sic et non*—that God cannot do what he does not will, he is consciously going against Augustine.[11]

Finally, Abelard draws on his favourite Latin church father, Jerome, in support of his view of a God who is rigidly bound to act according to reason. He turns to him in order to dismiss a voluntarist objection to NAG (see below, pp. 62–63), and he takes Jerome's celebrated denial that God could restore a woman who had lost her virginity—the cause of a controversy in the eleventh century—as evidence that God, who is the highest reason, *cannot* will *or act* against reason, glossing it with the extract from the Life of Jerome, quoted in *Sic et non,* which reaches the anti-Augustinian conclusion that God cannot do what he does not will.[12]

Before beginning to study NAG, it is important to make clear what it argues for and, especially, what it *does not* argue for. There are two different meanings of 'A cannot do other than he does'. It can be taken as an assertion of straightforward necessity: whatever *A* does, he does, not as a matter of contingent fact, but as a matter of necessity. But there is a different way to understand 'A cannot do other than he does' (and even, allowing that he is speaking loosely, 'A does whatever he does necessarily'). It can be taken as a statement about A's lack of alternative possibilities for action. When *A* chooses action 1 rather than action 2 (or action 3, 4 . . .), then it is necessary that he make that choice, but it is not necessary that the choice between these actions ever faces him.

Under the "no alternative possibilities" interpretation, then, the choice which is 'necessarily' made—the chooser cannot choose otherwise, given that this is the range of alternatives—does not happen as a matter of necessity, because the range of alternatives might have been different. Assume that my computer is mechanically infallible: when I press a certain combination of keys, there is only one word or picture that can appear on the screen; there are no alternatives so far as the computer's action is concerned. But, of course, so long as I am assumed to be free, there are many possibilities about which keys I press and thus which words or pictures actually appear on the screen.

NAG—as the name is supposed to emphasize—is an argument for God's lack of alternative possibilities when he chooses, not for the straightforward necessity of his actions. Abelard's conception of

God, as acting always in the best way according to an independent standard of goodness, forces him, he believes, to deny that God can choose between alternative courses of action but not to deny that it is open what these alternatives might be. Although Abelard does not himself spell out this distinction (and quite often talks of his argument showing that God acts 'necessarily'), his arguments are ones to establish no alternative possibilities, not straightforward necessity. According to some views about the relation between God and his creation, NAG does, indeed, arguably imply straightforward necessity, because everything whatsoever that happens in the world—from the movements of the stars to the innermost thoughts and intentions of each individual human—is chosen by divine providence. There is, on these views, nothing outside God which can choose between genuinely alternative possibilities, and since, by NAG, God cannot do so either, it follows that there is only one way in which things can be. Whether Abelard, as is often thought, held such views will be discussed in the final section of this chapter.

THE *THEOLOGIA CHRISTIANA*

This is how, in the *Theologia Christiana,* Abelard sets out the central thread of NAG (the numbers in square brackets are for ease of reference in the discussion that follows; where a number is repeated followed by *a* or *b*, the section following it is a variant of the one bearing the plain number):

[1] For if we propose that <God> could do more or fewer things, or could cease from those which he is doing, we shall indeed greatly derogate from his highest goodness. [2] It is indeed clear that he can do nothing except good things. If he were not to do good things when he could, and were to withdraw himself from doing some things which ought to be done, who would not blame him for being envious or wicked, [3] especially since no effort in doing anything weighs him down—[4] he to whose will everything is equally subject, according to what is written <in

the Psalms>: 'He said, and they were done; he ordered, and they were created.' [2a] Moreover, who would deny that everyone wills to act as well as he or she can and that everyone ought to act as well as he or she can? If we make this judgement with regard to ourselves, how much more should we make it with regard to the being which is supremely good, [3a] and whom the effort of no activity can weigh down? [4a] How does God will and be able, if he does not complete the act? [5] Or how is he just, if he does not do what he ought to do and also can do? [6] But even if he were to do less well than he could, he would not be perfectly good. [7] Therefore God does all that he can, and as well as he can. [8] Nor, however, can he cease from the things he is doing, so that he then would not do them when they ought to be done. Were he to cease from good things which he could do, when they ought to be done, from this he would certainly be shown not to be perfectly good.

[9] Besides, he cannot lack whatever are naturally within him. [10] If, therefore, it is necessary that he is the most good and benign, and he cannot diminish in his goodness, good will is present in him naturally and substantially and not, as in us, as an accident. [11] And so he cannot give up the good will he has, which it is also fitting to grant is God. Therefore he cannot lack whatever good will he has. [12] Therefore it is necessary that he wills all that he wills. [4b] But his will cannot be without its effect. Therefore it is necessary that whatever he wills he brings into effect, when we take his will in the sense of that which pertains to his disposing of things. [13] Therefore for these reasons it seems that it should be affirmed that God could in no way do more than he does, [14] or do better, or [15] cease from these things, but that [16] he necessarily does all things as he does them.[13]

Before considering what Abelard's arguments are, two preliminary points are necessary, and a third is appropriate. The first is about Abelard's views on God's relationship to time. He does not appear to think of God as timelessly eternal. In the *Sententie*, it is stated

that 'whatever was or is or will be is altogether present to him',[14] but
this Boethian idea does not imply that God really exists in an eternity simultaneous with our past, present and future.[15] Indeed, the
same passage suggests, rather, that God exists unchanging through
all time so that he will be what he was and is until the end of time.[16]
A little earlier it is explained that God does not come to know anything new: 'He knew from eternity that I would read today, and he
will know for eternity that I read today.'[17] Similarly, in the *Logica ingredientibus* Abelard writes that, although we say that God knows I
am sitting now and, when I stand up, that I am standing now, there
is really no variation in him, but we are speaking of him in a human
way, as if he were variable as we are.[18] In fact, in most of his discussions about God's power as well as his knowledge, Abelard is willing
to speak in this human way, as if God acted in time, willing now this
and now that. But such expressions are always just a way of putting
the real position, which is that God has held his providential plan
unchangingly for ever, and will continue to do so, although it un-
folds moment by moment in time for us.

The second preliminary concerns translation. The Latin verb *facere* means both 'to do' and 'to make', and so the question Abelard
poses—*utrum plura facere possit Deus uel meliora quam faciat*—might
be translated either 'Whether God could do more or better things
than he does' or 'Whether God could make more or better things
than he makes.' For most of the discussion here (and entirely in the
Theologia scholarium), Abelard seems to be talking about what God
does. But when he thinks about whether God can *facere* better—as
opposed to more or other—things than he does, he shifts to considering whether God can *make* things better.

There seem to be two main arguments, expressed in the rather
rhetorical paragraphs just cited (numbers in bold in square brackets
refer back to the numbers of sections inserted into the quotation).
The first begins from the premise implied by [1] and frequently in
the course of the argument, that

1. God is supremely good.
Abelard then argues [2] that

2. If God fails to do good things he can do, he is not supremely good (indeed, he is evil).

The context, and the comment which follows, show that, although Abelard says just 'good things', he means the best things—and the same is true for his subsequent references to good things in the argument. This view is reinforced by the consideration [2a] that even humans are obliged to act as well as they can and will to do so. But [3, 3a] because he acts without any difficulty and [4, 4a] always efficaciously,

3. God can do all good things.

From (1) and (2) it follows that

4. God does not fail to do good things he can do.

And from (3) and (4) it follows that

5. God does not fail to do any good thing.

Abelard also suggests [5] that the same line of argument could be run by describing God not as supremely good but as (completely) just. He then proposes [6] a stronger form of (2):

6. If God fails to do the best he can do, he is not supremely good.

Substituting (6) for (2), he can now [7, 14] conclude that

7. God never fails to do the best thing.

Abelard then adds [8, 15] the germ of an argument he will develop in the *Theologia scholarium* (see below, pp. 60–61), that, given that he is doing what is best, God cannot stop doing it and do something else, unless and until it is best to do something else.

The second argument begins from the premises [9] that

8. God has all his attributes necessarily

and [10]

9. One of God's attributes is to have a good will.

The argument that follows [11, 12] is not, as it might seem at first sight, that because God necessarily has a good will, whatever he wills, he wills necessarily—such reasoning is obviously fallacious. (Humans are necessarily rational, but it does not follow that the way they use their reason is necessary.) Rather, interpreting the text charitably, Abelard's point is that [11] because

10. It is an essential attribute of God that he has, not simply a will, but a *good* will
it follows [**12**] that

11. Necessarily, whenever he wills, he wills what is good for him to will.

Abelard takes it to follow that, on any occasion, there is just one way in which God can will. Given his assumption all along that God's willing what is good does not mean merely willing some good thing but rather willing the best, this inference is understandable, but it needs to be backed up, as Abelard will do later, by an argument to show that there is always just one best thing for God to will. Since, as already established [**4b**], God's will always has its effect, Abelard is able to conclude that [**13**] God can do no more, nor [14] do better than he does, nor [15] cease from what he is doing, which he summarizes by saying [16] that God does necessarily whatever he does.

Neither of these arguments is yet fully worked out, and Abelard will develop, especially, the first one in the *Theologia scholarium*. The second argument here makes very clear how, although Abelard talks in terms of God's acting necessarily, he is simply trying to establish that, necessarily, he chooses the best alternative course of action, not that his actions are simply necessary.[19]

After setting out these arguments, Abelard immediately goes on to consider (5.33) a line of objection to his conclusion that seems to be of his own devising. The argument concerns a *damnandus*, 'someone who ought to be damned'. Abelard seems to have in mind that the person concerned will as a matter of fact be damned because his or her deeds will deserve damnation.[20] The objector begins from a premise about the relationship between (13) 'This man is saved by God' and (14) 'God saves this man'. He says that everyone will accept the argument that from

13. This man is saved by God
it follows that

14. God saves this man.[21]
He then proposes a transfer of possibility principle:

15. 'The antecedent is not possible unless the consequent too is possible' which is justified by the claim that what something

impossible follows from must itself be impossible.[22] From this principle (15), along with (13) and (14), there follows

16. If it is possible that this man is saved by God, it is possible
that God saves him.

By contraposition, it follows that

17. If it is not possible that God saves him, it is not possible that
this man is saved by God.

But the consequent of (17), that it is not possible for this man to be
saved, implies that 'free will perishes and the man is commanded in
vain to do the things that pertain to salvation, since he cannot at all
be saved nor do the things by which he might be saved.'[23] Since it is
unacceptable that anyone could be in such a position, Abelard implies, the consequent of (17) is false and so, therefore, must be the
antecedent. And so it is possible for God to save this man—who will
in fact be damned—and so to do something that he does not do.[24]

Abelard then raises (5.34–35) another problem. If God cannot
make a thing better than it is, then it cannot be made better by him
or in any way become better. Yet no human (*aliquem nostrum*) is so
perfect that he or she cannot become more so.[25] Plato does, indeed,
seem to support the idea that everything is as good as it can be, Abelard goes on to say, when he writes in the *Timaeus* (29d–30a) that
God is in no way envious and so he willed to make everything as
similar to himself as its nature would allow. 'But this view is far both
from the truth and my opinion', he adds (5.36), and promises to explain why.[26] Returning to the first objection, Abelard generalizes the
point. If God cannot desist from what he does, then whatever he
does, he does necessarily. 'For if he cannot not do those things, then
indeed it is necessary that he do them, and so it is necessary that
they be done.'[27] And so, if someone is made good by God, it is necessary that he is good, and therefore he *cannot* be damned. (In putting
this objection to himself, which he will go on to reject, Abelard
seems deliberately to be moving from the position that God has no
alternative choices, which he has established, to the view that he acts
from straightforward necessity, which he has not established and
does not accept.) The conclusion that there is someone who cannot

be damned is of course unacceptable, and Abelard goes on (5.38–40) to give a number of authoritative statements, mainly from Augustine, which show that God could have acted differently from the way he did.

It is at this point that Abelard inserts his prayer, after which, making it clear that he is just asserting what seems to him the truth, he proceeds to propose (5.42–44) the view of God who wills necessarily whatever he wills and does necessarily whatever he does (5.42: *ut quae uult, necessario uelit, et quae facit, necessario faciat*). The discussion then turns (5.45–56) to the necessity of God's willing and making the world, and why he did not make it straight away. Only very near to the abrupt end of the text as we have it does Abelard return to consider the arguments he has raised against the position he is championing. He focuses straightaway on the most general form of the first objection: that, if God always acts of necessity, then what happens when he so acts will also be necessary—since it is necessary that he save this man (because all he does is necessary), it is necessary that this man is saved. (Necessity in all these cases means the absence of alternative choices, not straightforward necessity.) He now resolves this problem by a reduction of necessity to natural exigency:

> God does necessarily all that he does, and yet it is not the case, as it has been said, that the things done by him are done necessarily. When we say that it is necessary that God saves this man, we take the force of necessity from the nature of the subject [*uim ipsam necessitudinis ad subiecti naturam reducimus*], which is God. It is as if we were to say that God is compelled by his own very nature to do it, so that his nature would in no way allow him not to do it as he does it. It is not, however, necessary that this man is saved by him, since in no way does the nature of the man who is saved require that he is saved. His nature, indeed, is mutable and not fixed necessarily in any condition [*in nullo suo statu necessario fixa*]: it is possible that it should not exist at all.[28]

What is not necessarily not the case is possible—that is to say, according to Abelard's reduction, whatever the nature of a thing does not require not to be (what might be called a thing's potentiality). The objection of the *damnandus* can therefore be resolved by a parallel reduction of possibility to potentiality, as Abelard goes on (5.58) to illustrate. When we say that it is possible for the man (who has been described as *damnandus*) to be saved by God, we mean that his nature permits him to be saved by God, which is true, since his nature does not require that he is not saved. But when we say that it is possible for God to save the man, we are saying that God's nature permits him to save the man, which it does not. Abelard gives as parallels the case of an utterance, which is audible, because in itself it has the potentiality to be heard (*est aptam ex se ipsa audiri*), although there is no one there to hear it, and of a field which is ploughable even before anyone has been created to plough it. This reduction of necessity to natural exigency and possibility to potentiality is characteristic of Abelard's approach to modalities. What exactly it involves—whether Abelard is content to leave creatures with a merely notionally open possibilities or, rather, he has a more robust idea of human freedom—will be explored after his more elaborated re-use of the same strategy in the *Theologia scholarium* has been examined (see below, pp. 77–87).

Hugh of St Victor and the *Theologia Christiana* Argument

The earliest discussion of Abelard's argument comes from a perhaps unexpected source. Hugh of St Victor, who took up a tradition of theology at the Abbey of St Victor begun by William of Champeaux, Abelard's teacher and enemy, was certainly no follower of Abelard's, and his attitude to the NAG, as to other of Abelard's theological innovations, was critical.[29] But, although he lacked any strong interest in logic or the ancient philosophers, Hugh was a sophisticated theologian, and he meets Abelard with detailed and reasoned objections. Scholars have always looked at what he wrote, a few years before his death in 1141, in his grand theological textbook, *De sacramentis*.[30] But his closest reaction is found in a report, corrected by Hugh himself, of his teaching, the *Sententiae de divinitate*. Its compilation has been dated to before 1130,[31] and the passage on God and necessity bears this out, since the views it examines are close to those Abelard puts in the *Theologia Christiana*, although he seems to have known more Abelardian material than our text of that work contains.

Hugh begins by rejecting the position—held by unnamed people 'who set up opinions in order to show off their brilliance rather than being mindful of the truth to be sought or the authorities of the holy fathers to be imitated'[32]—that God's 'power is equal to his wisdom, in such a way that neither exceeds the other' because 'whatever God can do, that thing he wills to do.'[33] This view is a direct consequence of NAG, which Abelard would bring out more directly in the *Theologia scholarium*, and Hugh goes on, indeed, to say that 'those who hold the above opinion, or rather, falsehood, try to prove that God could do neither anything *other*, nor *otherwise*, nor *better* than he does.'[34]

According to Hugh, the argument that God can do nothing *other* than he does is that 'if God were to do other than he does, he would do other than he has foreseen. If he were to do other than he has foreseen, he would do contrary to his prescience, and this cannot be.'[35] This argument, which is answered merely by a cross-reference to the discussion of prescience, does not correspond to anything in the *Theologia Christiana*, though perhaps it reflects an earlier version of one of the subsidiary points that is considered in the *Theologia scholarium* (see below, p. 72). The view being attacked is, indeed, clearly that God's actions are straightforwardly necessary. By contrast, the position that God can do nothing *otherwise* than he does turns out to be that God has no alternative choices, and the argument for it is Abelard's NAG. If there is reason why God should do this now, there is not reason why he should not do it now, because there cannot be reason for two opposites, and so if there is reason for one to be done, there is not reason for the other to be done. But if there is no reason for God to do what he is not doing now, then

God cannot not do what he is doing.[36] Against this position, Hugh advances a powerful argument. The first stage is to make a distinction between a compelling (*cogens*) reason, and a 'suffering' or permissive (*patiens*) one. A compelling reason is what applies when one course of action is necessarily rational and the opposite not, as with a commandment such as 'Love your neighbour'. It is always reasonable to love one's neighbour, and never reasonable not to do so. A permissive reason is what applies where both a certain course of action and its opposite can be rational, according to the judgement of the agent: if I sit, that is well done; but if I choose not to sit, that too is well done. Those who propose the position under attack treat all of God's actions as subject to compelling reasons, but in the second stage of his argument Hugh insists that, by contrast, everything that God does with regard to his creation is subject only to permissive reasons. God therefore acts rationally whether he does what he does or not.[37] Hugh is therefore attacking Abelard's unstated assumption (which will be identified and justified in the *Theologia scholarium*) that for God there are never two courses of action which are equally good. But Hugh goes further. According to him, it is not just the case that, as for us, two courses of action are sometimes equally good. God, he insists, could always, with reason, do the opposite of what he does. Hugh gives no argument for this extreme view, which seems to indicate some kind of voluntarism.

The argument Hugh gives for the third view he is attacking, that God could not do or make anything *better* than he does, bears a strange and interesting relation to the second objection Abelard raises in the *Theologia Christiana* (5.34–35) to his own position on divine necessity (see above, pp. 55–56). Hugh seems to be arguing against a rather fuller version of this reasoning, but one that may have been garbled (or which he garbled). First, he gives the position of his opponents the view that 'God can do or make nothing better than he does or makes', which, he says, they support with the passage from the *Timaeus* about God's being free from envy—the very passage Abelard cited, but went on to say is wrong if it is taken to mean that everything is as good as it can be.[38] Hugh retorts that God does good to his creatures, not because he is under an obligation to do so, but from benignity. Hugh then gives another argument put by those he is attacking: 'Those I was referring to also say that the universe could be better than it has been made, because it is not repugnant to its nature for it to become better, but that God could not make it better than he made it or will make, for the reasons already given, just as an utterance is audible although there is no one who could hear it, and a field can be ploughed even if there is no one who could plough it. When no animal exists, both the field can be ploughed and the utterance be heard.'[39] This argument itself is not found in Abelard, but the underlying idea of reducing possibility to potentiality is, of course, very much his, as are the examples of the audible utterance and the ploughable field. Indeed, it is plausible that this is how he would have gone on, in the *Theologia Christiana,* to explain why he rejected Plato's position that the world could not be made better. God could not make or have made it better, because he can do nothing other than he does, but in itself the world could be better. Hugh dismisses this view, saying that, on the contrary, God could always increase the capacity of the universe for goodness and make it better, though in itself the universe might not be capable of more good than it has been given.[40] Such a rejection is not surprising, given that Hugh rejected NAG, which underlies the position.

The Argument in the *Theologia scholarium*—I

In the *Theologia scholarium,* Abelard gives his most precise and best-defended exposition of NAG. He concentrates on the logical steps that lead from the position that God always does the best to the conclusion that God can do only what he does. There is one important preliminary to understanding how he puts the argument here. The way in which he speaks (as in the quotation below) of God 'desisting from' or 'not desisting from' what he is doing may seem strange. If God is presented as acting and choosing to act in time, when we talk about whether God can do other than he does, we are not talking about whether he can ever stop doing something he has started—it would be absurd (except perhaps during an English summer) to think that, if God is making it rain now, he can never desist from making it rain. We are talking about whether, although God is in fact making it rain at this moment, t_1, it would have been possible for him to have been making it dry at this same moment, t_1. Abelard's use of the rather clumsy language of desisting and not desisting from an action might be put down to his discomfort with the idea of alternative synchronous possible states of affairs, such as that it is raining at t_1 and possibly it is dry at t_1. But the point he wants to make about God need not involve synchronic possibilities. Abelard is thinking about God as choosing to act in this or that way, and in his usual manner he is talking about God as acting in time, even though, strictly speaking, he does not (see above, p. 51). Choosing to act precedes the action, even if only momentarily. Suppose I choose to do x. I make this choice (at the latest) at t_0, and then I do x at t_1. At t_0, I may be either doing x, in which case I do not desist from doing x, or doing something else, y, in which case, following my choice, I desist from doing x and do y instead. Abelard's language, therefore, needs no excuses. In order not to complicate the presentation unnecessarily, the argument below has God simply doing or desisting from what he does, x, at t, but may more precisely be understood as just explained in terms of God's choice at t_0 to act at t_1.

Abelard's main argument (3.27–28) takes up and develops what had been just a sideline to the discussion in *Theologia Christiana*:[41]

> For if we suppose that he could do more or fewer things, or stop those that he is doing, we shall indeed be detracting from his highest goodness. For it is obvious that he can do nothing except good things, nor anything except for those things which it is fitting for him to do and which it is good that he does. Similarly, it is obvious that he can neither desist from doing any things, so that he stops doing them, unless they are fitting for him to desist from, and it is good that he desists from doing them. It is not fitting for him to do and desist from doing the same thing, nor is it good. Indeed, there is nothing about which

it is fitting at one and the same time that it be done and that it be desisted from being done, and it cannot be good that what is good to be done stops being done, because the only thing contrary to good is evil. Nor can there be a rational cause which is the basis for why the same thing should be done and desisted from being done. If, therefore, since it is good for something to be done, it is not good for it to be desisted from being done, and God can neither do nor desist from doing anything except what it is good that he does or desists from doing, then it seems that God can do or desist from doing only what he does or desists from doing, because that alone is good for him to do or desist from doing. For if it is good for him to desist from doing what he desists from doing, it certainly is not good for him to do that very thing, and consequently he cannot do it.

The argument here seems to be:

18. God does x at t. [premise]

19. God cannot do anything at any time which is not good to do at that time. [premise: supposedly Christian doctrine]

20. If it is good for x to be done at t, it is not good that x be desisted from being done at t. [premise]

21. It is good that x be done at t. [18, 19]

22. It is not good that x be desisted from being done at t. [21, 20]

23. God cannot desist from doing x at t. [19, 22]

24. God cannot do other than x at t. [18, 23]

The same reasoning applies, of course, to any instant of time, and so it shows that God cannot ever do other than he does.

If 'good' in this argument is taken to mean just 'has some degree of positive value', so that although it is good for x to be done at t, it is consistent to say that it is better for y to be done at that time, then Abelard's reasoning makes little sense. Clearly, then, by 'good', here, he means 'the best', just as he did in the *Theologia Christiana*—and this is brought out by the way in which, a little further on, Abelard speaks in terms, not only of what it is good for God to do, but also of what it is right that he should do (*quod fieri ... oportet*), what it is just that he should do, and what he is required to do (*facere debet*).[42] Most important, he links what it is good, right, just and requisite for God to do or desist from with having a 'reasonable cause' for doing or desisting from it: 'Indeed, there is nothing that he does or desists from doing, except from the best, reasonable cause, although it may be hidden from us.'[43] Abelard clearly considers that, for each action of God's, there is a reason—that it is the best, justest, rightest, most requisite action—for him to do it, and that this reason is independent of him.[44] It is this position which will allow him to defend the most obviously questionable premise in the argument, (20).

(20) should, in the light of the explanation above, be read as: 'If it is best (right, most just, etc.) for x to be done at t, it is not best (right, most just, etc.) that x be desisted from being done at t.' This conditional is based on the assumption that whether x is the best (etc.) thing for God to do at t is independent of whether it is actually done at t by God. One line of objection that Abelard anticipates is a voluntarist one—and this line of thought may have entered into Hugh of St Victor's claim that God acts only according to permissive reasons. Suppose that it is God's choice to do something that makes it good and fitting: x is good and fitting if and only if God chooses x. In that case, (20) can be rejected. It would still apply to an agent except for God. But, in God's case, if he is now making it rain here, that is good and fitting, because it is what he chooses; but if he had just desisted from making it rain and were making the sun shine here, that would be good and fitting, because it would be what he would be choosing. Abelard rejects the basis for this line of attack:

> In everything which God does he pays such attention to what is good that he may be said to follow in each thing he does, not the desire of his own will, but rather the value itself of the good. This is the reason behind what Jerome writes commenting on Daniel, in his exegesis of the third vision, where Nebuchadnezzar speaks about God in the following way: 'He does according to his will in heaven and on earth, and there is no one who may resist his hand and say: "Why have you done so?"' 'And this',

says Jerome, 'he says like a man of the world. For God does not do a thing because he wishes, but because the thing is good, God wishes it. Nebuchadnezzar spoke in such a way that, whilst he attributed power to God, he seemed to fault his justice because he (Nebuchadnezzar) had undeservedly suffered punishments.' When Jerome says, 'For God does not do a thing because he wishes, but because the thing is good, God wishes it,' it is as if he were to say: God does not act as Nebuchadnezzar judges that he does, in the manner of those who, in what they do, pay attention not so much to what is good but as to satisfying their will, whatever it may be. About such people it has been written: 'I will this, I order it so. Let my will take the place of a reason!' (Juvenal 6.223). Rather, he should be said to will that each thing happens, because he sees that it is good that they happen.[45]

According to Abelard, then, God does not make his will take the place of reason: rather, he chooses what things to do because he sees 'that it is good that they be done.' Abelard therefore believes that there is a standard of goodness *in a certain sense* independent of God, and in accord with which he acts. The sense in which the standard is independent is that God cannot change it. Abelard would certainly not hold that it is independent in the sense of lying outside God, whom he recognizes as the supreme good. The idea of this sort of standard is important not only for meeting the voluntarist objection. It also shapes Abelard's whole approach to the problem and, in particular, how he understands (1) ('God is supremely good'), the premise on which his argument is based.

Even supposing that voluntarism can be rejected, (20) seems to have another, more obvious weakness. Just as two runners sometimes must share the prize because they cross the finishing line at exactly the same moment, so it seems that there might be situations where two or more different actions are the best (rightest, justest, etc.), since they are equally good and better than all other actions. (This objection seems to have been one which Hugh of St Victor mainly had in mind when he attacked Abelard's position in *Theologia Christiana* by distinguishing between compelling and permissive reasons.) Whether in response to Hugh's or other similar criticisms, or as a result of his own reflection, Abelard now sees that he must state and answer this objection:

> But perhaps you will say that in the same way as what he is doing now is just, good and reasonable, so it would be equally good were he to desist from doing this—A—and do something else—B. Well, if what he desisted from doing (A) when he chose B were equally good, there was absolutely no reason why he should have desisted from A and chosen B. 'There was', you will say, 'because—since both together ought not to have been done, and it was equally good that A or B should be done, whichever of them were done would be done with reason.' But truly, according to this reasoning, what was done and what was not done equally ought to have been done, and it was equally good that A was done as B. Now, when that which is done is good, and it has a reasonable cause for which it should be done, whoever does not do what he is aware should be done by him acts irrationally indeed. And so we fall back again into the difficulty noted above. Now, if you say about B, the thing which was not done, that it was not good that it should be done except in such a way that A, the other thing, should stop, clearly by this very reasoning one will not be right to grant without qualification that it would be good for the one which was done, A, to be done, since it has been agreed that A and B are equally good to be done. Has God therefore done what it was not good to do? Perish the thought! And if only that which he does is good to be done by him, then indeed he—who can do nothing except that which is good to be done by him—can do only that which he does.[46]

This answer is based on his fundamental idea that, in doing the best, God is acting according to a reasonable cause. Were it ever to be the case that two courses of action, A and B, were equally good and fitting, then there could be no good reason for God to do one and not the other. And so there can be no dead heats with regard to divine choices for action. There is a single best choice, which God makes. A very strong principle of sufficient reason applies where God's actions are concerned.[47]

Abelard also anticipates three further main sorts of objection. The first is based on a scriptural quotation—'Who can resist his will?' to which Abelard links a comment of Augustine's: 'He is called "omnipotent" not because he can do everything, but because he can do whatever he wills and nothing at all can obstruct the effect of his will.'[48] This position is taken to imply that God can do what he does not, because, were he to will to do it, nothing could resist his will. Abelard rejects the position, because it would also entail, for the same reason, that God could sin. (His objection should have been that the position is incomplete. Abelard himself does not doubt the total efficaciousness of God's will: his controversial view concerns the limits set by God's nature on his will, a topic the position in question does not cover.) Abelard adds, with the quotation from Augustine in mind, that 'when they say that he is called "omnipotent" because he can do whatever he wills, they clearly connect his power and his will in such a way that, where his will is lacking, his power is also lacking.' This a bizarre interpretation of what Augustine says. Augustine's point is that, whatever it is that God wills, he can do; that is to say,

25. x (God wills x -> God can do x).

Abelard certainly accepts (25), but from it he derives: x (If God does not will x -> God cannot do x). That is to say, he asserts, not Augustine's conditional, (25), but the bi-conditional

26. x (God wills x <-> God can do x).

But (26) does not, of course, follow from (25). (26) is, however, precisely Abelard's own position, which he has stated very directly in the previous paragraph, and which follows from (25) along with the conclusion of NAG (God can do only what he does) and the obvious principle, given his omnipotence, that God does all he wills to do, and so if he does not do something, he does not will to do it.[49]

Another objection to Abelard's view is based on his position that God acts necessarily (that is, without alternative choices). If so, it is argued, God deserves no thanks, 'since when he acts he is led to do these things which he cannot stop doing, driven by a certain necessity of his own nature rather than by his free will.'[50] Abelard's answer is to distinguish between acting under coercion and acting necessarily. An agent is acting under coercion when he is compelled to act in a certain way, whether or not he wishes. No thanks are due to such an agent. God does not at all act under coercion, although he does act necessarily. Abelard accepts that this means that, in some sense, God is compelled to act as he does, but he argues that when someone is compelled to do what he wills to do, there is no coercion.[51] Abelard gives, as a parallel, the necessity that God is immortal: this necessity of God's nature is not disjoined from his will, because he wills to be what he necessarily is. It is the same with 'this necessity of his nature or goodness' (*haec . . . quaedam naturae uel bonitatis eius necessitas*), which is not separate from his will. If he is so good that he, not unwillingly but spontaneously, wills what is best, then the fact that it is not an accident that he does so but a result of what he is essentially (*substantialiter*) makes him all the more worthy of love and honour.[52]

The most important objection Abelard considers is, as in the *Theologia Christiana,* the one which concerns the *damnandus,* to which he adds a subsidiary problem that is solved in the same sort of way. One difference in his treatment is that he links it—though in a way that turns out to be potentially misleading—to his wider ideas about the analysis of modal expressions. A sketch of these views, as developed in the *Dialectica* and the *Logic ingredientibus,* will therefore help to clarify the discussion.

ABELARD ON MODALITY

Abelard was very attentive to the ambiguities in modal discourse.[53] The sentence

27. It is possible for the standing man to sit (*Possibile est stantem sedere*)

can be understood as either

28. It is possible for it to happen as this proposition says: 'The standing man sits'
or as

29. The thing which is standing can sit at some time.[54]

He calls the distinction between (27) and (28) one between the compound and divided sense—terms that he learned from Aristotle's *Sophistical Refutations,* although he had already made the analysis in the *Dialectica,* apparently before he had he read this text of Aristotle's.[55] He also describes the same distinction as one between understanding modalities *de sensu* and *de re* (very similar to the *de dicto* / *de re* distinction among contemporary logicians). When a modal sentence is read *de sensu,* the modal operator is applied to the whole non-modal sentence from which it derives (and so, in the language of contemporary logic, it has wide scope, ranging over the whole proposition). Thus, in the present case, the non-modal proposition 'The standing man sits' is said (falsely) to be possible. When a modal sentence is read *de re,* the modal operator is applied to the thing concerned (and so has narrow scope). In this case, the thing is the standing man, and the sentence states that it is possible for him to sit.

In the *Dialectica,* Abelard argues that the *de sensu* reading leads to mistakes in attributing truth values. Moreover, sentences interpreted in this way are not really modal: in modal sentences, we do not just say that one thing inheres in another but explain how it inheres—necessarily or possibly. But, read *de sensu,* a supposedly modal sentence predicates simply, rather than predicating a modal qualification, 'possible' or 'necessary', of the original, non-modal sentence.[56] Abelard repeats this view in the *Logica ingredientibus,*[57] although there he looks carefully into how different modal sentences are to be understand *de re* and *de sensu.* In the *Dialectica* he gives a general account of what is meant by 'possible', in which he clearly has in mind the *de re* interpretation:

> 'Possible' and 'contingent' have exactly the same meaning—for here we take 'contingent' as being, not what actually happens, but what can happen, even if it never happens, so long as the

nature of the thing is not repugnant to its happening. So, when we say, 'It is possible that Socrates is a bishop', it is true, although he never is one, because his nature is not repugnant to <being a> bishop. We gather this from other things of the same species, which we see actually participating in the property of <being a> bishop. For we judge that whatever happens to one in act can happen in all the individuals of the same species.[58]

This paradigm was probably not the only one Abelard used in order to think about modality, but it seems to have been the one he preferred.[59] In particular, this understanding of possibility helped him to deal with counterfactual possibilities. Abelard did not like to admit that, if one state of affairs is actual, then an alternative state of affairs is possible—though he could envisage alternative divine presciences according to the different ways contingent things might happen.[60] In his *de re* reading of 'It is possible for the standing man to sit', (29) above, Abelard seems deliberately to avoid committing himself to synchronic alternative possibilities by putting in the word *quandoque* ('at some time'). That is to say, it appears that, rather than allowing an interpretation of (27) as

    30. That which is standing at t_1 can sit at t_1,

by adding the *quandoque* in (29), Abelard is insisting that the *de re* reading of (27) is

    31. That which is standing at t_1 can sit at some other time.

If this is Abelard's meaning, then he would, at least here, be following an Aristotelian approach to necessity, according to which what is, when it is, necessarily is, and so there are no synchronic alternative possibilities.

In one sense, then, (31) does capture Abelard's meaning in (29). When Abelard puts to himself explicitly the question of whether, if someone can do something (such as sit) at any moment of his life, he can do it at that moment when he is not doing it (sit when he is not sitting), he avoids an affirmative answer.[61] But he does so because, in answering this question, he is forced to think about states of affairs, whereas he happily allows for synchronic possibilities so long as he can, as he prefers, focus on things and their potentialities. (31) is not, then, an entirely satisfactory exposition of (29), where Abelard's point is that the man has as part of his nature the potentiality to stand, which he might in principle exercise at any time. Using this conception of possibility, Abelard will go so far as to say that it is possible for a blind man to see, although there is no possibility that, having become blind, he will see again. It is possible for him to see because seeing is not repugnant to human nature, and this potentiality-based view leads to a conception, not of alternative possible states of affairs, but of alternative possible life stories. This man, as it sadly happened, became blind, and it will never be the case, now, that he sees again. But his life might have gone differently, and he might never have become blind.[62]

THE ARGUMENT IN THE *THEOLOGIA SCHOLARIUM*—2

It will be clear from the discussion above that what was described as the 'reduction of possibilities to potentialities' in the *Theologia Christiana* was a general feature of Abelard's treatment of modalities. This approach is also followed in the *Theologia scholarium*. The objection about the *damnandus* is given almost exactly as before, except that the term *damnandus* is used in the argument itself:

> For who does not know that this man who is *damnandus* can be saved, or that this man who is good can be made better than he is ever going to be, though both these things cannot happen save only through God. For if this *damnandus* were entirely unable to be saved, or to do those things through which he would be saved by God, he could not be blamed at all nor considered guilty that he does not do those things which he could not do. Nor would those things through which he would have been saved have been rightly commanded by God, since he could by no means do them. Now, if he *were* able to be saved by the Lord through the works he might perform, who would doubt but that God could save him—he who, however, is never to be saved (*numquam saluandus est*). For how could he be saved by God,

unless it was also the case that God could save him? What indeed is it for him to be saved by God other than for God to save him? So, if it is possible for him to be saved by God, how should it not be possible for God to save him? For when the antecedent is possible, so is the consequent, because something impossible never validly follows from what is possible, since it is obvious that what something impossible follows from is itself impossible. Who would deny that from the antecedent 'Now this man is saved by God' there follows 'God saves him', since, as I have said, for the *damnandus* to be saved by God is entirely the same as for God to save him? Since therefore it is possible for the *damnandus* to be saved by God, who will deny that it is also possible for God to save him? God can therefore do what he will not at all do, and it is clear that what I have already reasoned above—that God can do only what he at some time does—is entirely false.[63]

For the sake of clarity, here are the steps of the reasoning, which are the same as in the *Theologia Christiana:*

32. If the *damnandus* is saved by God, God saves the *damnandus.* [premise]

33. 'When the antecedent is possible, so is the consequent.' [transfer of possibility principle]

34. If it is possible that the *damnandus* is saved by God, it is possible that God saves the *damnandus.* [32, 33]

35. It is possible that the *damnandus* is saved by God. [Christian doctrine]

36. It is possible that God saves the *damnandus.* [34, 35]

37. God does not actually the save the *damnandus.* [meaning of *damnandus*]

38. It is possible for God to do what he does not do. [36, 37]

Despite the closeness of the way in which the objection is stated, the reply to it begins here quite differently from that in the *Theologia Christiana.*[64] Abelard gives examples of pairs of synonymous sentences which, when a possibility operator is added to them, cease, he claims, to have the same truth value. The two pairs are 'a speaking man is silent' and 'a man who is speaking is silent'; and 'that which is white is black' and 'whiteness and blackness are in the same thing at the same time'. Abelard explains that

39. The speaking man is silent

is impossible, but

40. The man who is speaking is silent

is possible; and that

41. Whiteness and blackness are in the same thing

is impossible, whereas

42. That which is white is black

is possible. These propositions, as will be clear from the section above, are in fact each examples of the phenomenon Abelard had analysed in his logical works: the compound (39, 41) sense and the divided (40, 42) sense of modal statements. The new element that Abelard adds here to this idea is that different formulations of the same non-modal proposition, when modalized, may lend themselves to being interpreted especially in one of the two senses, divided or compound.

Unfortunately, these comments of Abelard's can easily be mis-leading. These analogies would appear to suggest that Abelard wants to reject (34) by arguing that the consequent and the antecedent should be understood in different senses—the antecedent as a true divided-sense proposition ('This man ought to be damned and it is possible that he will be saved') and the consequent as a false, compound-sense one ('The following is possible: this man ought to be damned and God saves this man'). But this cannot be Abelard's in-tention, since he goes (3.49) on to make it clear that both antecedent and consequent are to be understood, exactly as suggested in the *Theologia Christiana,* as divided-sense *de re* modalities and that the consequent does not follow from the antecedent because each con-cerns a different thing: the antecedent is about possibilities for the *damnandus,* hence what human nature allows, whereas the conse-quent is about possibilities for God, hence what is allowed by divine nature:

When we say that he can be saved by God, we refer the pos-sibility to the capacity [*facultatem*] of human nature, as if we were to say that it does not go against the nature of man that he should be saved, because in himself he is changeable so that he might consent either to his salvation or to his damnation and he might offer himself to God as one to be treated in the one way or the other. When, however, we say that God can save the man who is not at all to be saved, we refer possibility to the very nature of the divinity: we are saying that it would not be repugnant to the nature of God for God to save him. This is entirely false. It does indeed go completely against the divine nature to do what detracts from its dignity, and what it is not at all fitting that <God> should do.

Abelard's explanation, then, relies—as in the *Theologia Christiana*—on the idea that, when the subject of a verb changes, as it does in the shift from passive to active, then the thing about which a divided-sense, *de re* possibility is asserted also changes, since the possibility is attached to the subject of the verb. The analogy with sentences interpreted according to divided or composite sense is merely intended to provide other examples of cases where statements which have the same meaning and truth values in their simple form diverge in meaning and truth value when modalized. Abelard's argument may still, however, seem far from convincing: the objections to it will be examined at the end of the chapter.

Abelard uses the same conception of *de re* possibility, determined by the thing to which it applies and not by a state of affairs, to tackle another objection (with no parallel in the *Theologia Christiana*, though a passage in Hugh of Victor's *Sententiae de divinitate* suggests that Abelard may have been thinking about the difficulty earlier on; see above, p. 57). The objection, which is not put very clearly, is that 'since God cannot be without what he has had in him from eternity, because it would not be fitting', the unacceptable conclusion seems to follow that 'the things God has foreseen and which he willed to be' happen of necessity.[65] At first sight, this seems to be a problem, not about God's omnipotence, but about his prescience: if God foresees all things, must they not happen of necessity? Abelard, however, considered this problem about prescience separately and believed that it rested on a logical confusion which he was able to unravel.[66] The two examples he considers here, though, are God's will to be merciful and his will to create the world. These are both volitions which God must have, because of his complete goodness, independent of anything which happens in his creation. Abelard insists that, in these cases too, God's lack of possibility to do otherwise does not deprive the things concerned of their own *de re* possibility to be otherwise. So far as the world and God's creatures are concerned, possibility applies to their natures, not God's, and there is nothing in the natures of his creatures which requires that they be pitied by God, or in the nature of the world, that it had to be created.

THE ARGUMENT IN ABELARD'S *SENTENTIAE*

The *Sentence* collections that report Abelard's teaching all explain his view that God cannot do other than he does. It is wisest, not to try and place these versions in a line of chronological development by Abelard of his views, but to see them as (in some cases rough) presentations of his thinking, already assimilated and perhaps adjusted by their audience. It is, in fact, the briefest of the reports, the *Sententiae Florianenses,* which gives the most, though still loosely, argued case—in effect, a different, simplified version of the argument in the *Theologia Scholarium:*[67]

43. God always acts according to reason. [premise]
44. God never omits to do anything without a reason. [43]
45. x is something that God omitted to do at t1. [premise]
46. There is a reason why God omitted to do x at t1. [44, 45]
47. God could not do x at t1. [43, 46]

In the *Sententiae Abaelardi* and the *Sententiae Parisienses,* there is a fuller exposition of authoritative texts that, apparently, contradict his view.[68] Against them is set, not so much a step-by-step argument, as the main lines of Abelard's position that 'since . . . all that he does, he does in the way that he sees they should be done, and he does just the number of things which it is fitting should be done, if then he were to do otherwise, or if he were to do more or less than he does, it would be unfitting.'[69] Both texts emphasize strongly God's providential planning of everything for the best: so, for instance, God foresaw that it would be fitting to choose Jacob and condemn Esau, and, given so, he could not have arranged events in anything other than this way. The *Sententaie Parisienses* go even further (they claim to be quoting Augustine, at least at the start, but no such quotation is to be found): 'All the things that are in this republic are so fittingly disposed and rationally foreseen from eternity that, were any one of them not in the way it is, it would not be able to remain fittingly, and the whole structure [*machina*] would perish—as if there were some structure put together so that, were the tiniest little stone to be taken away, the whole structure would tumble down in ruins.'[70] All three *Sentence* collections also emphasize the importance of Abelard's reduction of possibility to potentiality in order to preserve freedom for human choices, and they use the example of the field that is ploughable though there is no one to plough it.[71]

Abelard also considers a related, but different problem, linked to the considerations raised in the *Theologia Christiana* about God making everything as good as possible.[72] If God cannot do other than he does, it follows that he cannot do better than he does. But it seems wrong to say that, for example, God could not have made man better than he is—a point raised already in the *Theologia Christiana*. Abelard deals with this implicit objection by distinguishing between a nominal use of 'better' (a better thing) and an adverbial use (doing something better). God always acts in such a way that he could not act any better (adverbially), but in doing so he produces some things that are better than others, just as a craftsman makes equally well a golden goblet and a glass one.[73] This distinction of Abelard's was accepted and taken up by writers such as Peter the Lombard, who emphatically rejected Abelard's main position.[74] In later medieval discussions, this issue was usually distinguished from the question of whether God can do other than he does, since Peter the Lombard had treated it in a separate distinction (1.44).

EARLY RESPONSES TO ABELARD'S ARGUMENT

The followers who compiled these three *Sentence* collections were, it seems, alone in receiving NAG with approval, one exception aside. A master Omnebene compiled, probably before Sens, a collection of *Sentences* heavily influenced by Abelard.[75] In discussing NAG itself, Omnebene does not come down on one side or another, but he later makes it clear that God cannot dispose more than he has disposed and cannot predestine or know more than he predestines or knows.[76]

Otherwise, Abelard's views continued to arouse opposition. When Hugh of St Victor put together his systematic theological treatise *De sacramentis* probably in the late 1130s, a few years before his death in 1141, he used material from the *Sententiae de divinitate*, including some of the passage on NAG.[77] But Hugh abbreviated and altered it, removing entirely the argument and counter-argument that related most directly to Abelard, that God could not do otherwise than he does, perhaps because he wanted to recycle the distinction between compelling and permissive reasons he had used to tackle Abelard's view into one between compelling and permissive justice, which was used later on to show why God's choice to save some but not all humans is just.[78] Also omitted was the examination of Abelard's characteristic thesis about the difference between active and passive possibility (the field which can be ploughed, though there is no one to plough it). True, Hugh no longer dismissed the argument based on the immutability of God's providence by referring back to the discussion on prescience, but he explained (215BC) how events could be different from what they are, and how if so God's providence would be different. But this response does not meet Abelard's argument, which is not about foreknowledge but about the immutability of God's will. Altogether, in adapting the material for his systematic treatise, Hugh seems no longer to be focussing on Abelard's particular arguments. Similarly, in another, later work that has been seen as directed against Abelard, *De potestate et voluntate Dei*, Hugh explains how God can be held able to do more than he does without thereby implying a lack of unity and equality between his will and power;[79] the only thing that this discussion has to do with NAG is that it assumes its conclusion to be wrong.

Perhaps, though, Hugh was aware of some of the developments in Abelard's thinking. In a passage in *De sacramentis* not anticipated in the *Sententiae de divinitate,* he writes (215D–216A): 'They say that single created things, considered in themselves, are less than perfect, but the totality of things has been brought to such a consummation of the good that it could not be better than it is.' Here Hugh may well be referring to Abelard's distinct discussion, found in the *Sententie,* about whether God could do better than he does, and his distinction between how individual things are better and worse, but all equally well made by God: a position which, though rejected by Hugh, found favour among other thinkers.

Two other systematic treatises probably written near the time of *De sacramentis* and influenced by Hugh as well as Abelard himself engage a little more closely with NAG. In the *Summa sententiarum,* from 1140 or earlier, the author, a little unclearly, distinguishes two strands of reasoning (69 BC).[80] First, whatever God does is good and just, and so God should not desist from doing it—and he cannot do what he ought not to do. Second, for the same reason, God cannot do what he does not do, because if it were what he should do, he would do it.[81] Both arguments are dismissed by saying that it is wrong altogether to apply the verb of obligation (*debere*) to God, and so we should say of something neither that God ought to do it nor that he ought not to do it.[82] Rather, 'He does nothing out of obligation but rather from goodness alone.'[83] The thought behind this objection is similar to that Hugh of St Victor developed earlier on in his distinction between compelling and permissive reasons, when he insisted that God acts only according to permissive reasons—a position that suggests a voluntarism which Abelard would reject.[84] The *Ysagoge in Theologiam,* written by Odo, an Englishman, probably before 1139, also draws from Hugh but is strongly influenced by many of Abelard's own teachings.[85] It gives a similar, though more rapid, account of the NAG and rejects it for exactly the same reason.[86]

Assessing the NAG Argument and Its Implications

Abelard's argument about God and alternative possibilities falls into two main parts. First, there is the main line of reasoning which leads to the conclusion that God cannot do other than he does. Although it would in future years be attacked as if it rested on an undetected ambiguity (see below, chapter 4), it does not. It is a valid argument, but one or another of its premises can be attacked quite easily. Abelard foresaw two of the main lines of attack—the dead heats and the voluntarist objections—and he tried to answer them. His answers, however, depend on a conception of God which many Christians would find objectionable, because it tends to reduce him to an abstract principle of justice, leaving little room for the personal, loving God of the Bible. Second, there is Abelard's treatment of the *damnandus* objection (and, attached to it, some other problems to which he gives the same sort of solution). Here it may seem that Abelard's solution really is just a sophistical one, based on an equivocation which he does not notice, or else that it is a half-hearted solution, since it allows the *damnandus* not a real but merely a notional freedom to achieve salvation.

Abelard's imaginary opponent has apparently established, from the premise (32)—if the *damnandus* is saved by God, God saves the *damnandus*—and the transfer of possibility principle (33), the truth of (34): if it is possible that the *damnandus* is saved by God, it is possible that God saves the *damnandus*. But, if Abelard were to accept (34), he would have to give up his view that God cannot do other than he does, since, because Christian doctrine holds that no one is ever denied the possibility of salvation, Abelard accepts that its antecedent (35) is true, and the truth of the consequent entails that God *can* do other than he does, since, *ex hypothesi*, he will not in fact save the *damnandus*. Abelard's solution is to say that in (34) the possibility in the antecedent is possibility for the *damnandus*, whilst the possibility in the consequent is possibility for God. Not only does this allow him to show how the antecedent can be true but the consequent false—and so that the whole proposition (34) is false. It also indicates implicitly why he is able to reject the apparently irrefragable reasoning from (32) to (34). The transfer of possibility principle (33) applies only if the possibility operator has the same force when modifying the consequent as it does when modifying the antecedent. But, because Abelard considers that the possibilities are potentialities of the subject terms, in the case of the antecedent the possibility operator has the force of ampliating the statement according to what is possibility-for-the man, whereas in the consequent it has the force of ampliating the statement according to what is possibility-for-God.

So far, it seems, so good. But *damnandus* is a word that presents hidden dangers. The word can be used attributively or referentially. Used attributively, the word *damnandus* says that the person to whom it applies has led a life such that he or she is worthy to be damned. In this sense, 'It is possible that the *damnandus* is not the *damnandus*' is false, because it would mean that it is possible for someone to be *damnandus* and not *damnandus*. This is not the sense in which the word is used in the *damnandus* objection, because, were *damnandus* being used attributively, the objector would not be entitled to assert the premise from Christian doctrine (35) 'It is possible that the *damnandus* is saved by God'. This assertion would amount to saying that it is possible that God saves someone who merits damnation. Some Christian thinkers, indeed, *would* hold that God could act in such a way, mercifully but unjustly saving an unrepentant sinner, but Abelard would entirely reject this view, and so he could have dealt very easily with the *damnandus* objection if it had been based on it.

Used referentially, *damnandus* picks out a person by the feature that he or she will, at the moment of death, have led a life that merits damnation. Since, after death, the person is no longer *damnandus* but damned, the word will be used to pick out someone by an attribute which the person will, in fact, have but does not have at the time to which the reference applies; in the same way, a biographer might write, 'The composer was born in 1685' (though even Bach did not write music in the cradle). The fact that, with hindsight, we can pick someone out in this way does not mean that the attribute applies to the person necessarily (Bach might have grown up tone deaf). It is in this referential sense that the premise from Christian doctrine (35), that it is possible that the *damnandus* is saved by God, is to be understood. Every person has the chance to be saved, even those who in fact turn out to lead a life which merits them damnation. The problem for Abelard is that, once it is clear that the objector is using *damnandus* referentially, his insistence that God cannot save the *damnandus* seems unjustified. Abelard argues that God cannot save him, because to do so would be go against his justice, but that is not what *damnandus* in the referential sense implies. To say that God can save the *damnandus* (used referentially) means that it is possible for God to save this person, whom we identify by the damnation-worthy life he in fact ends up by leading, if he did not lead such a life—just the same conditions under which the *damnandus* could, as Abelard accepts, be saved by God.

Has Abelard slid from using *damnandus* referentially in 'It is possible for the *damnandus* to be saved by God' to using it attributively in 'It is possible for God to save the *damnandus*'? Perhaps a more charitable interpretation is to say, rather, that Abelard's underlying view—for which various passages about the perfect ordering of God's providence might be used as testimony—is that any person, and so the *damnandus* understood referentially, will be saved only if God has, for reasons to us inscrutable, chosen him for salvation. On this reading, the requirement that God, by justice, damn the *damnandus* would not be the demand that, if it turns out that he has lived a life worthy of damnation, he should be damned (which need not turn out to be pertinent if, as here, *damnandus* is understood referentially, not attributively). Rather, it is the demand that, because this person is one who, in God's best providential plan, will be damned, God will damn him after he has led, as he cannot but do, a life worthy of damnation. Despite this underlying position, Abelard, according to this interpretation, still wishes to keep in line with the Christian doctrine that it is possible that any person (including the *damnandus*) is saved. He is able to do so through his reduction of possibility to potentiality. As illustrated by the examples of the field which is ploughable although there is no one to plough it, and the sound which is audible although there is no one to hear it, some things have potentialities which cannot in fact be actualized. In this reading, the *damnandus* would have the potentiality to be saved by God (and so, in Abelard's terms, it is possible that he is saved by God), in the sense that as a human being he is the sort of thing which is potentially saveable. The problem with this reading is that possibility in this sense is purely notional. To say that it is possible for the *damnandus* to be saved means just that some other humans (but not the *damnandus*) are saved, and the *damnandus* is a human. To accept that it is possible for the *damnandus* to be saved only in this sense does not fulfil the spirit of the Christian doctrine that salvation is not closed to anyone. Moreover, it represents Abelard as a strict determinist. All things happen exactly as God has planned them, and God, as NAG establishes, has no alternative choices.

There is, however, a different interpretation which can be given of Abelard's reply to the *damnandus* objection, which vindicates Abelard's reasoning while at the same time making him a defender—as his ethical writings would suggest—of human freedom of choice and not a denier of it. NAG, as has been emphasized, does not in itself establish that God acts of necessity; it merely establishes that God has no alternative possibilities in acting: presented with choices, he cannot but choose the best, and there is always one best choice for him. The distinction between what is possible for the *damnandus* and what is possible for God with respect to the *damnandus* needs to be seen in terms of the alternative choices available in each case. Used referentially, *damnandus* picks out someone who will in fact lead a life worthy of damnation but might not have done so. He, therefore, has the possibility of acting in such a way that his life is worthy of salvation—in which case he will be saved by God. It is true, then, to say that it is possible for the *damnandus* to be saved by God. But God has no alternatives with respect to this *damnandus*. There is nothing, Abelard believes, which God—as opposed to the man himself—can choose to do to make his life not the evil one it turns out to be. The man will, in fact, die worthy of damnation, and it is not possible for God not to damn him, since that is what justice requires. Abelard is not denying that, because of the man's choices, it is possible for things to have been other than they turn out to be and for the man to die in a state worthy of salvation—in which case God cannot but save him: that is what is meant by saying that 'it is possible for the *damnandus* to be saved by God.' But this does not involve any alternative possibilities for God, and so it is not possible for God to save the *damnandus*.

To put it, for the sake of clarity, in anachronistic terms: if the underlying discussion were about straightforward necessity—about whether or not God necessarily does what he does—the objection would be asking whether, if God damns this man in the actual world (as is indicated by the description *damnandus*), then he damns this man in every possible world. Were Abelard to answer affirmatively, he would have to accept, against Christian doctrine and his own deepest beliefs, that the man is necessarily damned: nothing he can do will enable him to be saved. Since 'he is saved by God' and 'God saves him' mean the same, their truth values will be the same in each possible world in which the man and God exists. Since, if God acts necessarily, 'God saves him' is false in every such possible world, so 'he is saved by God' will also be false in every possible world. It is because the discussion is not about straightforward necessity but about alternative possibilities that Abelard's distinction can be upheld. The question is not about what is or is not the case in different possible worlds but about what powers something in the actual world has by its choices to make actual in the future a different possible world. The *damnandus* has the power—which he does not use—to choose in such a way as to make actual one of the possible worlds in which he lives so as to merit salvation. God, however, has no power to choose so as to make such a possible world actual. If, however, such a world is made actual through the choices of another agent, he has the power to choose to save the *damnandus* (and, indeed, he has no power not to make this choice).

Some Christian thinkers would query Abelard's argument, because they hold that, after the Fall, no one can be saved without the help of divine grace, which God grants individually. Without going to the extreme of those theologians who hold that God can act mercifully but against justice and save even someone who dies after a wicked life and in an unrepentant state, they would say that the *damnandus* does not have power, simply by himself, to make the choices which would actualize the possibility that he is saved; he also needs God's individual assistance in granting him the necessary grace. He could be saved, then, only if God did something which he does not do: that is to say, grant him the necessary grace. If God cannot do other than he does, then, on this view, the *damnandus* is necessarily damned. Abelard, however, entirely rejects such a theory of grace. He does not deny the necessity of grace for salvation, but he holds that no individual intervention from God is needed. God simply makes available to all freely the grace they need to act so as to be saved, if they choose to take it up.[87] He does not give or withhold grace in a way that would affect the decisions the person takes on his or her way to damnation or salvation.

Even allowing for his theory of grace, however, there is an obvious riposte to Abelard's view, as explained here. Granted, the moral choices which lead to the salvation of this or that person must be made by the individual, not by God. But this does not mean that God cannot intervene in all sorts of ways to make it easier or harder for the person to accept the grace that is freely offered and lead a life worthy of salvation. God could, at least in principle, it seems, so arrange matters that this person is not subjected to such and such a temptation or receives support in continuing a meritorious way of life. Indeed, at the extreme, cannot God choose that an infant die soon after baptism, without any chance to sin? These points would suggest that there are alternative ways that God can act towards the *damnandus*—that it is not the *damnandus* alone but God too who has the power to make choices which would lead to the actualization of the possible world in which the *damnandus* is saved. This objection, however, ignores the central point of NAG, that, at every juncture, God cannot but choose whatever course of action is the best. Take the case of the *damnandus*. Every action of God's towards him is the best action, all things considered, which could be taken, and the only action God could have chosen. Many of these actions may not be the best for the *damnandus* himself, but they will always be the best absolutely. It may be, for instance, that God exposes him to a temptation which God foreknows he cannot resist, but this is because there is a reason for doing so in the plan of the universe as a whole (this is exactly the case with Adam and the Fall). God therefore acts, and cannot but choose to act, towards every *damnandus* in the best way, consistent with the overall good of all things. The fact that the *damnandus* presents himself to God, on death, having lived a life worthy of damnation is due, not to any choice God had the power to make otherwise, but only to the *damnandus*'s own failure to exercise his power to choose a good life, whatever the difficulties providence placed in his way.

Does not the fact that God chooses which people to create mean that, nonetheless, ultimately it is God who chooses those who will be damned and those who will be saved? If, like Leibniz, Abelard had envisaged there being possible individuals down to every detail of their lives and God's choosing between them, then this objection would be relevant. But there is no sign that he ever thought in this way. He did, indeed, believe that God created individuals as being good or just to a greater or lesser extent, and this choice he saw as part of God's rational, providential plan and so as having no alternative, because it is in every case the best choice. As he writes in the *Sententiae:* 'God could not make [Peter] better or juster, because . . . <in that case> he would make him better or juster than is fitting.'[88] But this does not imply that God chose exactly which good deeds Peter would do and which sins he would commit. Although Abelard holds that God could not have made Peter better or juster, he accepts that Peter could have been juster than he was and that this would have been by or through God.[89] As he explains (using a version of some favourite examples): 'Just as this field can be ploughed by that boy and through him—it is apt for that—but he cannot plough it. I can receive a hundred *solidi* from you, and yet you, however, cannot give them to me.'[90] One way of understanding what Abelard means here would be to take the possibility of Peter's having been better or juster than he was as purely notional: although Peter himself could not have been better or juster than he was (because God could not have made him so), the potentiality for a human being to be just or good is greater than that which Peter realized, and so, considering possibility as potentiality for members of a species, Peter *could* have been better or juster. But there are the same strong reasons against taking possibility in this merely notional way as there were in the case of the *damnandus*. Moreover, the fuller account of Abelard's reasoning given in the *Sententiae Parisienses* brings out clearly that what is in question here, as in the case of the *damnandus,* is the genuine, though *ex hypothesi* counter-factual, possibility of Paul's having used his free will differently from how in fact he used it:

> He could have been juster, and through God, and yet God could not make him juster. It is true that Peter could be juster and through God, because God made Peter a creature such that he would be apt to receive many things from God, should he give them. Furthermore, it is shown that Peter could have been juster in this way. Because Peter was changeable [*mobilis*] and he could be withdrawn from that which he was, because he could withdraw himself from the good, in which he was, to evil. And, when he had got rid of this evil, he could receive justice from God.[91]

The comment about Peter's aptness to receive things from God might at first suggest that merely notional possibility is involved, but the explanation that follows shows not. It would not be enough for Abelard to have said that Peter might have freely made juster choices than he did, since this would not explain how this justice would have been from God. Rather, Peter can freely decide to sin, and freely decide to repent, at which juncture he will receive more justice from God (he is *more* just, it seems, not because he achieves a higher level of justice, but because he receives justice from God both originally and again after he has sinned). All this is in Peter's power, but not God's. God cannot make Peter sin or make him repent but must simply do whatever is best, depending on how Peter makes his choices.

How, then, are those passages in various of Abelard's works, alluded to above, which explain how God providentially ordains all things for the best, compatible with this interpretation? For example, the Christian in the *Collationes* (probably written a few years before the *Theologia scholarium*) declares (almost certainly here speaking for Abelard) that 'God's highest goodness, which permits nothing to happen without a cause, arranges even evil things so well, and also uses them in the best way, so that it is even true to say that it is good for there to be evil, although evil is in no way good.'[92] There are the passages in the *Sententia* collections mentioned above (see p. 74). And Abelard points to a very striking example of such divine arranging when, in the *Commentary on the Hexaemeron,* he poses the question of why God forbad Adam and Eve to eat from the Tree of Knowledge, when he foreknew that they would break his commandment and so sin. The answer is that, after having been redeemed by Christ, humans are better than if they had never sinned (Abelard even quotes from the Easter Liturgy of the Candle: *O felix culpa que talem ac tantum meruit habere redemptorem*). Through making them have to struggle, sin has made humans more meritorious and pleasing to God than if they had for ever remained without sin.[93] Even more striking in its description of an over-arching divine providential scheme is a passage, given to the Christian, near the end of the *Collationes,* at a point where he seems to be giving Abelard's own views. He brings up, as in the *Theologia Christiana,* Plato's idea that God does all things in the best way. He goes on: 'Whatever things are done by whomever, they take place rationally and well in the way in which they actually happen, because they happen as part of the design (which is the best) of divine providence— that is to say, because they have a rational cause for why they are brought about, *even if the person who does them does not do them well or rationally and, when he does them, he does not have in mind the cause which God has in mind.*'[94]

This passage (and its continuation), in especial, take the idea at the basis of NAG, that God must always choose the best, and apparently apply it to all things that happen, threatening to make NAG

entail the straightforward necessity of all events.[95] But there is clearly
an important exception which Abelard has in mind. It is central to
Abelard's ethics that humans decide between sinning (intending—
in his later technical usage, consenting to—acts which show con-
tempt of God) and avoiding sin.[96] With this in view, even when
Abelard's Christian most emphasizes God's providential planning,
he makes sure, as in the italicized passage above, to underline that it
does not extend to the intentions of the agents who carry out the
providentially ordained acts; and it is solely through their good or
bad intentions that people are saved or damned. He draws attention
to the same point a few lines later, when he says:

> It is evident, therefore, that whatever happens to be done or
> happens not to be done has a reasonable cause why it is done or
> not done, and so it is good that it should be done or good that it
> should not be done, *even if it is not done well by the person who
> does it, or if the person who does not do it acts evilly in not doing it—
> that is, he fails to do it from a bad intention. And so it is good that
> even evils themselves exist and are done, although evils themselves
> are by no means good.*[97]

Moreover, Abelard is careful to phrase his comments on divine
providence negatively: it is a matter, not of God's ordaining or bring-
ing about that things happen, but of his *permitting* them: 'Nothing is
done unless God permits it (nothing indeed could be done if he is
unwilling or resists it).'[98] The picture, then, is not of a God who has
a set plan which he actualizes in his creation but of one who re-
sponds to the situations produced by the exercise of human free
will, intervening where needed to ensure that the result is the best,
given that humans have made the choices they do. (This is to put it,
as Abelard usually speaks, as if God acted like an ordinary agent in
time, whereas, strictly speaking, there is one, immutable and eternal intention, based on his foreknowledge, according to which he
acts.) Even so, the claim that everything other than agents' intentions is subject to God's permission might seem to have the strange
and implausible consequence that there is a disconnection between

intentions and outcomes, so that the thwarting of intentions would be the rule rather than an exception. But Abelard's view need not have this consequence. First, God is presented as using evil intentions for good ends in a subtle way: rather than sending a thunderbolt to strike the murder weapon from the assassin's hand, he allows the murder to take place but somehow arranges a providence which is better than it would have been because this evil has happened. Second, although Abelard does not enter into such details—his discussion of this whole area is suggestive rather than full or precise— he could well have a principle that, for the overall best providence, causal laws should in general be allowed to operate normally and human intentions be realized, unless thwarted by other human intentions or natural causes. God would thus permit many circumstances that are less good than if he had thwarted certain actions and their natural consequences, because the overall benefit of giving such permissions outweighs the individual costs.

It has become common for both less and more specialized writers to treat Abelard's NAG argument as if it showed that God acts from straightforward necessity and that therefore the course of providence is entirely determined.[99] He is presented as a Stoic *redivivus*.[100] But it is far more plausible, and renders his defence of the argument coherent, to accept that Abelard wishes only to deny God alternative possibilities, and that, although he allows for the workings of providential design, it is within a framework in which humans, unlike their creator, have freedom to choose.

Part II

ABELARD'S PAST AND ABELARD'S FUTURE

INTRODUCTION TO PART II

The last two chapters examined aspects of Abelard's own present. As well as giving some of the information needed for studying his works, and considering the problems of interpreting it, they suggest a more general moral about methodology. Historians of philosophy should certainly attend to the fourth dimension (to be discussed in detail in chapters 5 and 6), the relationship between past thinkers and our own present, but they should also be careful not to neglect the first dimension, the present of the thinkers themselves. If they just hand over the task to intellectual historians, they are in danger of losing any claim to be engaged in history, and they will have to be content with whatever philosophical suggestions or stimulation texts from the past happen to give them. In that case, they will no doubt be serious and professional philosophers. But, in their attitude to history, they will be dilettantes. The history of philosophy, however, can be, and should be, a proper, professional specialism.

This chapter and the next will consider the two other dimensions, the past philosophers' own past and their future. The aspect of Abelard's future explored in chapter 4 will already be familiar: his argument, examined at length in the previous chapter, that God cannot do other than he does. As will be shown, it is one of Abelard's arguments which has a particularly long and traceable history. The choice of focus for chapter 3, on Abelard's past, requires a little more explanation.

Historians of philosophy are often wary of going too deeply into some aspects of the past of the thinkers they are studying. Their caution does not apply to every aspect of it. On the one side, they usually accept the need to identify and study direct textual connections—those passages where the writer being studied discusses a text from the past explicitly or clearly uses it though without mentioning the author. On the other side, historians of philosophy often engage in 'philosophical comparisons', looking at how certain topics are treated in different periods, looking at the similarities and differences between, for instance, the moral theories of Plato, Augustine, Abelard, Aquinas, Hume and Kant, without claiming that these authors had in each case read or known of the earlier ones' theories.

These are important aspects of the second dimension, but there is another too, a sort of 'historical comparison', which is often regarded as part of the scholarly trappings worn by intellectual historians with pride, but as something to be disdained by the historian of philosophy. This method of enquiry differs from the study of textual connections, because it looks beyond passages explicitly cited, and differs from comparing across time, because it makes an historical claim about influence. It can be used to compare any two philosophers, provided that there are grounds to believe that one of them knew at least some of the work of the other, even if only indirectly. For example, with regard to the moral philosophers listed above, as well as the philosophical comparison across time between their systems, in some cases, an historical comparison could be made—as, for example, between the ethics of Plato and Augustine. Augustine certainly knew something of Plato's ideas on ethics, though it is very unlikely that he had read, even in translation, the whole of any text actually written by him. Such historical comparison would begin from whatever textual connections were to be found, many of them indirect, but would not limit itself to considering the explicit remarks in Augustine about Plato's ethics. Rather, it would attempt to chart which parts of Platonic moral thought Augustine knew and how, and then to discern how he reacted to them, borrowing, adapting, rejecting. There would, of course, be an element of uncertainty, and sometimes the most that can be said is that Augustine was thinking in a Platonic manner, which perhaps went back, directly or indirectly, to Plato himself.

Abelard's relation to his most important sources from the more distant past offers many opportunities for the study of textual connections, since most of his logic is explicitly or implicitly a commentary on texts by Aristotle, Porphyry and Boethius, often involving an intricate relationship with Boethius's own commentaries on Aristotle and Porphyry, and as a theologian Abelard is very fond of citing directly and sometimes explicitly both philosophers such as Plato and Cicero and church fathers, especially Augustine and Jerome.[1] (One of his most remarkable productions, indeed, *Sic et non*, is a collection of explicit citations, arranged so as to show how discussion of central doctrinal issues might proceed.) Any careful reader of Abelard will find thought about these textual connections an integral part in the process of analysing his texts. And there are, of course, many pertinent philosophical comparisons across time which can be made with Abelard, though they tend to be with figures of later centuries, such as Ockham or Kant (see below), rather than with ones from his past.[2]

There is, though, just one thinker who provides an opportunity to look, in a single case, at all these three sorts of relation—textual connection, historical comparison, philosophical comparison—with Abelard. He is Anselm of Canterbury, a figure from his very near past, since, although he was born circa 1033, nearly half a century before Abelard, his last book, *De concordia*, was not finished until 1107–8, when Abelard was already establishing himself as a logic teacher.

CHAPTER THREE

ABELARD AND ANSELM

Few doubt that Anselm was the outstanding Latin philosopher of the eleventh century and the only one to rival, and very possibly excel, Abelard in both logical acuity and profundity of thought. But the connections between the two men's thought are fewer and less direct than might be expected. The following pages attempt to discern, chart and analyse them. They begin by considering the extent to which Anselm's texts were disseminated in Abelard's milieu, then study Abelard's explicit references to Anselm and then move on to two areas—divine omnipotence and necessity, and ethics and moral psychology—where it is difficult to draw the boundaries between direct but inexplicit textual connection, historical comparison and philosophical comparison.

ANSELM'S TEXTS AND IDEAS IN ABELARD'S MILIEU

There was, in the past, a tendency to consider that Anselm's influence on the earlier twelfth-century Paris schools, and on Abelard himself, was very limited. When, nearly sixty years ago, Sofia Vanni

Rovighi showed that Anselm was widely read in the twelfth century, she concentrated on Honorius Augustodunensis, the Cistercians and the Victorines. Abelard entered her account only negatively, since she explicitly denied that he was influenced by Anselm's ethics (on the mistaken grounds that for Abelard there were no universal criteria for rightness and wrongness).[1] Nowadays, however, it is generally recognized that some of Anselm's work and ideas were known in Abelard's milieux and that he might perhaps have been an important influence on Abelard himself.[2]

One reason to believe that links with Abelard are probable is the evidence that Anselm was studied by Abelard's own teachers and by other thinkers with whom he interacted. It seems that *Cur Deus homo* was particularly well known in early twelfth-century north French theological circles.[3] Abelard's first teacher, Roscelin, writing to Abelard in about 1122, refers to *Cur Deus homo*.[4] Ralph of Laon, brother of the more famous Anselm of Laon, with whom Abelard briefly and abortively studied, uses the same text, though what he borrows, approvingly, is Anselm's explanation of a view he rejects.[5] The *Sententie divine pagine*—probably from the Parisian schools in the 1130s or 1140s, at or near the time when Abelard was teaching there—refer to *Cur Deus homo* and other works of Anselm, though the author is confused about which.[6] But other works of Anselm's, besides *Cur Deus homo*, seem also to have been known. William of Champeaux, Abelard's most important teacher, shows many points of contact with Anselm, which may indicate familiarity with some of his work.[7] Hugh of St Victor, a contemporary with whom, as the previous chapter shows, Abelard had intellectual contacts, was familiar with the moral theory of Anselm's dialogues, though he understood it in his own way.[8] Probably at much the same time, the writer of a work already mentioned in connection with NAG (see above, chapter 2, p. 76), the *Ysagoge in Theologiam*, which is much influenced by Abelard, also uses Anselmian ideas.[9]

Moreover, recent research on manuscript diffusion has provided further evidence of the general availability of Anselm's writings in Abelard's time. Unfortunately, the standard edition of Anselm by Schmitt does not provide an adequate basis for studying the diffusion of his works. But Richard Sharpe has shown that Anselm was an author in demand, whose works were often copied and distributed even before he was ready with them.[10] A considerable number of copies survive from Anselm's lifetime and shortly afterwards, and the fact that most of them contain multiple works of Anselm's makes it likely that an author who certainly knew one or two of Anselm's writings would have had access to more of them.

All in all, therefore, even before an examination of the internal evidence, it seems likely that Abelard would have known something of Anselm's thought and perhaps read one or more of his texts, although it is improbable, to judge from his contemporaries, that he knew his work thoroughly and accurately.

Abelard's Citations of Anselm

There is, in any case, no doubt that Abelard knew about Anselm and some of his work, since there are three passages where Abelard names Anselm and one which contains very close parallels with one of his works. Of the three namings, one is merely a very respectful mention of Anselm as 'the magnificent doctor of the Church' (in the context of denouncing Roscelin to Bishop Gilbert of Paris for, among other things, defaming such a person).[11] Abelard also wrote to Roscelin himself at this time, but only Roscelin's reply survives. Roscelin's letter, occupied mainly by acid criticism of its recipient, also contains a sarcastically respectful attack on Anselm's views about divine necessity. The complicated relations between Anselm's position, Roscelin's attack and Abelard's own views are discussed below (see pp. 101–2).

The other place where Abelard names Anselm seems directly to engage with the discussion in one of his texts. It is in the *Theologia Christiana,* and it appears again in the final version of the *Theologia,* the *Theologia scholarium.* Abelard is discussing various attempts by others—all of which he finds unsatisfactory—to provide an analogy for the Trinity: 'There was also a writer who, very recently, seemed to preserve the unity of the substance and to draw a stronger likeness to the things we have been talking about. He was Anselm—the Metropolitan of Canterbury. . . . For this archbishop takes a spring, a stream and a pool as if they were three things of the same substance: the spring from which there is the stream is like the Father from whom is the Son, the pool which comes from the spring and the stream is like the Spirit, who proceeds from the Father and the Son.'[12] Abelard is clearly referring to a passage in *De incarnatione Verbi,* where Anselm makes this comparison, playfully calling the river 'the Nile' and concluding that 'the spring, stream and lake are therefore three, and there is one Nile, one river, one nature, one water, and it cannot be said that they are three. For there are neither three of the Nile nor of the river nor of the water nor of the nature, nor three springs or streams or lakes. Therefore one is here said of three and three of one, but not the three things of each other.'[13] Abelard goes on to report that 'he also takes the stream being in a pipe as like the Son in human nature, as if we were to call the incarnate Word the enpiped stream', summarizing a point Anselm goes on to make.[14] Abelard then explains why these analogies are misleading:

One and the same substance is not that of the spring and of the stream and of the pool, but the same water at succeeding times is made first the spring and then the stream and finally the pool. And so it is no wonder if at succeeding times the same substance of water should present itself in different ways, although the substance of the spring and the stream and the pool is never numerically the same, in such a way that it could truly be said: 'Now the water of the spring is the water of the stream or of the pool'—in the way that we always say that the substance of the Father is the substance of the Son and the Holy Spirit. Rather, perhaps this likeness might especially support the heresy which mixes together the properties of the persons depending on the times, so that it says that the same person is the Father when he wishes, and when he wishes the Son or the Holy Spirit.[15]

Scholars are not agreed on how to judge Abelard's tone and intention. Michael Clanchy, who has written a vividly illuminating bi-

ography of Abelard, believes that the passage shows Abelard's love
of mockery and also his unbalanced, even insane state of mind in
the period after he had been condemned at Soissons.[16] According
to Clanchy, Abelard began by teasing his audience, making them
expect that he was about to denounce the stupidity of Anselm *of
Laon*—a respected figure whom he was known to despise—then as-
tonishing them by announcing that the even more eminent Anselm
of Canterbury was his target, and then ridiculing the language of
Anselm's analogy and suggesting its association with drains and
sewage. Other Abelard specialists have disagreed.[17] No one, though,
has pointed out the strangest thing about Abelard's criticism. Read
on its own, Abelard's critique sounds philosophically convincing.
The point of the analogy is to convey how God is one substance but
three Persons. The choice of the spring, the stream and the pool
is inappropriate, Abelard contends, because 'the substance of the
spring and the stream and the pool' is not numerically the same.
One bit of water (*eadem aqua*) is successively the spring, then the
stream, then the pool. But Anselm has anticipated such an objection, according to which the analogy breaks the Trinity into parts:

> If he objects that neither the spring nor the stream nor the lake
> on its own, nor any two of them, are the complete Nile, but parts
> of the Nile: let him conceive that this whole Nile, from when it
> began until when it ends, exists for as it were the whole of its
> span, because this whole is not simultaneous in space or in
> time, but through its parts, nor will it be complete until it ceases
> to be. For it has in this way a certain likeness to speech, which,
> while it is coming as it were from the spring of the mouth, is not
> complete, and when it is complete no longer exists.[18]

Although Anselm's idea is not completely clear, he is certainly
not trying to say that the parts of the Nile are one in substance (or
analogous to something one in substance) because the same bit of
water makes each of them up successively. Rather, he is suggesting
that, because of the way it constantly changes as the water flows
through it, the Nile never really exists as a whole. The reader is asked

to perform a thought experiment —Anselm is the great medieval philosopher of thought experiments—and, suspending time, to conceive the Nile as one. Since, according to Boethius's commentary on Aristotle, there is really no arrangement of parts in the river (and certainly not if, by freezing time, the flow of water is stopped), Anselm can reasonably contend that the Nile is just one indivisible block of water, and so one as a substance, though it takes the form of a spring, a stream and a lake.

Abelard's criticism is, therefore, very wide of the mark, and yet the verbal similarities suggest he must have known this text. The most charitable explanation is that he may not have had to hand the whole passage. Perhaps, though, Abelard was unscrupulous and hoped that few readers would recall and understand what Anselm had really said.

ANSELM AND ABELARD ON DIVINE OMNIPOTENCE AND NECESSITY

Abelard—so the last chapter explained—developed at length an unusual view about God's power. He accepted, of course, that God is omnipotent, but he argued that, as completely wise and good, God never has any alternative choices, since he cannot but act in the best way at every juncture. Anselm had already thought about some of the same issues. With regard to the definition of omnipotence, there may be reason to think, as Matthias Perkams has suggested, that Abelard's discussion in the *Theologia Christiana* (and the *Theologia scholarium*) is textually connected.[19] In the *Proslogion,* chapter 7, Anselm raises the question of how God can be considered omnipotent, when he cannot do all things: he cannot, for example, lie, nor can he make what is true false. Anselm answers by saying that these are cases, not of power (*potentia*), but of lack of power (*impotentia*). He goes on to explain that it is a feature of ordinary language sometimes to use a positive expression, as here, where a negative one would be more accurate: when someone says that something is not the case, we say, 'It is as you say', when strictly, we should reply: 'It is not as you say it is not.'

Abelard's way of posing the problem is similar in its wording to Anselm's. Anselm (speaking directly to God) writes: 'Sed omnipotens quomodo es, si omnia non potes?', whilst Abelard has: 'Quaerendum itaque primo uidetur quomodo uere dicatur omnipotens, si non possit omnia efficere.'[20] Abelard goes on, like Anselm, to say that, in the cases where God cannot do something, what he is without is not power (*potentia*) but a lack of power (*impotentia*—Anselm's word) or *debilitas*. Anselm says of the things that God cannot do that 'whoever can do these things can do what does not serve him well and what he should not do.'[21] Abelard enunciates a more general principle, along similar (but, as will emerge, not entirely similar) lines: 'According to the philosophers themselves and to normal usage in speech, only what pertains to the well-being [*commodum*] or worthiness [*dignitas*] of a thing is considered to be its power [*potentia*].'[22]

There are, however, some striking differences between the two discussions. Anselm is concerned exclusively with God's inability to do things which are, in themselves, wrong. Abelard, by contrast, asks how it is that an omnipotent being cannot act in various ways that are normal for corporeal things—walk, talk, speak and sense. He does, later, mention (but only in passing) the point that God cannot lie.[23] In order to answer the question he has posed, he needs to add to his argument an element not found in Anselm: the idea that potency should be understood relative to the sort of thing concerned—as the principle cited above illustrates. God does not lack power because, for example, he cannot walk, because, whereas humans need to be able to walk, God, who brings about all things simply by willing, has no need to do so.[24] Abelard even goes on to suggest that, in one sense, God might be said to be able to do all that humans do, since he uses them as his tools.[25] Moreover, in his discussion Abelard refers explicitly to Aristotle's *Categories* for the notion of impotency as the opposite of potency,[26] and so it may well be that his own thoughts, based partly (no doubt like Anselm's) on

Aristotle led him to these views on divine omnipotence, without his having read the *Proslogion*.[27]

Anselm's most important discussion of God and necessity (as opposed to the necessity of God's existence) is found, however, in another of his works, *Cur Deus homo,* where he tries to show that there are *necessary* reasons why the Incarnation and the Crucifixion had to take place. These reasons rest on a satisfaction theory of the Incarnation: only the sacrifice of a man who was also God could repay what was due to God because of Adam's sin and so allow God's plans in creating humans to be fulfilled. In this case, there are good grounds to think that Abelard knew at least some of the positions Anselm takes in the work, if not the text itself. In his *Commentary on Romans*, Abelard includes a long passage in which he explains how the incarnation and crucifixion of Christ brought about human salvation.[28] There are some fairly close verbal parallels here with *Cur Deus homo,* and, more important, Abelard is in full agreement with Anselm in his rejection of the view which had been dominant, according to which the devil had rights over mankind, though he does not mention Anselm's name.[29] Then, before presenting his own theory, he writes:

> If, then, Adam's sin was so great that it could not be expiated except through the death of Christ, what power of expiation will the act of murder committed against Christ have? So many and such crimes committed against him and his followers? Did the death of his innocent son so please God the Father that through it he is reconciled to us—who, by sinning, committed the fault on account of which the innocent Lord has been killed? Only because this would be the greatest of sins, and so he could have forgiven the other one much more easily! Only were he not able to do such good until evils had been multiplied! . . . Indeed, how cruel and evil it seems, that someone should require the blood of an innocent as a price, or that in any way it should please him for an innocent to be killed; still less that God should have so welcomed the death of his son that through it he was reconciled to the whole world.[30]

This passage seems, at first sight, to be a sarcastic attack on Anselm's satisfaction theory of the Redemption, and so it has tradition-
ally been held to be. If so, it is not a fair attack, because it does not
state Anselm's views clearly and fully before attacking them. But, as
the last example shows, Abelard may have been an opportunistic
rather than a fair opponent. In recent decades scholars have abandoned the traditional view that Anselm is targeted here. Rolf Peppermüller considers that Abelard may not have known, or at least
not directly, *Cur Deus homo,* and so may not have intended these remarks against the satisfaction theory.[31] David Luscombe, by contrast,
believes that there are parallels which show that Abelard must have
known *Cur Deus homo,* but he rejects the view that he is attacking it:
'He seems more concerned to heighten his readers' curiosity and to
prepare them for his own presentation of the redemption in the
solutio which follows immediately.'[32] Given such disagreements,
sorting out exactly what relation Abelard's rather rhetorical discussion at this point bears to Anselm's may turn out to be impossible,
but it is hard to deny that he had some knowledge of the contents of
Cur Deus homo.

What, then, did Abelard think about Anselm's claim to have
given *necessary* reasons for the Incarnation? As well as the likeli-
hood, just argued, of more or less direct knowledge about the claim
from *Cur Deus homo,* in a letter written to Abelard himself, Roscelin
names *Cur Deus homo* and summarizes just this aspect of Anselm's
approach ('God could not save men except as he did, that is unless
he became a man and suffered all that he suffered'), then cites Leo
the Great and, especially, Augustine to show that this view is unacceptable.[33] Abelard himself may already have raised the issue in
the letter to which Roscelin is replying.[34] He certainly complained
strongly about Roscelin's critical attitude towards Anselm (in his
letter to Bishop Gilbert; see above, p. 95). The most obvious conclusion would be that Abelard accepted Anselm's view that God could
not save man except as he did. Indeed, a few years after this exchange with Roscelin, Abelard formulated in the *Theologia Christiana* the view, studied in the last chapter, that God in general cannot
do other than he does, which would entail that, in the particular case

of the Incarnation, God had no alternative possibilities. This is David Luscombe's position. Abelard, he considers, not only had the same view as Anselm on this question but—in the absence of any evidence to the contrary—should be presumed to have learnt it from him: 'When we take into account the strikingly unusual character of their common viewpoint . . . we must conclude that an onus of proof lies on those who disbelieve that Abelard was powerfully persuaded either by Anselm or at least by reports of a teaching that was so singular that only a very badly informed master could have been unaware of the identity of its foremost exponent.'[35]

Others, though, have seen the matter differently. Richard Weingart had previously argued that Abelard believed that God *could* have redeemed humanity in some other way.[36] This judgement seems, in part, to be based on a misunderstanding of Abelard's dialectical way of presenting his argument in the *Theologia Christiana*,[37] but Weingart also notices another passage in that work which might indicate that Abelard would be likely to oppose Anselm's views. In the *Theologia Christiana* (and, copied from there, the *Theologia scholarium*), Abelard, in Weingart's words, 'disclaims any interest in necessary reasons, avowing a preference for "worthy" reasons': 'We rely on worthy reasons [*honestae rationes*] rather than necessary [*necessariae*] ones, because among good people always what is more commended for its worthiness is put in the first place, and the reason is always stronger which tends to worthiness rather than to necessity.'[38] Abelard, Weingart therefore surmises, would have had 'a bias against [Anselm's] intent of demonstrating the necessity of Christ's death.'[39] Over thirty years later, without apparently knowing Weingart's work, Matthias Perkams drew attention to the same passage in Abelard and its implications for his relationship with Anselm. In Perkams's opinion, although Abelard does not cite Anselm here by name, 'it is very probable that here Abelard has [Anselm's] method in mind.'[40] Abelard is thus, Perkams says, taking up a position opposed to Anselm's, though the distinction relates to differing ways of going about theology.

In face of these different views, a first step is to establish what in fact were Anselm's views about the necessity of God's actions (including the Incarnation), and the extent to which Abelard's were the same: to make a philosophical comparison, so as to clear the ground for an historical one. Anselm, it has already been said, claims to provide necessary reasons for the Incarnation, and he also makes the claim that humans must necessarily have been saved by Christ.[41] Yet it seems clear that he does not think that this event was absolutely necessary, in the sense that it could not possibly have happened otherwise, since it is one of his fundamental beliefs that Adam had the alternative not to sin, in which case humanity would not have needed to be saved by Christ. More generally, Anselm holds that rational beings were created with the freedom to choose between alternative possible actions, and it is to show how this freedom of choice comes about that he posits the existence of two wills in each, one to the beneficial (*commodum*), one to rightness (*rectitudo*).[42] Since, however, Anselm bases his conclusion about the necessity of the Incarnation on general principles for thinking about divine action, it might be argued that God himself never has alternative possibilities but that his creatures do. Katherin Rogers has proposed an interpretation on these lines, coming to the conclusion that God 'brings about the best "actualizable" world, that is, the best world He can, taking into account created choices.'[43] This view would be remarkably similar to Abelard's, according to the interpretation argued in the previous chapter. But the view does not in fact accord with Anselm's own comments. Whereas Abelard was willing to accept that God acts by necessity, in the sense that he cannot do other than he does, but with the proviso that this necessity does not involve his being compelled in any way, Anselm reasons that, because necessity involves either compulsion or prohibition, it cannot be applied to God at all. He even goes so far as to say that 'nothing is necessary or impossible except because he wishes it so.'[44] Moreover, as Brian Leftow has pointed out, there is nothing in Anselm's argument to exclude God's having chosen to create a universe which was inhabited by different sorts of creatures than Adam and his descendants.[45]

A careful look, however, at the principle on which he argues that God cannot have become incarnate shows that Anselm's position is even further from Abelard's than these points suggest. Anselm draws out this principle—which is needed because his argument is directed against those who will believe only what is rationally demonstrated—from an argument about the nature of God. 'No unfittingness in God,' he says, 'even the slightest, should be accepted by us, and no reason, even the slightest, should be rejected. For, *just as in God an impossibility follows from any unfittingness, however small, so necessity accompanies any reason, however small, so long as it is not defeated by a greater one.'*[46] What claims does Anselm make here about God and necessity? The first is that, necessarily, God does not do anything which is unfitting, even slightly. The second is that where there is one reason, or a reason stronger than any other reasons, for God to act in a certain way, it is necessary that he act in this way. At first sight, these claims seem rather like those which Abelard would make about God's always acting according to reason and always doing what is best. They do, indeed, derive from the same underlying thought, that God is entirely good as a necessary part of his nature. Yet these two claims do not show (and are not intended to show) that God has no alternative possible choices. Rather, they assert that there are certain choices which, necessarily, God cannot make: choices which are unfitting (God necessarily chooses in accord with rightness) and choices which go against the strongest reason for action (it is impossible for God to be weak-willed). Anselm does not propose the strong principle of sufficient reason adopted by Abelard, which rules out the possibility of cases where God can choose between alternatives, because each is equally good. There may, for Anselm, be more than one action open to God which is fitting and the reasons for which neither trump nor are trumped by the alternatives. His claim, however, about the Incarnation is that— as he establishes by the end of the first book of *Cur Deus homo*—any explanation other than the Christian one entails that God acts unfittingly, and that, as the second book goes on to show, a series of reasons explain the details of the Christian story of redemption; because these reasons are not defeated by other reasons, they have the force of necessity. Roscelin was not, therefore, unfair to Anselm in

his letter to Abelard, when he quoted against him Augustine's statement that God could have redeemed us in some other way. Anselm
would not be able to accept this view, since he considers that any
way of redeeming mankind other than by the Incarnation would
have been unfitting and so impossible for God.

Abelard seems to have remembered Roscelin's Augustinian
quotations against Anselm, because he cites three which he took
from *De trinitate* in the *Theologia Christiana*.[47] Here they are arguments for the position—that God can do otherwise than he does—
which Abelard wishes to reject. Yet, when in the *Sententiae* he discusses explicitly whether God could have redeemed humanity other
than he did, he replies: 'He could indeed have done this [the Re-
demption] in many ways, but none of them would have been so fitting.' This comment is an accurate summary of the central point
made by Augustine in one of these *De trinitate* passages which Roscelin had quoted against Anselm and which Abelard cites in the
Theologia Christiana: 'God, under whose power all things equally lie,
did not lack some other possible way <to liberate us>. But there
was no more fitting way of healing our wretched state.'[48] How can a
thinker who believes that God cannot do otherwise than he does
say that God could have redeemed humanity in many ways other
than through the Incarnation? Abelard himself immediately explains it: 'But, I think, what this possibility refers to has been sufficiently determined above. Whereas it suffices for us to do something well, for him who is supremely good it is not befitting or
appropriate that he does anything except in the way in which it can
best happen. But this redemption could not have been brought
about in any better way than—or even so good a way as—if the Son
of God became man.'[49] The passage to which he refers about the
type of possibility involved is the following, from a little earlier
where he was talking about whether God could have made Peter
juster than he was: 'The authorities I have cited should be understood in such a way that the possibility refers to the things, not to
God; just as, when we say, "The chimaera is thinkable [*opinabile*]",
this is linked back not to the chimaera but to the people who are

thinking <about it>, so that "The chimaera is thinkable" means
"People can think about the chimaera". Similarly, God, who raised
up Lazarus in body, could have raised up Judas in mind: this "could"
refers to that man's nature, not to God himself. The others too
should be expounded in the same way.'[50] In the *Sententiae Parisienses,* the parallel passage to this one (which is clearly very abbreviated in the *Sententiae,* since the authorities discussed are not in
fact cited there) makes an explicit reference to Augustine's comment that another mode of redemption was possible for God and
says that 'possible' must here be understood in this special way.[51]

Abelard, then, is able to accept, as Anselm could not, the Augustinian view that God could have redeemed humanity in many different ways, by making a move similar to that which allowed him to
answer the *damnandus* objection to his view that God cannot do
otherwise than he does (see above, chapter 2, pp. 53–56, 66–73). But
he has to add one more piece to his argument. In the case of the
damnandus, he needs to show that, although God (who cannot do
otherwise than he does) cannot save the *damnandus,* the *damnandus*
can be saved by God. But here he has to show, even more paradoxi-
cally, that God, who cannot choose other than what is most fitting,
could choose what was not most fitting (another manner of redemption). He therefore adds the idea that sometimes words which seem,
on the surface, to attribute possibility to the referent of the word of
which they are predicated really attribute it to something else. When
we say that a chimera is thinkable, we are attributing the power to
think, not to the chimera, which does not exist, but to the people
who think about it. Similarly, in the case of the possibility predicated
of God with regard to redeeming humans in another way, it must be
taken to apply, not to God, but to humans. Once this extra piece is
added to the argument, it becomes exactly parallel to the reasoning
used in the case of the *damnandus.* In that case, it seemed initially
plausible to understand the possibility as merely notional, so too
here it might seem as if Abelard's agreement with Augustine were
merely verbal, since humans, although potentially redeemable in
many ways, could be redeemed only in the one, most fitting way in

which God could not but redeem them. But that interpretation of Abelard was rejected (see above) in favour of one which gave a genuine role to human freedom, and a similar interpretation is preferable here too. Abelard's view, most plausibly, is that humans might, through their freely chosen acts, have done differently from how they in fact did, in such a way that it would have been most fitting for God to choose another way of redeeming them, and so he would have chosen it.

The upshot of this philosophical comparison between Anselm's and Abelard's views on the necessity of the Incarnation is that, although Abelard in general allowed less freedom of action to God than Anselm did, his way of conceiving possibility in terms of potentiality gave him a genuine, and not purely verbal, way of accepting the Augustinian view, against Anselm, that, in some sense, God could have redeemed humans in a different way. What this implies about the actual, historical influence of *Cur Deus homo* on Abelard it is hard to say. It is probable that he knew the work, or at least its main theses, and perhaps this knowledge emboldened him to develop his extreme view about God's lack of alternative choices, although Anselm did not share it (nor, presumably, did Abelard think he did, since he described his own position as one which had 'few or no supporters').[52] At the same time, Abelard believed that his understanding of possibility enabled his own position, though more extreme, to be reconciled with patristic authority, in a way that Anselm's could not be. It would be wrong, then, to see him as counterattacking Roscelin by reasserting Anselm's view; he seems to believe, rather, that he has improved on it. With regard to the supposed attack in *Theologia Christiana* on the Anselmian method of necessary reasons, it is hard to make a connection with *Cur Deus homo,* despite the explicit use of the term *rationes necessariae,* because the topic under discussion is different. Abelard is saying that it is better to use fitting rather than necessary reasons to show the unity of God. If the comments are aimed against Anselm, then Abelard is attacking rather the method of the *Monologion,* where Anselm does try to develop rational proofs from first principles of God's unity as well as his triunity; but he would be using the methodological language of *Cur Deus homo* to do so. But where an apparent attack is so oblique, there must be doubt whether any was intended.

ANSELM'S *ETHICS* AND ABELARD

Abelard has long been recognized as a moralist, author of at least one treatise dedicated to the subject and often called his *Ethics*.[53] But the credit for being the first ethical philosopher of the Middle Ages would now usually be attributed to Anselm. Although the works in which Anselm discusses moral psychology and ethics—principally the three dialogues, *De veritate, De libertate arbitrii* and *De casu diaboli,* and his final work, *De concordia*—are more closely and obviously linked to biblical problems than Abelard's *Scito teipsum* (*Ethics*) or *Collationes,* recent studies have shown how he develops in them a reasoned and subtle view of moral action, freedom, good and evil.[54] Did Abelard look back to Anselm's moral philosophy, borrowing from it or reacting to it? The question seems to be a particularly pertinent one, since there are some important similarities between their approaches to the subject which have led each of them to be seen as medieval forerunners of Kant. Yet it turns out to be far from easy to find any clear lines of influence.

The most plausible case for borrowing comes, not from one of Anselm's more obviously ethical works, but from his *Monologion.* In his *Collationes,* Abelard proposes two sets of definitions. Into the mouth of his philosopher—a pagan who follows natural law— he puts a classification of the virtues which is taken mainly from Cicero, and which is accepted by his interlocutor, the Christian. The Christian then undertakes the task which the Philosopher could not undertake of defining the meaning of 'good' and 'evil'. Abelard seems to have had in mind that, whilst there was no attempt to define 'good' in the pagan philosophical texts, his Christian near contemporary Anselm had offered a definition, since, as the comparison in table 1 makes clear, there are a number of verbal parallels with the passage where he does so in the *Monologion.*

Table 1.

Per aliud enim videtur dici bonus equus quia fortis est, et per aliud bonus equus quia velox est. Cum enim dici videatur bonus per fortitudinem et bonus per velocitatem, non tamen idem videtur esse fortitudo et velocitas. Verum si equus, quia est fortis aut velox, idcirco bonus est: quomodo fortis et uelox latro malus est? Potius igitur, quemadmodum fortis et velox latro ideo malus est quia noxius est, ita fortis et uelox equus idcirco bonus est quia utilis est. Et quidem nihil solet putari bonum nisi aut propter aliquam utilitatem, ut bona dicitur salus et quae saluti prosunt, aut propter quamlibet honestatem, sicut pulchritudo aestimatur bona et quae pulchritudinem iuvant.[a]

CHRISTIANUS: Quantum estimo, difficile diffiniri ea censuerunt quorum nomina uix umquam in una significatione consistere uiderint. Quippe cum dicitur bonus homo uel bonus faber aut bonus equus et similia, quis nesciat hoc nomen 'bonus' ex adiunctis diuersum mutuare sensum? Hominem nempe bonum ex moribus dicimus, fabrum ex scientia, equum ex uiribus et uelocitate uel que ad usum eius pertinent. Adeo autem ex adiunctis boni significatio uariatur, ut etiam cum nominibus uitiorum ipsum iungere non uereamur, dicentes scilicet bonum uel optimum furem eo quod in hac malitia peragenda sit callidus uel astutus. . . .

Quantum tamen michi nunc occurrit, bonum simpliciter, idest bonam rem dici arbitror, que cum alicui usui sit apta, nullius rei commodum uel dignitatem per eam impediri necesse est. E contrario malum idest malam rem uocari credo, per quam alterum horum impediri necesse est. Indifferens uero, id est rem, quae neque bona est neque mala, illam arbitror per cuius existentiam nec illa conferri neque impediri necesse est, sicut est fortuita motio digiti uel quecunque actiones huiusmodi.[c]

For a horse seems to be called 'good' through one thing because it is strong, and called 'good' through another thing because it is swift. For although it seems to

So far as I can judge, they considered it difficult to define things the names of which, they saw, hardly ever comprise a single meaning. Indeed, when a person be good through strength and good through swiftness, yet strength and swiftness do not seem to be the same thing. But if a horse, because it is strong or swift, is good for that reason, how is a strong and swift thief evil? Rather, therefore, just as the strong and swift thief is evil because he is harmful, so the strong and swift horse is good, because it is useful. And indeed nothing is usually though good except on account of some utility, as health and that which favours health is said to be good, or on account of some intrinsic worth, as beauty and what helps beauty are considered good.[b]

is said to be 'good', or a craftsman to be 'good' or a horse to be 'good' and so on, then, as everyone knows, the word 'good' changes its sense according to the words attached to it. Without doubt, we say that a person is good because of his behaviour, a craftsman from knowledge, a horse from its strength, speed and what makes it useful. The meaning of 'good' varies so much according to the words attached to it that we are not afraid to join it to words for vicious things—as when we say that a thief is 'good' or 'the best', in that he is skilled or crafty at carrying out this wickedness. . . .

But, as it strikes me now, I consider that something is said to be 'good' unqualifedly—that is, 'a good thing'—which is fitted for some use, and there is no thing, the dignity or convenience of which is necessarily obstructed by it. By contrast, I believe that something is said to be 'evil' unqualifiedly—that is, 'an evil thing'— through which either of them is necessarily impeded. I consider something to be indifferent—that is, to be a thing which is neither good nor evil—through the existence of which it is not necessary that these are either brought about or impeded, like the chance movement of a finger or any sort of action like this.[d]

Notes:
a. Anselm, *Monologion* 1; Anselm 1946a, page 14, lines 19–28.
b. The translation is my own.
c. Abelard, *Coll.*, secs. 201, 203–4.
d. The translation is my own, as given in *Coll.*, ed Marenbon and Orlandi.

Not only are there verbal parallels here which make a textual connection plausible. Abelard also seems to have grasped Anselm's line of thought and followed it, but changing and sharpening it. Anselm is posing himself the question of what the word 'good' means. A simple way of answering would be to say that it means whatever are the qualities on account of which we call something 'good'. But in that case, he points out, 'good', even used of the same object, seems to have more than one meaning, since a horse is good both because it is strong and because it is swift. Moreover, if 'good' means strong and swift, then whatever is strong and swift is good; but a thief who is strong and swift is not good. Anselm then gives a better answer. To call something 'good' means that it has value either as a means to some end (*utilitas*) or as an end in itself (*honestas*).

When Abelard's Christian defines 'good', two of his ideas and examples are the same as Anselm's: that in the case of a horse goodness is a matter of its strength and speed, because they make it useful; and that a thief who thieves well is evil. He makes a subtler point about this, though, than Anselm. Abelard is willing to allow the meaning of 'good' to be varied by the words it is used to qualify (an idea he found in Aristotle), and so the Christian can say—in accord with normal usage—that a good thief is a thief who is good at thieving: 'good thief' has the sense 'good *qua* thief'. Abelard also introduces the idea that 'good' has an absolute sense, and it is this which the Christian proceeds to define, in a way that seems to draw on Anselm's definition of 'good' in terms of good as a means or an end, but to refine it. A good thing has to be fitted to some use—that is to say, be a means to something, and it must not necessarily impede the intrinsic worth of anything or its well-being (*commodum*). *Commodum* is not a word Anselm uses in the parallel passage of the *Monologion,* but it became a central term in the three ethical dialogues he went on to write, and Abelard might have been thinking of Anselm when, already in the *Theologia Christiana,* he used the word whilst considering what features count as a power (*potentia*) of a thing.[55] In this passage, then, Abelard is not, in the end, thinking like Anselm. But it makes very good sense to see the passage as taking its start from Anselm, especially since Anselm was probably the only Christian moralist he knew who had already tried to define 'good'.

There are other aspects of Abelard's ethical theory, however, where, although there is no obvious textual connection with Anselm, he seems to be following a very similar pattern of thinking to his predecessor's, although he puts it in his own terms. Are these cases of influence or merely of congruence between the two thinkers? Consider these two cases, which concern two central ethical issues, intention and reluctant action.

Abelard held that intentions, rather than acts or their consequences, are the proper object of moral evaluation.[56] He took this view to the extreme, by insisting that, in themselves, acts are indifferent. As he put it in the Collationes: 'Actions are judged good or evil only according to the root of the intention, but they are all in themselves indifferent'.[57] Anselm is also recognized as an intentionalist, but he is usually supposed to have been less extreme than Abelard, because he held that certain sorts of action are always bad.[58] Yet, in his discussion in De conceptu virginali, Anselm's view turns out, even in this respect, to be near to Abelard's. He states explicitly that no action is unjust in itself, but only because it is done with an unjust will.[59] This, he says, is clear in the cases of actions, which can include even murder (he gives the example of Phinees, grandson of Aaron, who showed his zeal by stabbing in a single blow both a fellow Israelite who was consorting with a prostitute and the prostitute herself), which can sometimes take place justly. But there are, he considers, some actions 'which can never take place except unjustly, such as perjury and some others which should not be named.' In these cases, it is not so easy to see why they are not unjust in themselves, but he goes on to explain why. Neither the action, nor indeed its effect, can be identified as the sin, since if the sin is identified with the action, it will disappear once the action has passed, and if it is the effect, then the sin will last as long as the effect, which need not be the case.[60] Ian Wilks has pointed to this passage as a place where Anselm shows himself willing 'to blunt the edge of his position', whereas Abelard 'shows no hesitancy in taking it to its logical extreme.'[61] But it is hard to see how Anselm's position is really less extreme than Abelard's. Anselm, indeed, provides a metaphysical argument to show that actions *cannot* be identified with sins (and so are not what are evaluated morally). The view that there are some actions which cannot be performed except with an unjust will does not conflict with Abelard's position that actions in themselves are indifferent.

This way of identifying what is to be judged morally is, then, very near to Abelard's, and the closeness between the two thinkers is even more marked with regard to how they treat reluctant action. For philosophers like Anselm and Abelard, who hold that moral badness is a matter of having a bad intention, there is a problem about cases where someone performs what would normally be considered a bad act but plausibly claims that it was performed unwillingly. Since there was no bad intention, because the agent did not want to perform the act, and acts themselves are not the object of moral evaluation, it seems that no blame can attach to the person concerned. Most would agree that, indeed, an agent who has been coerced to act is not blameworthy. But unwilling actions are often uncoerced, and it does not seem then that the agent should escape moral responsibility—where, for instance, as in Anselm's example, a man lies in order not to be killed.[62] He does not will to lie, in the sense that he would far prefer not to be in a position where he needs to lie to save his life, yet many moralists, Anselm included, would hold that he is blameworthy. But how can an intentionalist do so?

Anselm's strategy is to deny that such actions are performed unwillingly. He insists that whenever we choose a course of action, we do so willingly: we will to will.[63] He accepts three ways in which one might *say* that the man who lies so as not to be killed wills to lie unwillingly. First, one can distinguish willing for something else and for itself. In this case, the person wills to lie, not for itself, but only for something else—to save his life. Second, one could say that the man does not will that he is in the position that either he lies or he is killed. Or, third, when there is something which we can avoid doing only with great difficulty, we say that we do it of necessity and unwillingly. In all three cases, Anselm believes that we do in fact will to perform the act we perform reluctantly.[64]

Abelard (whose treatment of this theme is far better known) gives the dramatic story of someone who is being pursued by his lord and kills him in order not to be killed himself.[65] He considers that, despite the circumstances, the man is guilty and that the correct moral choice would have been to let himself be killed rather than to kill someone else. On the face of it, his solution to the problem of explaining this blameworthiness is the opposite of Anselm's. Unlike Anselm, Abelard accepts that the reluctant agent does not will to perform his act—he considers it absurd to suggest that the fugitive wills to kill his lord, when it is the very last thing he wants to do. But he introduces another concept, that of consent. I consent to an action if I do it (or am ready to do it unless thwarted), even if I do it unwillingly. The fugitive consents to kill his lord. Or, when I arrange for my son to be substituted for myself as a prisoner, so that I can raise funds for my ransom, I consent to his imprisonment but I certainly do not will it.[66] Abelard also insists that it is by our consent or our withholding of consent that we are judged by God.[67] Although verbally the position seems quite far from Anselm's, in effect they are close: for Anselm there is a will, though not for itself, and that is sufficient for the person to be judged by it; for Abelard there is not a will, but consent (which is just like Anselm's will for something else).

These are, then, parallels in thought between Anselm and Abelard. But there is no textual connection, and the case for making an historical as opposed to a purely philosophical comparison is weak. It is possible, certainly, that Abelard had read some or all of *De conceptu virginali* and *De libertate arbitrii* or knew of some of their positions indirectly, but the solid evidence of his knowledge of Anselm suggests that he was acquainted with doctrines and passages here and there, not that he was thoroughly steeped in Anselmian teaching. Where there is no verbal similarity and Abelard arrives at views similar, but not identical, to Anselm's, the most probably explanation is that he reached them without Anselm's help and that the resemblance is not a result of influence, though it is not exactly coincidental either, but the result of two brilliant thinkers working with similar sources (Augustine especially), in not dissimilar intellectual milieus.[68]

The same point should be made, but even more emphatically, with regard to the broader and deeper comparison of Anselm and Abelard as supposed precursors of Kantian ethics. As formulated in the three dialogues, Anselm's ethics centres on the notion of justice, which is defined as 'rightness of the will kept for its own sake' (*rectitudo voluntatis propter se servata*).[69] Many recent interpreters have developed at length the parallel between this idea and Kant's doctrine that the will alone is what can be judged as morally good, if and only if it wills in accord with duty, rather than inclination.[70] Abelard's ethics too has been seen as Kantian. A mainly German tradition of scholarship has seen as the point of similarity the way in which both thinkers make the will to act in the right way (according to God's commands for Abelard, according to duty for Kant) the basis for moral evaluation.[71] Independently, a leading anglophone specialist has identified the two approaches as similar because 'Abelard and Kant locate moral worth in features of the way the agent conceptualizes her performances, and each thinks that goodness is characterizable in terms of the form such conceptualization takes.'[72] Do these apparent shared anticipations of Kant mean that Abelard owed the underlying direction of his moral thought to Anselm? In his recent discussion, Ian Wilks has identified Anselm and Abelard as marking two stages, on a road from Augustine to Ockham, in the development of an intentionalist moral theory, 'revisited' centuries later by Kant. But wisely he refrains from positing any actual historical influence in this direction from Anselm to Abelard. The one writer explicitly to put the similarity between the moral philosophy of Anselm and Abelard in terms of their having both anticipated 'the fundamental thoughts of Kantian Ethics', Stephan Ernst, goes on to argue that each thinker arrives at his proto-Kantian insights from a different direction.[73] As a philosophical comparison, of course, juxtaposing the two medieval thinkers with each other, and both of them with Kant, can be illuminating just because it brings out the specificities of each theory. There is no scope, however, for an historical comparison of Anselm and Abelard with regard to the bases of their moral theories.

There is no easy and certain conclusion to be reached about the historical relations between Anselm and Abelard. On the one side, there is the solid ground of explicit citations and the rather less firm area of other possible textual connections. On the other, there is the open space for philosophical comparison, which throws each of these thinkers' arguments into a sharper focus but does not establish anything certain about actual influence. The marshy area between threatens to swallow the historian foolish enough to venture into it. The best conjecture may be that, although Abelard almost certainly knew more about Anselm's thought than twentieth-century historians imagined, he was content to take an idea from him here and there, and to score a point against him when he thought he could, without ever especially trying to gain an accurate and full knowledge of this great, near contemporary's ideas.

CHAPTER FOUR

AN UNPOPULAR ARGUMENT (II)
From the Lombard to Leibniz

In chapter 2, the genesis of Abelard's argument about God's in-ability to do other than he does (NAG) and the reactions to it during or just after his lifetime were examined. Although it has different versions and comprises different arguments, the central reasoning, as put forward in *Theologia scholarium,* is as follows:

1. God does *x* at *t*. [premise]
2. God cannot do anything at any time which is not good to do at that time. [premise: supposedly Christian doctrine]
3. If it is good for *x* to be done at *t*, it is not good that *x* be desisted from being done at *t*. [premise]
4. It is good that *x* be done at *t*. [1, 2]
5. It is not good that *x* be desisted from being done at *t*. [3, 4]
6. God cannot desist from doing *x* at *t*. [2, 5]
7. God cannot do other than *x* at *t*. [1, 6][1]

Since the same reasoning applies to all that God does, the argument shows that 'God can only do or desist from things just in the way and at the time that he does, and not otherwise or at another time.' This claim figures in the list of heresies attached to Bernard of Clairvaux's letter denouncing Abelard.[2] We know from a passage quoted by Thomas of Morigny that Abelard defended this position in his (mostly lost) *Apologia,* though not how he did so.[3] In the *Confessio fidei 'Universis'* Abelard says, however: 'I believe that God can do only those things which it befits him to do, and that he could do many things which he does not do.'[4] This seems, at first sight, to be a denial of the position which he upholds everywhere else, and as such to fit the contrite mood of this statement of faith, which might even—so its editor has speculated—be 'a document demanded, or required by convention, from Abelard in the course of the proceedings of an inquisition against heresy.'[5] Yet Abelard still asserts here his fundamental view that God can do only what it befits him to do, and he could, without rejecting his usual position, agree to the formula that God 'could do many things which he does not do', since it merely rules out the position that God's acts are strictly necessary, which Abelard never held, not his view that God has no alternative possibilities.[6] Admittedly, he usually puts this second position by saying that God cannot do more than he does or cannot do what he does not do—almost exactly what, verbally, he denies in the *Confessio.* But it is tempting to think that Abelard exploited the ambiguity of the expressions so as to satisfy his inquisitors without compromising his own beliefs.

It might be expected that such a controversial view would have had no future in theological discussions, especially since it had been condemned. In fact, as it would turn out, this view was discussed by medieval theologians perhaps more than any other of Abelard's, but always only to reject it—in most cases without seriously considering the arguments Abelard made for it. One of the first thinkers to examine it after Abelard's death is, however, a remarkable exception.

THE *SENTENCES* OF ROLAND

Peter the Lombard appears in this chapter's title because the discussion of the NAG argument in his *Sentences* explains in large part both the fortune of Abelard's idea—discussed by most of the thirteenth- and fourteenth-century scholastic theologians—and, as will become clear, its misfortune. But a far more careful and thorough discussion of the argument is found in a work from roughly the same time, the *Sentences* of Roland, a Bolognese master who, in many respects, was a follower of Abelard's.[7] His *Sentences* are thought to date from between 1149 to the late 1150s.[8]

Roland's discussion is unlike any of the earlier or later ones in the dispassionate detail with which he discusses and expounds the argument.[9] Whether God can or cannot do more than he does is considered as a genuine *quaestio,* with arguments for and against; and, although Abelard is not named, the main arguments for the position that God cannot do more than he does are his. Roland may well have known the *Theologia scholarium,* but his knowledge of Abelard's position was not limited to that work, since on one occasion he gives a quotation found only in the *Theologia Christiana* and often he includes details which are not in any of Abelard's surviving works.[10] Some of the examples discussed (Judas, God's choice of Jacob over Esau) are found in Abelard's *Sententiae.*[11] Roland may have had a fuller source for Abelard's teaching than any now available or may have been reacting to Abelard's position as developed by his followers (although there are no other records of such a development).

Roland begins by considering the position that God *cannot* do more than he does (that is, Abelard's view). First, he cites four authorities that seem to support this negative answer: all are quotations used by Abelard, though only one is cited by him directly as an authority for the negative answer.[12] Then he gives the rational arguments for this view, and here, without mentioning his name, he rehearses Abelard's basic argument in two forms (which Abelard himself did not so clearly distinguish). If God does not do something, then either it is not fitting or it is unjust for him to do it. Just as he cannot walk or sin, because it is unfitting for him to walk or to sin, so he cannot move a stone from where it is, because it is unfitting for him to move it. That it is so is evident from the fact that he does not do it. 'Were it fitting that he should move it, he would move it.'[13] The same reasoning is applied with regard to the act's justice.

Roland then goes on to capture, though with an example not otherwise known, and more clearly, exactly Abelard's strong principle of
sufficient reason. Consider an action of God's, such as creating a
soul. With regard to this action, there were two possibilities: that
God create it (as he did), or that he not create it.[14] Faced with a choice
of two evils, God can do neither of them; faced with an evil and a
good, he will desist from the evil. If there are two unequal goods,
then he will do the better. But suppose that the two goods are equal,
then 'there will be no reason why he should do what he does and
desist from what he desists from, and so what God does, he does
without judgement and reason'[15]—a consequence that is clearly considered impossible.

There follow a variety of authoritative quotations for the position that God can do other than he does, some of them given by Abelard himself, and rational arguments for this position, including
Abelard's own example of the *damnandus*.[16] At this point, Roland
considers that he has given enough authoritative texts and arguments to bear out both sides of the question,[17] but what follows is
not, as might be expected, Roland's own solution to the problem.
Rather, Roland goes on to elaborate the views supporting the position that God cannot do other than he does—views which he describes as those of 'certain people who are at odds with the Church's
way of thinking' (*quidam a ratione ecclesie dissencientes*)—a clear reference to Abelard and his followers and, in the light of the condemnation, a remarkably gentle one. They will be called here the
'Abelardians', though Roland does not mention Abelard by name.
First, Roland explains how the Abelardians show that the authoritative quotations used against them can be interpreted in a way consistent with their position.[18] Abelard himself did so for one of the
authorities cited also by Roland,[19] but Roland ignores this authority
and offers explanations for the other citations: these explanations
are not found in any of Abelard's surviving works but are Abelardian
in manner.[20] Then he goes on to show how the Abelardians also
counter the arguments from reason for the view that God can do
other than he does. When, begging the question, the objector says
that God could make it rain today, although in fact it will not rain,

the Abelardians answer simply by saying that 'given that he will not make it rain, he cannot at all make it rain.'[21] To the objection (which is not raised in this form in Abelard's own work) that, if God cannot do other than he does, then it is pointless to ask him to grant eternal life, the Abelardians reply that we should do so, all the same, so that people do not think we are wicked and lacking in faith.[22]

Roland then comes to the *damnandus* objection, which he reports fully and thoroughly. But he goes on to give as the Abelardians' answer a line of argument which does not immediately correspond to that in the *Theologia Christiana* and the *Theologia scholarium:* '[The Abelardians] say that what [the objectors] have said, 'The *damnandus* can be saved', is true, yet they say it is not the case that he [God] will be able to do what he could not do now, because, were he to save the *damnandus,* the *damnandus* would have charity with perseverance, and [God] always has this power—that is, the power to save someone who perseveres in charity. For which reason, if he were to save the *damnandus,* it does not follow that he could do something, which he cannot do now.'[23] This view recognizes that there are indeed two possible states of affairs, that the person described as *damnandus* dies in a state of sin or that he dies in a state of grace, and that God will damn him in the former case and save him in the latter one. But this does not mean that God has the power for alternative actions which Abelard wants to deny. The answer may seem to go off the point, by considering whether God has the same powers at one time as at another. But the 'now's here are modal, rather than temporal, and the point of the answer is that, whether the person dies unrepentant or not, there is a set way God must respond, a one-way power to damn him if he is damnable and a one-way power to save him if he perseveres in charity. Roland's presentation of the Abelardian argument also shows explicitly its connection with his theory of grace. The Abelardians, he says, insist that the *damnandus* can have the grace of perseverance from God 'because God sets grace before all people.'[24] In short, the way Roland presents the Abelardian reply corresponds very closely to the manner in which it was argued above (chapter 2, pp. 77–87) that the arguments found in the *Theologia scholarium* should be interpreted.

Roland goes on to give the Abelardians' response to the objections that, on their view, God acts of necessity and that his power is limited: the fact that God cannot not do x does not mean that he does x of necessity, as is shown by the example of the generation of the Son; nor is his power limited, since otherwise it would follow that his power is limited because he cannot know more than he knows.[25]

Only now does Roland give his own view, which claims that God *can* do other than he does.[26] First, he shows how the authoritative statements cited by the Abelardians to support their position can be interpreted so that they do not imply that God cannot do other than he does.[27] He then turns to the argument about God's creating or not creating a soul. He considers that, in this case, both alternatives are goods and equal goods: 'Some say that to create is a greater good. We say that, in themselves, to create and not to create are equal, and yet it is not without reason that God does the former and desists from the latter. For in him there is a hidden justice, because of which he should choose the one and desist from the other.'[28] An example of this, he adds, is found in the election of Jacob and reprobation of Esau: God *could have* equally reprobated Jacob and chosen Esau, but 'it was not done without the hidden justice set up in God that he chose the one through grace and reprobated the other through justice.' This argument reveals a hidden assumption in Abelard's reasoning. Abelard thinks that there must always be a reason why God does x rather than desists from doing $x,$ and he concludes that this reason must lie in the nature of the action: were to do x (for example, for God to create this soul) and not to do x equal goods, then God would act without a reason in choosing either. But this cannot be, and so they must be unequal goods and God cannot but choose the greater one. Roland's suggestion is that there might be *no reason in the nature of the action itself* for a choice. For God to create or not to create this soul are equal goods. But God can, nonetheless, choose one alternative *for a reason*—a hidden reason within him. Roland does not elaborate further on this idea, but what he might have in mind can be illustrated by a human example and without the apparatus of hidden reasons. Suppose that for me now to write the next paragraph or to go to the University Library are, in themselves, exactly equally good actions. Given their equality, then even if I make myself like God by binding myself to choose the best, I can freely choose one or the other. Yet, in the pattern I go on to construct of all my actions, I can make the choice of, say, going to the library rather than continuing writing a choice made according to reason. For me, living in time, it would only be subsequent to my action that the reason for it was constructed. But for God, who—according to Abelard's own proper way of thinking about it—decides all things immutably for eternity, the reason would be constructed by him simultaneously with the action.

Finally, Roland answers two arguments not found in the same form in Abelard. The first is that God cannot do what he does not will to do and that his will is immutable; if his immutable will is to do x, then he cannot not do x, and so he cannot do any things from which he desists. The second is that God cannot act against how he has disposed to act and that he has disposed from eternity to do x—so he cannot not do x without acting against his disposition.[29] Roland answers by saying that 'He cannot do any things from which he desists' is true in the compound sense but not in the divided sense. God cannot do and desist from the same action, but what he does he could not do, and what he does not do he could do. Similarly, God cannot dispose not to do x and do x, but, given that x is what God has disposed to do, God can nonetheless not do x.[30] This use of distinctions to disambiguate propositions, however, serves less to show up any serious flaws in his opponents' argument than to assert the only sense in which Roland is willing to accept their statements.

Peter the Lombard

Disambiguation plays a much more pervasive role in the extremely influential discussion of NAG by Peter the Lombard in his *Sentences*, although it is arguably no more pertinent to Abelard's reasoning than in Roland.

Peter the Lombard was as unlike Abelard in intellectual temperament as can be imagined. The theological synthesis he achieved in his *Sentences,* compiled circa 1155, came to be used from early in the thirteenth century as the textbook for theology in the universities because it presented a balanced and, in most respects, impeccably orthodox synthesis of the main problems of theology—not virtues even the most enthusiastic follower would claim for Abelard's work. But the Lombard knew at least some of Abelard's teachings. In a very few areas, he may have been influenced by them.[31] With regard to God's power, he devoted a whole section of his discussion to presenting NAG and refuting it. Since every major medieval theologian from the thirteenth century onwards commented on the *Sentences,* the argument is very frequently discussed by later medieval writers, although, because the Lombard does not mention his name (the view is just that of 'certain people'), Abelard was in general spared the credit, or rather the blame, for it. Peter the Lombard thus determined both the form of NAG that was discussed in later medieval centuries and, as it turns out, the method by which it was attacked. For whereas on many questions the Lombard's own arguments were quickly left behind by commentators, on this question his basic approach continued to be followed.

NAG is presented in the *Sentences* like this:

> *The opinion of some who say that God can do nothing except what he does.* Some people, however, glorying in their own views, have tried to restrict God within a measure. . . . For they say: 'God cannot do other than he does, nor do better than he does, nor omit any of the things he does.' They attempt to support this opinion of theirs with verisimilar arguments and made-up reasons, as well as scriptural testimonies, saying: God cannot do anything except what is good and just to be done; but only what he does is good and just to be done. For if something other than he does is good and just for him to do, he does not therefore do what is good and just for him to do. But who would dare to say this?[32]

The underlying idea behind this reasoning is clearly Abelard's: God can choose only whatever action is the good and just one. The Lombard puts it, however, in a rather different way. He proposes that

6. God cannot do anything unless it is good and just to be done (by him)

and that only what God does is good and just to be done, that is to say, there is nothing apart from what God does which is good and just to be done by him, and so

7. God does everything which is good and just to be done (by him).

(7) is supported by the contention that its denial means that God does not do what is good and just for him to do—a clearly unacceptable statement. From (6) and (7) it seems to follow that God cannot do other than he does. To spell out the implied reasoning: since 'cannot' implies 'does not', (6) and (7) together establish that God does all and only the things that are good and just. But these things, according to (6), are the only ones God can do, and so God can do only what he does do. This presentation differs from Abelard's own (and from that of Roland, who knew Abelard's thinking more directly, it seems),[33] because it does not talk in terms of God's deciding to do or desist from a given action. Moreover, it gives no suggestion that Abelard has arguments (against voluntarism and for a very strong principle of sufficient reason), based on his conception of God, which support the unusual views that underlie his reasoning.

As his introductory comments will have already indicated, the Lombard does not believe that the Abelardian argument he has presented (anonymously) is at all convincing. He continues: 'To these we reply, opening up the twofold understanding of the words and uncoiling what has been coiled up by them, in this way. When "God cannot do except what is good and just" has the meaning "God cannot do anything except that which, if he did it, would be good and just", then it is true. But God *can* do many things which are neither good nor just, because they are not nor will be, nor are they done well or shall be done well, because they will never be done.'[34]

The Lombard's central distinction, then, is between what is not good and just if God does it (which God cannot do) and what is not good and just (which God can do). Behind this central distinction lies that between the false proposition

8. This is possible: God does x and x is not good and just
and the true one:

9. x is not good and just, and it is possible that God does x.
The difference between (8) and (9) is, of course, that between understanding the negation of the main premise of the NAG argument, (2) (God cannot do anything at any time which is not good to do at that time), in the compound (8) or the divided (9) sense, and there is irony in the fact that, although this distinction goes back to Aristotle, it was Abelard who rediscovered it and for whom it was a favourite move in argument.[35] The Lombard, who often shies away from such logical subtleties, is here attacking Abelard with his own weapons. His contention is that Abelard has been taken in by the very sort of ambiguity he himself loved to uncover. Understood as ruling out (8), (2) is true, but in this sense it asserts merely that, as the Lombard puts it, whatever God actually does is good and just:

2* God can only do what, if he does it, is good and fitting.
(4) does not follow from (1) and (2*), as it does from (1) and (2). Rather, what follows is

4* The following is good and fitting: that, if God is doing x at t, God does x at t.
It is no longer, therefore, possible to deduce (5), and so the argument does not go through. If, by contrast, (2) is understood as ruling out (9) as well as (8), and so understood as

2** The good and fitting thing is the only thing God can do,
then the argument is valid. But the Lombard believes that, in this sense, (2) is not true.

The Lombard continues by playing variations on the same theme, considering various ways of putting basically the same argument, starting out from premises based on God's justice ('He cannot do except what his justice requires'), his rightness ('He cannot do anything except what he should') and his rationality ('He can do only what there is reason for him to do'). These premises are each

subjected to analyses parallel with that just studied. Each is found
to be ambiguous, with one interpretation asserting, truly, the impossibility of God's actually doing something unjust, or which does not
befit him, or which is unreasonable, and the other claiming—falsely,
says the Lombard—that God can do only what he in fact wills to do
because of his justice, rightness or rationality.[36]

From the Lombard's discussion, it seems that the Abelardians
have made a basic error in argumentation. They have not noticed
that the first premise in their argument is ambiguous. It has a
meaning in which it is true and one in which it is false, and the conclusion they urge follows only when it is understood in the false
sense. But this impression is misleading. Abelard has not made an
error in argument, because he would hold that these premises are
true in both senses. Not only is (2*) true, but also (2**): whatever is
the good and fitting thing for him to do at a given juncture is the
only thing that God can do then. The reasons why Abelard holds
(2**) are precisely the positions which he uses to answer the two
first counter-arguments he anticipates—those based on voluntarism
and 'dead heats'. To each he opposes the idea that there is a reason
independent of God which he must follow in acting, a reason such
that there could never be any case where one action was not, in
itself, the best and therefore that which God must choose. Of course,
this is a highly contentious view of God, which few Christian thinkers would accept, and those who reject it would not affirm (2) in the
sense (2**). The Lombard does not explicitly go into which of the
assumptions behind Abelard's counter-arguments he would reject,
but from the remarks he makes in the course of analysing the variety
of forms of (2), put in terms of justice, rightness and so on, there are
some hints. At one point, he says, 'Although there is a reason within
him [God] for which he does some things and desists from doing
others, he can, however, according to the same reason desist from
what he is doing and do what he is desisting from.' This sounds as
if the Lombard would not accept Abelard's principle that there can
be no dead heats. The Lombard is not putting forward the idea of
a voluntarist God, who makes things good by doing them. Along
with Abelard, he accepts that God has to have reasons—and, unlike

Roland, he seems to be thinking of independent reasons—for acting as he does, but he thinks that the same reasons might authorize
alternative, equally just and fitting actions. In place of Abelard's very
strong principle of sufficient reason ('God performs only the action
which is better than any alternative action') he would put the less
strong: 'God performs only the action which is no worse than any alternative action'.

In one sense, then, the Lombard does not do justice to Abelard's
position, since he does not give the details of his argumentation and
his answers to the objections he has anticipated, and he omits entirely the incisive counter-argument about the *damnandus* and Abelard's unexpected but characteristic way of rebutting it. In another
sense, though, the Lombard is not unjust. Abelard's argument does
make it appear as if, from (2) ('God can do only what is good and fitting') and its variants—statements which seem, on the surface, to be
ones which any Christian would accept—it follows, by a process of
rigorous logical argument, that God cannot do other than he does.
The Lombard shows that, understood in the sense which most
Christians would choose, (2) does not entail this consequence; it entails it only if it is understood in a sense which most Christians
would reject.

The Influence of the Lombard's Approach

With one important exception, thirteenth- and fourteenth-century
theologians seem to have known about NAG only what they read in
the *Sentences*. They did not, then, attribute it to Abelard or to anyone
in particular, and they did not know of the details of the argument,
merely the basic idea that, because God does only what is good, just
and fitting, he cannot do other than he does. They followed the Lombard in thinking that this position was based on an ambiguity, and
they picked up on his central distinction in their analyses, although
often the exact way in which they explained this ambiguity differed
a little from his. Consider, for example, two treatments of the prob-

lem early in the tradition, when the question at issue is still very clearly (though anonymously) Abelard's argument.

In his *Summa aurea* (1229—longer version), William of Auxerre says that the problem can be solved by distinguishing between the verb 'is' as signifying 'actual inherence' and 'natural coherence'.[37] In the first sense, it seems, '*A* is *F*' means that it is actually the case that *A* is *F,* and in the second sense, that it is possible for *A* to be *F.* William uses this analysis to dispose of the Abelardian argument put in much the same form as by the Lombard (6 and 7). There is an ambiguity, he says, in the meaning of 'is' in (6) and (7). If 'is' is taken to signify 'actual inherence', then (6) is false. There are, then, in his view, things which are not actually good and just, which God could do—and, presumably, although he does not state it, they are things which God does not in fact do and which, were he to perform them, would be good and just. If 'is' is taken to signify 'natural coherence', then (6) is true, but, read with 'is' in this sense, (7) is false. 'Natural coherence' seems to mean compossibility, and so, in this sense, what 'is' good and just is what possibly is good and just. Whatever God can do is possibly good and just—in the sense, presumably, that it would be good and just if he did it (the Lombard's central distinction), but, as this sense suggests, there are things possibly good and just which God does not in fact do. By contrast, Abelard would, of course, insist that (6) is *true* when 'is' signifies actual inherence as well as when it signifies natural coherence, and that (7) is true when 'is' signifies natural coherence as well as when it signifies actual inherence. It sounds, from the little he says, as if William would reject Abelard's position on broadly voluntarist grounds—there are things which are not actually good and right but which would be so if God did them. Maybe, though, his point—in line with one of the Lombard's ideas—is that only things that are actually done are good and just, and that, for God, there are dead heats, alternatives between various courses of action, capable of being good and just, one of which becomes so actually when he chooses it. As in the Lombard, the illusion that the problem rests entirely on an ambiguity in the linguistic expression of the logical structure of the argument

spares the critic from making explicit his deeper reasons for rejecting Abelard's argument.

In the *Summa fratris Alexandri,* a vast textbook of theology compiled by the followers of Alexander of Hales a decade or so later
(1236–45), the Abelardian argument is presented, following the
Lombard, in a form similar to that in William of Auxerre, and the
analysis of why it fails is conducted along the same lines, although
the terminology is different: 'The word "is" can copulate (i) a present
which is indeterminate or habitual [= William's "natural coherence"], or (ii) a present as it is now or in act [= William's "actual inherence"]. Taken in sense (i), <the proposition "God can do only what
is good and just"> is true, and its sense is: God can do only what
would be good and just, if he did it. Taken in sense (ii), it is false,
and its sense is: God can do only what is good and just as it is now.'[38]
The writers of this *Summa* spare themselves the trouble of going on
to tie up the refutation neatly, in the way William did. But they consider a way of putting the Abelardian position, which receives a very
interesting reply, not found in the *Summa aurea* or the Lombard, or
indeed in Abelard himself and his early critics. Suppose that God
can do something from his power which he cannot do from his justice, and consider the case when that power is exercised in an act.
'Either the act is just or unjust. If it is unjust, then God can do what
is not just. If it is just, then he can do only what is just.'[39] The reply
which might be expected, given the way the *Summa* has handled the
positions so far, is that 'God can do what is not just' is ambiguous
and in the sense of 'God can do something which would not be just
if God did not do it' can be accepted as true. Instead, the authors
move away from pure linguistic analysis to make a different distinction, about God's justice: 'God's justice in one way connotes what
befits divine goodness [*condecentiam divinae bonitatis*], and, in this
way, whatever he can do by power, he can do by justice, that is, by fit-
tingness with <his> goodness, for it befits the highest goodness that
it should be able to do whatever power enables it to do [*quidquid
posse potentiae est*]. In another way, it connotes congruence with merits, and in this way he cannot do by justice—that is, according to
congruence with our merits—everything he can do by power.'[40] This

answer takes a much more definitely voluntarist line than any of the others considered up until now. The authors contend that there is no difference between what God can do and what it is just, in one sense, for him to do, precisely because, in this sense, since he is the highest good, whatever he can do is just. Whereas, for Abelard, to say that God can do only what is just means that his ability to act is limited by justice, here the implication is the opposite: the range of just acts is to be extended to everything that God can do. This is true, though, for justice only in one sense. In the sense of 'justice' in which an action towards us is just because it is what we deserve, God is able, by his power, to act unjustly. (By contrast, Abelard's general approach is to insist that there is no such gap between senses of 'justice', so that God's actions are bound to follow a single conception of justice.)

From the mid-thirteenth century onwards, there was a tendency for direct discussion of the problem raised by Abelard, as presented by the Lombard, to be pushed aside, so as to devote this distinction of the *Sentences* to questions on other topics, such as the infinity of God's power. For example, all four questions in Bonaventure's commentary (1250–52) are on this subject, but he then adds some *dubia* about the Lombard's text, where he both justifies the Lombard's central distinction and distinguishes between justice *ad condecentiam* and justice *ad merita,* in the same way as in the *Summa fratris Alexandri.*[41] Bonaventure's Dominican contemporary Albert the Great keeps close to the Lombard's solution, explaining it along the same main lines as William of Auxerre and the *Summa fratris Alexandri* and making the distinction between different types of justice.[42]

Another famous theologian who does, briefly, treat the Lombard's version of Abelard's question directly shows, by the manner in which he does so, how in fact it all but vanished from the agenda for discussion by the fourteenth century. In his commentary on the *Sentences* (1317–18), near the beginning of his first question on book 1, distinction 43, William of Ockham puts the argument that 'God cannot do anything except what is right to be done by him, but nothing is right or just to be done by him except what he does; therefore he can do nothing except what he does'[43]—the Abelardian argument, as presented by the Lombard. A number of pages later, at the end of the *quaestio*, he returns to the point and briskly rejects the Abelardian reasoning 'because, although God cannot do anything except what it is just to be done, something which is not now just to be done, because it is not done by God, can, however, be just to be done if God were to do it. And so such a mixing of possible and non-modal premises is not valid, but it is not our business to discuss why here, since this pertains rather to logic.'[44] Ockham is making the Lombard's central distinction, but he uses his theories of modal logic to support the point. As he explains in the *Summa logicae*, in a first-figure syllogism where one of the premises is non-modal and the other asserts possibility in a composed sense—that is to say that the possibility operator ranges over the whole proposition—one cannot draw a possible proposition as a conclusion.[45] The sort of syllogism he might have in mind to illustrate the discussion about God's power could be:

10. No unjust act is possible for God.
11. Every sparing the guilty is an unjust act.
12. No sparing of the guilty is possible for God.

This is invalid if (10) is taken in the composed sense to mean (10c) 'The following is impossible: "God does something unjust".' The syllogism would be valid were (10) taken in the divided sense— where the possibility operator has narrow scope—to mean (10d): 'With regard to every unjust act, it is impossible for God to do it.' But whereas (10c) is true, Ockham would reject (10d) because, as he says, an act which is unjust now might be just were God to perform it.

The most revealing feature of Ockham's discussion, though, is not the little he says but where he places it. The Abelardian reasoning is one of the opening arguments, which have to be answered at the end of the *quaestio*. Whereas in the thirteenth century dealing with these arguments was one of the important functions of the *quaestio*, by Ockham's time they were merely a relic of its earlier form, and their statement and rejection provided a formal frame for the discussion, organized in whatever way seemed most suitable, of the real questions at issue. For Ockham the real question is whether

God is a free efficient cause and not a natural one, and whether this can be shown by natural reason or is the doctrine of the faith. It was Scotus—whose arguments are attacked here—who had made this a central issue, and the Abelardian argument, which made God into a non-natural but unfree agent, became an irrelevance. Duns Scotus does not in fact put forward these arguments in discussing this distinction. Indeed, rather strangely, he devotes book I, distinction 43, to talking about the goodness of the world, a topic which, as he says, the Lombard treats in the next distinction. When he comes to distinction 44, the question Scotus proposes may seem as if it relates closely to the Abelardian argument: 'whether God could make things otherwise than it has been ordained by him that they are made.' This question turns out, however, to treat a distinction that had been widely used in talking about God's power from the early thirteenth century onwards: that between God's ordained and absolute power. In its earlier theological use, up to the time of Scotus and in some later thinkers, these labels distinguish between what God does (his ordained power) and what he could but does not do (his absolute power). It belongs, then, to a way of looking at the world which Abelard's NAG argument rejects, by insisting that there is no difference between what God does and what he could possibly do under the same circumstances. Further development of the distinction (beginning with the canon lawyers and, among theologians, with Scotus), which allowed God to act at times according to his absolute power, underlines the distance between later medieval attitudes to divine power and Abelard's impersonal God, reminiscent of Plato's demiurge, acting according to determinate rational causes.[46]

AN EXCEPTION TO THE RULE: THOMAS AQUINAS

Despite the apparent influence of Abelard's NAG argument, it would seem that, in fact, it fared hardly better among later medieval thinkers than the rest of his ideas, which simply remained unknown. The argument was transmitted only through the Lombard's

incomplete account, was treated as an example of obviously fallacious reasoning and, by the fourteenth century, had even in that
form become a relic of earlier discussion. But one theologian and
philosopher is exceptional in treating Abelard's central idea, though
not the details of NAG, seriously and in providing a powerful
counter-argument. And he is the most famous of all the scholastics,
Thomas Aquinas.

Aquinas's first treatment of the Abelardian argument, in his
Commentary on the Sentences (1253–56), is nearer to the usual approach than his later discussions of it. Concentrating on the formulation of the problem in terms of justice (the question is: does God
act out of the necessity of justice?), like other theologians he uses
the Lombard's central distinction,[47] and he makes the distinction
between justice as 'retribution for what is deserved' and as 'what
befits [*decentia*] divine goodness'.[48] Unlike other writers, however,
Aquinas recognizes that there is more than a logical confusion here.
Granted the Lombard's central distinction between God's not being
able to do anything which would not be just, if he did it—which is
clearly acceptable—and God's being determined by justice to do
one thing, so that he could do no other, it still remains to provide an
argument to show why the second interpretation expresses a falsehood. And Aquinas goes on to give one. Some human choices concern actions which, in their own nature, are indifferent, such as to
sit or not to sit. Which choice is just under such circumstances depends on the circumstances, and so, Aquinas believes, the human
agent is not in these cases compelled to one or the other by necessity
of justice. By contrast, some sorts of action are good or bad in themselves: a person cannot, for instance, lie without going against justice, and so the human agent, Aquinas implies, is constrained, if he
or she is not to act badly. But, he says, because whatever is ordained
as good or just in created things is entirely from God's will which so
ordains it, God does not do anything from the necessity of justice
where he could not equally do something else. This argument therefore accepts voluntarism, at least to a degree, by contrast with Abelard. The point of Aquinas's example of types of human action may
be to suggest that we can gain some idea of God's lack of necessity

in acting justly in every case by considering a similar lack of necessity for us with regard to indifferent sorts of action. Abelard, however, does not seem to have made any such distinction: of every action, it can be asked whether it is the best, and if and only if it is such, a just agent is bound to perform it.[49]

In his later treatments of the problem, however, in his disputed questions *On Power* (1265–66) and in the first part of the *Summa theologiae* (1266–68), Aquinas completely leaves behind the usual treatment of the topic and provides a counter-argument which is more adequate as a response to Abelard, even though Abelard probably would not have accepted it. Moreover, Aquinas seems even to have had an idea that Abelard was the originator of this view. In the *Questions on Power* he writes about the error 'of certain theologians who considered the order of divine justice and wisdom, according to which things are made by God, and they said that God cannot act except in accord with it, and so they came to saying that God can do only what he does. And this error is attributed to Master Peter Almalareo.'[50] This garbled name could indicate that Aquinas did not know about Abelard's position only from the Lombard's *Sentences* and that he had found some other source of information about it after his early years, when he wrote his commentary on the *Sentences*. Or perhaps Aquinas connected in his mind some information about Abelard's heretical views, which was current in the later Middle Ages, with the view he read about in the Lombard's *Sentences*.[51]

Whereas in his *Sentences* commentary Aquinas based his rejection of NAG on a willingness to accept a more voluntaristic view than Abelard, in the two later works his strategy is, rather, to show why the very strong principle of sufficient reason does not apply to God. There is no trace of voluntarism. So, in the *Questions on Power*, God's will is seen as moving towards its natural end, in the same way as any other will does. 'It is necessary', he says, 'that any will'— God's included—'should have some end which it naturally wills, and the contrary to which it cannot will.' He continues, 'And along with the will's necessarily willing its natural end, it also wills of necessity those things without which it cannot have the end, if it knows that [i.e. that it cannot have its end without them], and these are commensurate with the end, as for instance if I will life, I will food. But those things without which the end can be had, which are not commensurate with the end, it does not will of necessity.' By 'commensurate with the end' Aquinas may mean here just 'required by the end'. For he goes on to say that the natural end of the divine will is its goodness, which it must will. But since he could manifest this goodness without these creatures—he could do it 'through other creatures ordered in a different way'—the creatures that there happen in fact to be are not commensurate with God's end, and so his will does not have to will them.

Understood in this way, however, Aquinas is merely asserting that God's goodness could manifest itself through different creatures (and so through different actions). But this does not meet Abelard's contention that, since he is always good and just, God's action must always be that one which is the best and most just and that there is only one such course of action. Either Aquinas has merely established that, by acting otherwise than he does, God could still manifest his goodness, but not so well as he in fact does, or, on the more reasonable interpretation that God could manifest his goodness *equally* well through other creatures, Aquinas is dismissing the very strong principle of sufficient reason, by which Abelard rules out such a possibility. He may be right to do so, but an argument to support his position is lacking.

In the *Summa theologiae,* however, he provides one. He writes that

the order put into things by the divine wisdom, on which is based what justice is . . . does not adequately correspond to divine wisdom in such a way that divine wisdom should be limited to this order. For it is clear that the whole rationale of the order which a wise person imposes on the things made by him is taken from its end. When, therefore, the end is proportioned to the things that are made for the sake of the end, the wisdom of the maker is limited to some determinate order. But the divine goodness is an end that exceeds created things beyond all

proportion. For which reason the divine wisdom is not determined to any certain order of things in such a way that another
course of things could not flow from it. And so it should be said
without qualification that God can do other things than those
he does.[52]

The most important notion here—and one which is perhaps
also implied by the use of the term 'commensurate' in the *Questions
on Power*—is that of being out of proportion. Aquinas is saying that
God does indeed will in accord with a rule of goodness and fitting-
ness but that this rule is set according to God's ultimate aim, which
is to manifest his own goodness. Were there a proportion between
God's goodness and the manifestation of it in a good and just universe, then there would indeed be just one best way of manifesting
it, one fitting action at each point. But because there is no proportion between infinite goodness and finite goodness, there is no reason to think that there are not many ways of its being manifested, all
equally good, though all completely inadequate.

This argument is an effective counter to Abelard's very strong
principle of sufficient reason, since it shows why two or more different outcomes in a situation can equally be the result of a reasonable cause, because of the gap between God's infinity and the finite
universe which expresses it. Abelard himself, though, would probably have rejected the idea that there is such a gap between divine
goodness and any possible non-divine manifestation of it. In making this argument, Aquinas is leaning heavily on the negative aspect
of his theology and moving closer than usual to the position of a
thinker like Maimonides, who denies that we can properly even describe God as 'good'.

ABELARD, WYCLIF AND DIODORUS: THOMAS NETTER AND CARDINAL BELLARMINE

In the early fifteenth century, when even second-hand discussion
of NAG had been pushed to, or beyond, the sidelines of *Sentences*

commentaries, Abelard's argument made an unexpected reappearance, in a different context, and firmly attached to its author. But Abelard's name was there to discredit both the argument and the recent thinker who was blamed for having revived it: John Wyclif (d. 1384). One of the most learned and vituperative of Wyclif's critics was Thomas Netter (or Waldensis), whose vast *Doctrinale antiquae fidei* was aimed, principally, at Wyclif and his followers, collecting copious quotations from patristic and earlier medieval writings to counter each of their supposed doctrines. It was written in the 1420s, after Wyclif—a controversial but respected thinker in his lifetime—had been condemned as heretical and the leader of his followers in Bohemia, Jan Hus, had been burned. Wyclif was attacked by his enemies, who distorted his subtle views on this topic, for teaching a thoroughgoing determinism, based on the idea that the way God has ordained the universe is the only way in which he could do so. As Netter puts it, summarizing what he believes to be Wyclif's view: 'God's omnipotence and his actual creation are identical, and God is omnipotent because he produces everything possible. I shall not (he says) discuss the intelligibility or the power of producing things that do not exist, since I hold that nothing can be produced except what exists.'[53]

Netter connected this supposed view with something which he had read in the collection of fourteen heresies attributed to Abelard, which he thought (wrongly) had been made by Bernard of Clairvaux, and which were read along with Bernard's widely circulated letter treatise against Abelard.[54] The third of the heresies in this list is Abelard's view about the impossibility of God's acting otherwise.[55] There follow five very short extracts from the *Theologia scholarium*. Netter uses these to argue that, although Wyclif is guilty of spreading the heresy, he has learnt it from 'the famous heretic Peter Abelard', and he quotes three of them—one which simply states the thesis that 'God can do only what he does at some time', another that 'God can do or desist from doing only what he does and do them only in the way and at the time he does' and another that, just as God begat the best Son he could, since otherwise he would have been guilty of envy, so he makes everything, so far as it can be, excellent.[56] Netter thinks that Abelard is playing the part of Absalom to Wyclif's Achitophel. Netter's method of refutation is not to analyse or invent arguments but to cite authorities, beginning with a comment against Abelard from Bernard's letter and continuing with a passage from Hugh of St Victor's *De sacramentis* written against Abelard's views. He also mentions, though he does not cite, the attack on Abelard's view in Peter the Lombard's *Sentences,* before going on to cite patristic authorities at length.[57]

In the second book of his *Doctrinale,* Netter returns to the links between determinism, Abelard and Wyclif, and now he links a third name to them. He recalls that, in the first book, he said that Abelard was the originator of this 'heresy of necessity'. But now he has found that he was not the first to put it forward, and he refers to a dialogue (about which he has read in Jerome) 'long before', between Chrysippus and Diodorus, in which Diodorus held that only what is true or will be true can be, whereas Chrysippus argued that things which will not happen can happen (this pearl can be broken, although it never will be).[58] Chrysippus, he remarks, took 'the Catholic side'.

Netter's book had many readers in the sixteenth century—it went through four editions—and they included Cardinal Bellarmine. When he turns, in his *De controversiis,* to discussing whether God has free will, he lists, among those denying it, not only Aristotle and Avicenna but, among the Christians, Abelard and Wyclif (on Netter's authority)—to whom he adds some of the leading Protestants: Luther, Bucer and Calvin. Bellarmine offers a series of arguments to support God's freedom of will.[59] The one which relates to Abelard's position—though Bellarmine does not link arguments to individual figures—presents his argument as claiming that God's will must conform to God's wisdom and that God's wisdom cannot fail to judge as best what is really best and should be done, so that God's will is not free, because it only ever has one choice. Bellarmine's answer is unabashedly voluntaristic. God's wisdom knows that whatever God wills to be done is the best and ought to be done.[60]

Although this fifteenth- and sixteenth-century interest in Abelard's position restored it to its author, neither Netter nor Bellarmine knew the details of the NAG argument, nor did they exercise
much ingenuity in thinking about the general position, as given in
the quotations in the *Capitula xiv haeresum*. But there is one very
important new feature in their approach. None of Abelard's earlier
critics had accused him of arguing that all things happen by necessity. Netter, however, makes the link between him and Wyclif (who,
equally wrongly, he thinks favoured such determinism) and, later
on, with Diodorus. Bellarmine adds a list of Protestants, all of whom
were suspected, not without reason, of limiting or denying human
free will. This misreading of Abelard's position—shared by many
interpreters today—would mould attitudes to his argument in the
century following.[61]

BAYLE AND LEIBNIZ

Among the readers of Bellarmine's *De controversiis* in the seven-
teenth century was Gottfried Wilhelm Leibniz. He made notes in
his copy, probably between 1680 and 1684. When he came to the
passage referring to Abelard's view that God cannot do other than he
does, he noted in the margin: 'This is false, otherwise nothing would
be possible except what actually happened.'[62] Leibniz followed Bellarmine, then, in seeing Abelard as a necessitarian, and he rejected
the position out of hand. When he wrote his *Essais de théodicée* (1710),
Leibniz would return to Abelard and to the NAG argument in particular. Given his vast library and learning, and D'Amboise and Duchesne's 1616 *editio princeps* of the works of Abelard (and Heloise),
which contains the *Theologia scholarium*, it might be expected that,
at last, Abelard's argument would be studied at first hand and
even, at last, appreciatively—given the apparent closeness between
Leibniz's position—that God, being supremely good, cannot but
create the best possible world—and Abelard's denial of alternative
choices to God, because he must always choose the best. Both hopes,
though, are disappointed.

Leibniz's first, fleeting contact with Abelard had come through Bellarmine. His somewhat deeper knowledge of him resulted from his reading of Bayle, against whose views the *Théodicée* was directed. In his great *Dictionnaire historique et critique* (1701—a shorter, first edition was published in 1696), Bayle discusses Abelard in the article devoted to him; briefly in the article on his editor, D'Amboise; (reporting the surprising accusation of materialist pantheism) in his article on Spinoza (Note A); and, more importantly, in the article on Chrysippus and that on Berenger (Berengarius of Poitiers, a follower of Abelard's).[63] Just as Netter had linked together Diodorus and Abelard as exponents of the view that all happens of necessity, so in the article on Diodorus (Note S) Bayle reconstructs—in more detail, and from ancient sources, rather than Jerome—the dispute between Diodorus, who thought that what does not exist at some time cannot possibly exist, and Chrysippus, who took the opposite view. He adds that Abelard, so it has been claimed, taught a doctrine similar to Diodorus's. It is in the article on Berenger, however, that Bayle presents (Note M) the most information on the NAG argument, which is taken entirely from the discussion and summary of the *Theologia scholarium* in Louis Dupin's *Nouvelle bibliothèque des auteurs ecclésiastiques*. Bayle ends by suggesting that he might return to discuss the argument in his article on Wyclif—thus making the same link which Netter made three centuries earlier.

Bayle not only was Leibniz's intermediary for his information about Abelard but also set out the context in which Abelard was placed, as someone who followed Diodorus's determinist view—a view which fitted well what he had read, years before, in Bellarmine (supposing he remembered it).[64] Almost directly after quoting at length from Note S of Bayle's article on Chrysippus, Leibniz adds that 'the renowned Peter Abelard was of a view near to that of Diodorus, when he said that God can do only what he does.' After a few remarks on Abelard, Leibniz goes on to quote Dupin's summary almost verbatim: 'The reason he gave for it was that God cannot do except what he wills; and he cannot will to do other than he does, because it is necessary that he wills whatever is fitting: from which it follows that all that he does not do is not fitting, that he cannot wish to do it and in consequence that he cannot do it.' Leibniz comments coldly on the idea, putting together with the summary of what Abelard wrote in the *Theologia scholarium* a remark Dupin himself had made about him ('il ne s'accorde pas avec la maniere de penser & de parler des autres'): 'Abelard himself admits that this opinion is peculiar to him, that almost no one agrees with it, that it seems contrary to the teaching of the saints and of reason and to derogate from the greatness of God. It seems that this writer was a bit too inclined to think and speak differently from everybody else.'[65] Then Leibniz offers his own analysis of where Abelard goes wrong. Continuing from the idea that he liked to speak differently from others, he accuses him of changing the meaning of words: 'Power and will are different faculties, and they have different objects too. To say that God can do only what he wills is to confuse them. On the contrary, among several possible things, he wills only that which he finds the best. For we consider all possible things as objects of his power, but we consider the things which actually exist as the objects of his ordaining will.'

Dupin, as quoted by Bayle, had summarized the *damnandus* argument, and Leibniz copies this account. But he believes that, through this counter-argument, Abelard is in fact tacitly admitting that God *can* do other than he does:

> Abelard recognized this himself. He puts this objection to himself. Someone destined for damnation [*un reprouvé*] can be saved. But he cannot be saved unless God saves him. And so God can save him, and as a result do something which he does not do. He replies that we can indeed say that this man can be saved with regard to the possibility of human nature, which is capable of salvation; but we cannot say that God can save him with regard to God himself, because it is impossible that God do what he should not do. But since he accepts that we can indeed say in one sense, speaking absolutely and setting aside the supposition that he is destined for damnation, that such a person, who is among those destined for damnation, can be saved—and that thus that which God does not do can be done—he could

therefore speak like everyone else, who mean the same thing
when they say that God can save this man and that he can do
what he does not do.

Leibniz's approach to Abelard's position might seem paradoxical
or even disingenuous.[66] Leibniz himself holds that God cannot but
create the best possible world, because by his nature he must always
do what is best. Yet he seems to criticize Abelard—indeed, to judge
that his position rests on merely verbal distinctions—for, apparently, holding the same view. Yet, given Leibniz's assumption that
Abelard wants to hold that all things happen of necessity, his comment is perfectly understandable. For Leibniz's own central, though
problematic, claim is that, although God must create the best possible world, all things do *not* happen of necessity. He supported it
with various arguments at different times, but his favourite one—
devised much earlier, and repeated in the *Théodicée*—relies on distinguishing between a realm of absolute possibility, which he sometimes talks about in terms of things being possible in their own
nature, from what it is possible should be brought into existence by
God, given that God must choose the best.[67] To hold, as Abelard
does, that it is possible for God to do only what he wills to do, and
that he must will the best, is to destroy the very distinction which
Leibniz wants to use to allow for contingency, since it leaves no
space for the possibility of anything other than what God wills. Yet,
from Leibniz's perspective, Abelard's own distinction, in his answer
to the *damnandus* objection, between what is possible for the man
and what is possible for God seems to capture very well his own central point that there is in some sense a possibility for the man which
is not removed just because it cannot in fact be realized in the best
possible world that God must create. This is why Leibniz takes Abelard's answer to the objection as an implicit admission that God *can*
do other than he does, since Abelard does indeed admit the possibility for the *damnandus* (in the referential sense ('speaking absolutely and setting aside the supposition that he is damned') to be
saved.[68] And, since Leibniz does not realize that the argument is

about alternative choices, the distinction between his saving's being by God and God's saving him seems purely verbal.[69]

There is, however, a deep irony here. Against the determinist view which Leibniz thinks, wrongly, Abelard is urging, he upholds for the *damnandus* the possibility of salvation just in the sense that there is a possible world in which he (or, more strictly speaking, his counterpart) is saved, but this possible world is one that God cannot actualize, and so cannot be actualized, because it is not the best. In Abelard's true and anything but determinist view, whilst God has no alternative choices with regard to the *damnandus,* the *damnandus* has the genuine possibility, which he might have actualized, had he so chosen, to be saved. But Leibniz is blind to his real argument because, through the intermediary of Bayle's *Dictionnaire,* and, ultimately, as a result of late medieval scholarship, he approaches Abelard as an epigone of Diodorus and a forerunner of Wyclif.

Part III

ABELARD AND OUR PRESENT

INTRODUCTION TO PART III

Slowly, the period examined in the last chapter, when Abelard's thought was known usually anonymously and, most often through distorted fragments, pre-judged as erroneous, gave way to one where more and more of his surviving texts were published and scholars tried, with more historical detachment, to understand his thinking. It was not, though, until well into the second half of the twentieth century that his complete known works were all available in print. By this time, there existed an extensive secondary literature about Abelard, his life and his ideas, but little if anything in the way of analyses which engaged philosophically with his reasoning, apart from a few studies of his views on universals. The re-discovery of Abelard as a philosopher that has taken place over the last forty years has various and complex origins.[1] Jean Jolivet's 1969 study of his theology in relation to the 'arts of language' (logic and grammar) was the first monograph on Abelard to pay detailed attention to his logico-linguistic subtleties, and these were also examined, from a different angle, by scholars from the Dutch school, such as Nuchelmans and De Rijk, and have been taken to a new level of technical insight and historical precision in the many detailed studies by Irène Rosier-Catach.[2] Yet the most important element in this re-discovery resulted from the development, from the 1950s onwards, whereby philosophers trained analytically (usually in anglophone philosophy departments) began to look, albeit in an unhistorical way, at philosophers from the past. This movement had a special importance for medieval philosophy (even though this was, and remains, an area many analytical philosophers are even keener to ignore than the rest of the past). Many of the characteristics of analytical philosophy, such as its emphasis on logic and semantics, attention to the precise form in which positions are stated, willingness to invent technical terms and tendency to set out arguments step by step, are closely paralleled in much medieval philosophy. Whole areas of medieval thought, especially in logic, which had been judged worthless or impenetrable were seen to be fascinating and sophisticated once the tools and approach of analytical philosophy were brought to bear on them.

More than anything else, it is the work of analytically trained philosophers which is now enabling Abelard at last to be understood and appreciated as a philosopher. Martin Tweedale's 1976 book on Abelard's theory of universals pioneered this approach. Given the technical complications of studying Abelard and the lack of translations, it is not surprising that some of those who have brought an analytical treatment to him are scholars like Klaus Jacobi and Simo Knuuttila, who combine an analytic training with the wider philological and historical grasp typical of the European tradition, or Alain de Libera, who brings together many strands, including an analytic one, in his approach.[3] Nonetheless, today's two leading experts on Abelard's philosophy (by contrast with those who look at his work and thought more widely), Peter King and Christopher Martin, have a more purely analytic training. Along with Abelard's own texts, their important and wide-ranging discussions of Abelard's semantics, philosophy of mind and metaphysics will be the focus of the two following chapters. The first of them looks at a dispute between King and Martin over Abelard's theory of meaning. On one level, through scrutiny of their arguments and consideration of some passages neither of them discusses, Abelard's complex and original position becomes graspable. On another level, the dispute provides the occasion to think about questions of methodology, since it concerns the plausibility of the link King makes, and Martin questions, between Abelard and the 'new theorists' of meaning of the 1970s and 1980s. The second of the chapters is more wide-ranging, but it revolves around the contrast between King's reconstruction of Abelard's metaphysics and a different interpretation of it, first proposed by Martin (and which I further developed), where the contemporary idea of tropes plays an important part. Here too questions about the advantages and limitations of using ideas from our philosophical present to understand Abelard are in the foreground.

CHAPTER FIVE

ABELARD AND THE 'NEW' THEORY
OF MEANING

PETER KING, ABELARD AND THE 'NEW' THEORISTS

One of the best-known, and best, studies of Abelard was never
published. Peter King submitted his doctoral dissertation 'Peter
Abailard and the Problem of Universals' to Princeton in 1982; it
has never been printed, although it is available in microfilm and is
widely cited.[1] King's seven-hundred-page study is complex and wide-
ranging, but its most striking claim is about Abelard and the philosophy of language. In the 1980s, the latest developments in the
philosophy of language were those that had just been made by Hilary Putnam and Saul Kripke. Although their concerns and theories
were not the same, they were seen as the originators of the 'new'
theory of meaning, in which direct reference plays a central part.
But according to King, this theory was hardly new, since Abelard
had succeeded in anticipating it almost a millennium earlier. King
has changed his mind about many things he wrote in his dissertation, but he seems to have stuck to the view of Abelard as an exponent of direct reference. In his entry on Peter Abelard in the *Stanford
Encyclopedia of Philosophy*, he writes that for Abelard

A name is linked with that of which it is the name as though
there were someone who devised the name to label a given thing
or kind of thing, a process known as 'imposition' . . . rather like
baptism. This rational reconstruction of reference does not require the person imposing the name, the 'impositor', to have
anything more than an indefinite intention to pick out the thing
or kind of thing, whatever its nature may be. . . . Put in modern
terms, Abelard holds a theory of *direct reference,* in which the extension of a term is not a function of its sense. We are often
'completely ignorant' of the proper conceptual content that
should be associated with a term that has been successfully
imposed.[2]

If King's account of Abelard's theory is correct, does he have
grounds for connecting it with the new theorists of the 1980s? Certainly, the comparison must be understood—more clearly perhaps
than King brings out—to be a partial one. The new theorists considered two questions. The first was about the meaning of proper
names and kind terms (the names of natural kinds, such as 'water'),
which they often answered by identifying the meaning of such
terms with their reference. The second was the question of how
their reference is determined.[3] It is their answer just to this second
question, about the determination of reference, which is the subject
of King's comparison with Abelard's semantics. And the comparison
must be made, King believes, not with Abelard's semantics as a
whole, but just with the part of his semantic theory concerned with
reference. Moreover, the comparison King makes concerns in the
main kind terms; about proper names, which are also discussed by
the new theorists, Abelard has much less to say.

Given these limitations of the scope of the comparison, however, King seems to have good grounds for the similarity he finds
between Abelard's views, as described above, and the contemporary
theory. The new theorists argued for a causal theory of how reference is determined, in opposition to what its exponents considered
to be the traditional view, the description theory.[4] According to the
description theory, the reference of natural kind names is estab-

lished by a mental representation: a descriptive thought in speakers' and listeners' minds, such as (to take an oversimplified example) *four-legged animal that barks* for 'dog'. The things that fit this description are those to which the word refers. The causal theorists do not, of course, dispute that there are thoughts associated with the words we speak and hear. But they deny that these thoughts determine a word's reference. According to the description theorist, when I say 'water', the name refers to water in virtue of a descriptive thought of some properties of water which I associate with it. By contrast, according to the causal theory, the word refers in virtue of a chain, in which the name is passed 'from link to link'. At the beginning of the chain is a 'hypothetical baptism' of the substance.[5] Abelard, by King's account, explains how reference is determined in just this way.

And the similarity seems to go deeper. The contemporary causal theorists argue in favour of their view that it allows our language to connect with reality—in the way we normally suppose it does—despite the inadequacy of many speakers' descriptive thoughts. The description theory, by contrast, results in many of our uses of words failing to have the references which we suppose them to have. Putnam is, as he admits, a horticultural ignoramus, who cannot tell the difference between a beech and an elm, and so the descriptive thought he connects with both beeches and elms is that of a common deciduous tree. Yet most people would accept that 'beech' refers to beeches, not elms, even when used by Putnam. We must acknowledge, he therefore argues, a division of linguistic labour in society. Some people, but not everyone, can tell beeches from elms, and a small number of people are experts who can discriminate between real gold and substances that appear to be gold. For those who cannot make these distinctions, it is enough that they accept that these words refer to whatever the experts hold is their reference. But the knowledge in a society sometimes may not be such as to allow anyone in it to have a descriptive thought which correctly distinguishes between what does and does not belong to a given natural kind. Before it was known that water was H_2O, it may not have been possible for anyone to tell the difference between water and a different chemical substance that resembled it exactly in appearance and effects. But, according to Putnam, if 'water' was chosen as the name for the substance which was in fact H_2O, then the word referred, even in that unscientific age, just to what was H_2O. Similarly, according to Abelard, says King, the impositor need not have anything more than an indefinite intention to pick out the thing or kind of thing, whatever its nature may be. As King (2010) quotes him writing: 'The inventor [of names] intended to impose them according to some natures or distinctive properties of things, even if he himself did not know how to think correctly upon the nature or distinctive property of a thing.'[6]

CHRISTOPHER MARTIN'S CRITIQUE

King's views about Abelard's semantics have been the subject of a searching critique by Christopher Martin.[7] Martin argues that King's reading is anachronistic (though he does not use this word), and that Abelard's conceptions about the relationship between words, things and thought should be seen rather as a development of the Aristotelian-Boethian tradition in which he and his contemporaries worked. Not only is this clash between two radically diverse readings important for the light it throws on a central strand in Abelard's thought. It also provides an excellent, real-life illustration to help think about one of the main methodological issues which faces all historians of philosophy. How should the dimension of Abelard or any other past thinker and *his* present be juxtaposed with the dimension of the thinker and *our* present? How far should readings of texts from the past be influenced by the desire to link the arguments there with discussions today and so make thinkers from distant centuries into our own philosophical interlocutors? The example is all the more helpful because, in different ways, both King and Martin are right, despite their differences.

According to Martin, King is mistaken to think that there are significant parallels between the causal theory and Abelard, because he misinterprets Abelard's views. Abelard, Martin argues, follows the tradition of Aristotle and Boethius, according to which words primarily signify '*passiones* of the soul', which Abelard identifies with *intellectus* ('understandings'). Only secondarily do they signify things. If this is so, then it seems to be wrong to assert that for Abelard 'the extension of a term is not a function of its sense', since a word is, for Abelard, imposed and used primarily in order to generate a certain understanding, and it is this understanding that decides its extension.

This approach, which puts meaning firmly 'in the head', is developed further, Martin explains, in Abelard's theory of *attentio*.[8] Here Martin is following the lead of Irène Rosier-Catach, who first noticed the importance of *attentio* in Abelard's semantic theory and showed how the idea probably was derived from Augustine.[9] According to Abelard, the human mind is capable of attending to different aspects of an object or an image—its various 'natures' (what is predicable of it in its own category) and 'properties' (properties of it belonging to another category). For example, Socrates can be regarded not just as Socrates but as a man, an animal and a bodily thing—these are his natures, since they, like Socrates, belong to the category of substance; and he can be regarded as a rational thing, a white thing and a medium-sized thing, according to his various properties in the categories of (in these cases) quality and quantity. Moreover, this varied *attentio* can be directed either at the object itself, if it is present, or at a mental image of the object. Our sensory awareness of the object either directly or through a mental image already carries in it a complete account of the thing's nature and properties, but only in a confused way. It is the ability to unravel this confused impression, distinguishing between the different 'natures and properties' of a thing, which constitutes reason, possessed by humans alone among animals.

Abelard's discussion of mental images has been used by King and other scholars, however, as a way of breaking the link between mental description and reference. They claim that, for Abelard, the image a person uses to think about something need not be like the thing in question.[10] We could, for instance, use a mental image of Socrates to think about Plato, or a mental image of a lion to think about a giraffe. If this is so, then it seems that reference is not determined by what is going on in speakers' or listeners' minds, because you and I could both be using 'Socrates' to refer successfully to Socrates, but I would be directing my mind's attention to a mental image of, say, Plato and you to a mental image of, say, a hippopotamus you saw in the zoo. But Martin argues powerfully that there is no textual basis for such a claim: although one can attend to an image in different ways, it must be a likeness of the object of thought.[11]

HOW PETER KING WOULD RESPOND

King has written no response following Martin's article, but he had, before the piece by Martin appeared, written another article about Abelard and language.[12] Here he draws attention to exactly the feature of Abelard's account of language that Martin uses to attack his views—his taking up the Aristotelian-Boethian position that words signify primarily understandings and that these are shared naturally by all humans. But King still keeps to his earlier views about Abelard and direct reference. He does so by means of another assimilation of Abelard to recent philosophy—here of the early rather than the late twentieth century. He explains that 'Abelard offers his breakthrough distinction between sense (*significatio*) and reference (*nominatio*).'[13] He then goes on to assimilate, as anticipated by his translation, this distinction to the one made by Frege between 'sense and reference', which 'is a staple of contemporary philosophy of language.'[14] Signification, he says, is 'a quasi-psychological property, like Fregean *Sinn*; it is a matter of the causal force a term has in giving rise to an understanding.' Nomination or reference is what links words to the world. King then goes on to present Abelardian reference in terms almost identical to those in his *Stanford Encyclopedia* article. A name acquires reference 'through imposition (*impositio*), a performative act akin to baptism, which by fiat associates a linguistic item with things in the world. . . . The reference of a common noun is determined by the nature of the thing to which it is applied: "human" is associated with whatever is a rational mortal animal, for instance, since that is human nature, though it would refer to humans even if we were ignorant of what human nature consists in.'[15] (King uses 'human' to translate the Latin *homo*.) And, as if to stress the affinities with Putnam and Kripke, King adds in a footnote: 'Thus "water" refers to whatever is H_2O, rather than XYZ, regardless of our knowledge of water's nature or our ability to identify samples correctly.'

In the rest of the article, King concentrates on the side of semantics concerned with signification and so with thoughts, arguing that Abelard devises a sophisticated theory of mental language. But, as the quotation above explains, these views are consistent with Abelard's also holding a theory of direct reference, in his account of nomination. It appears then that, according to King's most recent account, Abelard has a Boethian semantics, which accords central importance to the thoughts of speakers and listeners and which can be seen as a mental language theory; and at the same time he is, so far as reference is concerned, akin to a direct reference theorist. If this is a fair reconstruction of Abelard's views, then it seems that King can meet Martin's criticisms by saying that his Boethian account of Abelard's semantics is correct, but just so far as sense is concerned; with regard to reference, Abelard holds to the causal theory, and it is only with this part of Abelard's theory that King is making his comparison.

There is, however, a very strong objection to this putative defence. The link between Abelard and the causal theory of reference is supposed to be provided by his account of imposition. But imposition is not linked by Abelard just to reference. Rather, to use Fregean language, it is linked to a theory primarily about the sense of the names which are imposed and only incidentally about their reference. Abelard's ideas on imposition should not, therefore, be grouped together with his comments on reference and contrasted with a supposedly different side of his semantics concerned with sense and developed through a Boethian theory of signification. Is

King, then, as misguided as Martin believes, though for somewhat different reasons? Matters do not turn out to be so simple. Following through to its end the trail of Abelard's thought about imposition, the cause of imposition and the semantic term he links with it, *sententia*, eventually reveals a real parallel with Putnam and Kripke, though one far less direct than King has suggested.

BAPTISM, IMPOSITION AND THE CAUSE OF IMPOSITION

Baptism, stripped of its religious connotations and understood as a pure naming ceremony, provides an excellent metaphor for the process by which, in the causal theory of reference, words are attached to things or sorts of things. In baptism, a particular name, such as 'Peter', 'Paul', or 'Mary', is attached to an individual person. The name is not supposed to tell anything about the person, but to act as a label, to pick out just that individual. For the direct reference theorists, this is just how names continue to refer to individuals and how they refer to kinds. And, for a baptismal naming to succeed, it does not matter what the baptizer is thinking, so long as the ceremony is performed correctly and the community thenceforth calls the person by the name. Similarly, for causal reference theorists, what gives a word its meaning is not what goes in people's minds but social, linguistic practice that establishes and continues a link between a given word and the thing or sorts of things to which it refers. By contrast, baptism is a rather bad metaphor for imposition as conceived by Abelard. For him imposition does not simply link words and things; it links words to things, in order to produce a thought in the listener's mind, and that thought is not just of the thing but of the thing *under a description*. In addition—this is a point which will be discussed later—what goes on in the impositor's mind has an important bearing on the nature of the imposition.

Abelard distinguishes between signification as a relationship between words and things, on the one hand, and signification as a relationship between words and the thoughts they produce in the listener (*significatio intellectus*—the signification of thought) on the

other. If one asks why names are imposed, 'the first and main signification is that of thought, because the word is attached to the thing
only so that it should produce a thought.'[16] This attitude is simply
the result of how signification was usually understood in the Middle
Ages: where 'w' is a significant word, 'w' signifies w = 'w' causes a
thought of w in the listener.[17] This consideration does not in itself
undermine King's position, but it does once the sort of thought
Abelard has in mind is taken into account. According to Abelard,
the thought produced is about the nature of the thing, so that in
principle someone who understands the name of a kind knows
something about its fundamental characteristics. The relationship
between the name imposed, the thing, its characteristics and the
thought of them is, however, quite complex.

The first link in the chain is the notion of the 'cause of imposition'. This cause of imposition is not some extrinsic reason why it
so happened that this word was attached to this thing (as, in a real
baptism, a person might be named 'Mary' because his grandmother
had that name or because of its religious associations). Rather, the
'cause of imposition' is the having of a characteristic or set of characteristics by the thing named which—in a way quite unlike what
happens in a baptism—are from then on linked to that name. This
idea comes out very clearly in the case of equivocal names (for example, in English, 'bank' as in 'bank of a river' and 'High Street
bank'), which have, says Abelard, more than one cause of imposition (so, in this case: *land at the edge of a river* and *establishment that
keeps (or endangers?) people's money for them*).[18] In the case of a univocal word, such as 'man', there is 'a single cause of imposition on all
genuine men. The definition, "rational, mortal, animal", which the
word has because of it, provides a firm proof.'[19]

In his discussion of universals, Abelard maintains that one reason why a word is a universal is that it has a 'common cause of
imposition'—that is to say, it does not just refer to many things of
the same sort, but it does so on account of what they have in common.[20] So the common cause of imposition of 'man' is what he calls
the *status* of man—that is to say, being-a-man or that-it-is-a-man,
which can be analysed into having certain features, such as being

an animal, mortal and rational.[21] But it is not at all the case that a description such as 'mortal, rational animal' is simply used to fix the reference of 'man' (as even a causal theorist might accept) or to determine its reference, as a descriptivist would think. The position is rather that the name 'man' is attached to that thing standing there and everything of its kind (which things they are is taken to be uncontroversial and obvious to everyone). This attaching establishes *not just* the word's reference *but also* the word's carrying a certain sense, linked to its cause of imposition. In the case of man, part of this sense is 'mortal, rational animal', although—as will be explained—it is not the whole of it. One of the clearest ways of seeing that the cause of imposition does not simply determine reference is to look at the passages where Abelard uses it precisely to explain the difference in meaning between words which have the same reference. Whatever is able to laugh (*risibile*) is also able to sail (*navigabile*)—the reference of these words is the same (all and only human beings). But the words 'sound differently' (that is, have different meanings—but see below on the misleading connotations of 'meaning') because of their different causes of imposition. Similarly, in Abelard's view, 'fate' and 'providence' refer to the same thing but have different causes of imposition. Here the 'cause of imposition' seems very close to the Fregean notion of 'sense', with 'fate' as morning star to the evening star of 'providence'.[22]

Here the examples of words distinguished in meaning by their cause of imposition are not kind names. But Abelard's approach to kind names is similar. He develops it through a word which he connects closely with the cause of imposition: *sententia.*

SENTENTIA AND DEFINITION

From its cause of imposition a word receives not just its reference but what Abelard calls its *sententia.*[23] As Abelard puts it, making the contrast between equivocal words, which have more than one cause of imposition and so more than one *sententia,* and univocal ones:

'An utterance is called single which has one *sententia* according to a single cause of imposition, such as "man", "white thing" or "Socrates". For, although they are imposed on diverse things, yet when they are pronounced they make known the same about the single things and they are imposed on them all according to the same nature or property.'[24] *Sententia* here, and in other semantic contexts, might be translated as 'sense' or 'meaning'.[25] Here, for example, are a couple of instances of this usage from early in the *Dialectica:* 'For why treat the signification [*significatio*] of a name, in order to open up its meaning [*ut eius sententiam aperiret*], when what it signifies does not exist?'; 'It is, however, worth investigating whether there can be a perfect and true meaning [*perfecta et vera sententia*] for things which are expressed in a faulty way, such as *mulier albus* ["white woman", but with "white" given a masculine as opposed to a feminine ending].'[26] 'Meaning', however, might have misleading implications. 'Meaning' is often equated in contemporary discussions with reference (the word used by Frege that is usually translated as 'reference', *Bedeutung,* has the normal sense in German of 'meaning'). Abelardian *sententia,* it will already be clear, is *not* reference. If two terms are extensionally equivalent, they have the same reference. But Abelard considers that two terms can be extensionally equivalent without having the same *sententia.* 'Mortal, rational animal' and 'two-footed animal able to walk' are, he says, 'equal in nomination' (that is, they have the same reference) but are diverse in *sententia.*[27] Similarly, he recognizes that, if we say 'corporeal substance', we thereby refer to the things which are designated by 'to be coloured', but this characterization is not 'according to the *sententia* of the name, since "coloured thing" does not have either substance or corporeal in its meaning [*significatio*].'[28] Indeed, often information that would, on its own, be sufficient to establish reference is not even part of a word's *sententia.* Abelard brings out this point when he is talking about *propria,* properties that, according to the terminology of Porphyry's *Isagoge,* belong to all and only the members of a given species. The *proprium* of man, in the Porphyrean tradition, is capability of laughter. Abelard writes in the *Logica ingre-dientibus* that

> if someone should say, in order to determine what a man is, 'an animal capable of laughter', through the term 'capable of laughter' he determines the content for the word 'man' with re-gard to things ranged under it but he does not open up the *sen-tentia* of the name. The sense of 'capable of laughter' is not contained in the *sententia* of 'man'. It ['an animal capable of laughter'] can therefore be a description of man in so far as the things contained by the term are concerned, but not so far as the *sententia* of the name is concerned.[29]

Is the *sententia* of a kind word then the definition of the species in question? The answer is not straightforward. Abelard distin-guishes between three sorts of definition. For what we might call 'weak definition'—sometimes Abelard does not recognize it as defi-nition at all but calls it rather 'determination'—the criterion is merely extensional equivalence. An example is the (quasi-) defini-tion of body as 'to be coloured'.[30] Then there is 'normal definition', corresponding to definition taken in the usual sense of the Aristote-lian and Porphyrean tradition. Such a definition is not only exten-sionally equivalent to what is defined; it is also, unlike weak or quasi-definition, framed from the essential characteristics without which a thing *cannot* be of a given kind. 'Mortal, rational animal' is, for example, such a definition of 'man', because animal is its genus and mortality and rationality are its *differentiae,* the essential proper-ties that distinguish men from other types of animal.[31] In Abelard's view, however, such standard definitions often do not contain all the essential properties of a kind of thing. There is therefore for Abelard also a stronger sense of definition, which excludes even 'man is a ra-tional, mortal animal'. On this, strictest sense, a definition is—in Abelard's phrase—'according to the *sententia* of the name': for ex-ample, when 'a coloured thing' is defined as 'that which is informed by colour', because '"coloured thing" seems to make known nothing other than this phrase does.'[32] This definition 'seems to hold the whole *sententia* of the name' as does the definition of 'substance' as 'a thing existing per se'.[33] Abelard is not sure whether to add the definition of 'body' as 'corporeal substance' to this list. He cannot be sure that the only *differentia* of body is corporeality. If there are more, then it does not hold the whole *sententia* of body, just as

> the definition 'rational, mortal animal' or 'two-footed animal able to walk' does not <hold the whole *sententia*> of 'man'. . . . Now since being two-footed, and being able to walk and being able to be taught and also perhaps many other forms are *differentiae* of man, and they are all said to be determined in the name 'man' . . . it appears that the whole *sententia* of 'man' is not enclosed in its definition but that it is defined according to a certain part of what makes it up. Therefore what suffices for defining does not suffice for constituting. For just as man cannot subsist without rationality or mortality, so neither can he in any way remain without other *differentiae*, by which equally his substance is completed.[34]

How an Impositor Can Establish a *Sententia* without Fully Grasping It

The *sententia* of a kind term is, therefore, what might be called its 'full meaning', its definition in this final, very strict acceptation, rather than in the usual sense of the word. To give the *sententia* of such a word, it is not enough to give a term that is extensionally equivalent (and in many cases, such as *risibile* with respect to *homo*, such a term is not part of its *sententia* at all). Nor is it enough to give a normal definition, which marks out a kind of thing by its essential features. The *sententia* contains all the essential features of things of that sort. But, if a word is given its *sententia* at imposition, how is it to be given unless the impositor knows all these features in every case—something which Abelard clearly thinks impossible, since he says that the essential features of some kinds are still unknown. An example of this state of ignorance is given in the case just discussed.

Abelard simply does not know whether body has more *differentiae* than bodiliness. Writing probably more than ten years after the *Dialectica*, Abelard makes a similar point, through the mouth of the Christian of his *Collationes* (sec. 206): 'Consider this: we all know, from our everyday use of language, which things are called "stones". But we have not, I believe, been able to find a word for what are the proper *differentiae* of a stone or the property of this species, by which any definition or description of "stone" could be completed.' Here speakers seem to be in an even worse position than with regard to 'body'. It is not merely that they do not know *all* the *differentiae* and so cannot give the full *sententia* of the word 'stone' and so define it in its strictest sense; they cannot even provide a normal definition of it.

It is precisely to answer this problem that Abelard enters on a line of thought that does, in an important respect, parallel the thinking behind the causal theory of reference—although Abelard is not thinking about reference. Immediately after the discussion of definition and *sententia* in the *Dialectica*, Abelard writes a passage parallel to the well-known one from which King quotes (see above, p. 150) to show Abelard's affinity to the causal reference theory: 'There will perhaps be a question about whether, as has been said, all its *differentiae* [sc. the *differentiae* of the species] are understood in the name of the species. For, if we consider the understanding of the impositor, this does not seem true, since perhaps he did <not> name all its *differentiae*, just as he did not name all <the thing in question's> accidents.' Then he replies: 'Although the impositor did not understand distinctly all the *differentiae* of man, he wanted the word to be taken according to all the *differentiae* of man, whatever they might be, although he conceived them confusedly. Or, if he imposed the name according to certain *differentiae*, the *sententia* of the name should consist only according to them and the definition of the *sententia* can be assigned only according to them.'[35] Abelard is concerned, very explicitly, with the *sententia*, not the reference, of a kind name such as 'man'. He offers two possibilities: his main theory and an alternative. In both cases, a decision made by the impositor determines what the *sententia* of this word will be. According to the main theory, the impositor of, for example, the word 'man' intends—with a man in front of him—that the *sententia* of the word should contain all the *differentiae* of man, that is to say, all the *differentiae* which attach to that thing, a man, standing in front of him, whatever they are, even though the impositor himself cannot discern them clearly and enumerate them. According to the alternative suggestion, the impositor discerns, for example, that the man standing in front of him is corporeal and rational, and he determines the *sententia* of 'man' as containing just corporeality and rationality.

In the better-known passage on the same theme from the *Logica ingredientibus,* Abelard confines himself to his main theory. He has been considering the idea that universal words, including kind names, signify Platonic Ideas in the mind of God. His view is that there might well be such conceptions in the divine mind, which represent perfectly the natures of different things—not just natural kinds but also accidents and *differentiae.* But since we do not have access to God's mind, the conceptions in it do nothing to explain the semantics of human language:

> It is right that these conceptions through abstraction of this sort are ascribed to the divine mind, not the human one, because humans, who know things only through the senses, scarcely or never rise to this sort of simple intelligence, because the external appearance of the accidents stops them from conceiving the pure natures of things. And so it happens that humans have opinion rather than intelligence with regard to things which do not lie beneath sense. Experience itself teaches us this. For when we think of some city that we have not seen, when we arrive there we find it other than we thought it to be. Thus also do I believe that we have opinion rather <than intelligence> of the intrinsic forms that do not come to the senses, such as rationality and mortality, being-a-father and sitting. But all the names of every sort of existing thing, in themselves, produce understanding rather than opinion, because the inventor intended to impose them according to some natures or properties of the

things, even if he himself was not able to distinguish well the nature or property.[36]

Abelard is talking more generally here, about names of all sorts (other than proper names), and rather more loosely, but the idea is the same as in the main *Dialectica* theory. The impositor need not himself be able to discern the different features of a type of thing which become part of the *sententia* of the word he imposes on such things. He need only intend that the *sententia* of the word include the nature or properties that things of the sort really have, and which he cannot clearly discern, for it to include them.

ABELARD AND THE CAUSAL THEORY OF REFERENCE, AGAIN

Abelard's main theory about the imposition of a word's *sententia* is both significantly similar to an aspect of the direct reference theory and also strikingly different from it. Abelard, Putnam and Kripke share the recognition that our ordinary language does a better job of talking about how the world really is than individual language users' limited knowledge of the facts would allow. From this, they con-clude that there must be some direct link between the things in the world and words, which is not mediated by our deficient under-standings. For Putnam and Kripke, the reference of, for instance, 'water' is determined as being everything which has the same chemical structure as that stuff there to which the impositor was pointing, although the impositor himself and many language users knew and even now know nothing about its chemical structure. For Abelard, the *sententia* of 'man' is established as being whatever re-ally are the *differentiae* of members of the kind to which that thing on which he imposed the word 'man' belongs. For Putnam and Kripke, the impositor's decision to make the word 'water' refer to that stuff (which in fact is H_2O) makes 'Water is H_2O' a necessary truth, but one that has to be discovered by scientific investigation. For Abelard, if a kind of thing, K, has the essential properties m to z, then they are all part of the sense of the word 'k', since the impositor imposed the name with the intention that it was in accord with all these essential properties, whatever they really were. It is for the science of subsequent generations to discover what the full sense of 'k' is. Propositions such as 'a k is *m*' or 'a k is *t*' are all analytic but will not seem to be so until the requisite level of scientific knowledge about K has been reached.

For Abelard's move to be successful, he needs the assumption that the world is in fact divided into natural kinds which each have a distinctive set of natures or essential properties and that, even though very often we do not know what they are (and have no grasp of the inner character of these and other properties), we usually faultlessly recognize which things belong to which kinds. Putnam and Kripke do not need, and would not make, the second of these assumptions, but their theory does involve the idea that there are certain natural kinds, such as water. Martin has remarked on how this essentialism shared by Abelard with Putnam and Kripke is a reason why King thinks that Abelard anticipated the 'new theory', but, he adds, 'The order of explanation connecting metaphysics to semantics is quite the opposite in Abaelard to that on which the new theory relies. For Abaelard "essentialism" does not follow from rigidity but rather guarantees it.'[37] Yet, in fact, this shared essentialism is linked to a way in which their theories are really alike, and it is at least disputable whether Putnam and Kripke draw deep metaphysical conclusions from their semantics, as Martin contends, or, like Abelard, start from a metaphysics which supports their semantics.

There is, however, as well as the underlying gap between a theory about sense and one about reference, another important difference. As Martin makes clear when he discusses *attentio*, Abelard believes that our sense perception of a natural thing, direct or through an imagination of it, does contain, though confusedly, an account of its natures and properties. Humans, he believes, have naturally accurate mental representations of the natural kinds they have observed, though these representations are confused, unless and until they are rationally analysed. Abelard would not accept that the only mental representation Putnam has of an elm is the description 'common deciduous tree'. No one is *that* much of an ignoramus! Even stay-indoors Putnam has a correct, but confused, mental representation of an elm. The same was true for the original impositor. When he gave a word its sense using an open formula— 'whatever its *differentiae* really are'—it was not as if these *differentiae* were entirely hidden from him. Confusedly and darkly he saw what the science of future generations would discern with clarity and order.

ABELARD AND CONTEMPORARY
METAPHYSICS

This chapter is about one side of Abelard's metaphysics: his ontology, that is to say, his account of how objects in the world are
made up. It looks, especially, at how Abelard's ideas in this field have
been linked by interpreters to discussions by contemporary meta-
physicians. Is he some kind of trope theorist?[1] Does he give Aristotelian thinking a decidedly modern, materialist and reductionist twist?
But the chapter's purpose extends beyond the methodological. It begins with a general presentation of the ontology found in the *Dialectica* and the *Logica ingredientibus,* which summarizes, clarifies and,
where necessary, corrects what I have written before. In weighing
up the case for linking Abelard with trope theory and criticizing the
most influential contemporary interpretation of his metaphysics, a
reductionist one, the next two sections present further evidence for
the reading presented in the first section and add detail to it. The
final section argues that, although the reductive interpretation of the
Dialectica and *Logica ingredientibus* is wrong, Abelard did in fact go
on to develop his ontology in a limitedly reductive manner. It thus

illustrates the value, as argued in chapter 1, of allowing for development in Abelard's thought over time in order to understand it.

ON WHAT THERE IS: A SKETCH OF ABELARD'S VIEWS

Thinkers in the early twelfth-century Paris schools based their account of the fundamental constituents of the world mainly on two
sources: Aristotle's *Categories* and Porphyry's *Isagoge*. It may seem
surprising that two logical textbooks should be sources for metaphysics, but then these thinkers were primarily logicians, and, in
any case, no ancient metaphysical writings were available. Abelard
followed his contemporaries in making these two texts by Porphyry
and Aristotle the basis for his thought about what there is. Although,
as will become clear, he was very willing to develop his own trains of
thought, his starting point was an extremely scrupulous regard for
the text of the *Isagoge* and the *Categories,* which led to a willingness
to question, though always respectfully, the interpretations of their
authoritative commentator, Boethius.

At the beginning of the *Categories,* Aristotle distinguishes between things said with and without combination (*complexio*): 'man
runs' as opposed to 'man' and 'runs'. He then proposes a fourfold
division of 'those things which exist', using the notions of what are
'said of a subject' (*de subiecto dicuntur*) and what are 'in a subject' (*in
subiecto sunt*), and their negations. He gives no further explanation
of what is meant by 'said of a subject', but he describes that which is
in a subject as being 'in something, not as a part, and not able to
exist without that in which it is.'[2] The divisions are exemplified as
follows. Man is said of a subject, a certain man, but is not in a subject. A certain knowledge of grammar is in a subject, the soul, but is
not said of a subject. Knowledge is both in a subject, the soul, and
said of a subject, knowledge of grammar. And this man or that horse
is neither in nor said of a subject.[3]

The text of the *Categories,* which starts from a discussion of language and uses the term 'said of' but says it is talking about 'those
things which exist', leaves interpreters uncertain whether the four-

fold division it is to be taken as of words, things or a mixture of the two. Boethius considers this division to be, in the first place, of words, but he takes it straightforwardly to reflect the way in which the things to which they refer are divided. He believes that there are things of each of the four types it distinguishes and that between them they include all things—just as all things, he considers, are included in Aristotle's more detailed scheme of categories: substance and nine categories of accident:

> Here Aristotle collects the multitude of all words [*sermones*] into a very small division. . . . For every thing is either substance, or quantity, or quality, relation [*ad aliquid*], or doing or being-done-to, or when, or where, or having or posture [*situs*]. Concerning which there will also be the same number of <divisions of> the words which signify these things. And this is the largest division, to which nothing can be added. But the smallest division is that which is made into four: into substance and accident, and universal and particular. For every thing is either a substance or an accident; either universal or particular.[4]

Abelard also reads Aristotle as talking about words. But he does not follow Boethius in thinking that all of it also reflects how things are divided. He thinks that only part of what Aristotle says applies also to things: 'And note that to be said of a subject, which applies to universals, is properly speaking <a property> of words. But to be in a subject, although it is attributed to words here, is, however, properly speaking <a property> of things, because it is things which are properly are said to be foundations or what is founded on them'.[5] It is not surprising that he gives such an interpretation. At least by the time he wrote the *Isagoge* commentary of the *Logica ingredientibus*, Abelard was what would now be called a 'nominalist': he held that no things are universals.[6] He gives arguments against the variety of theories by which other philosophers tried to show that universals do really exist, claiming to have shown that it is impossible for anything to be one and many in the manner of a universal. Although the debate in which he engages is principally about genera and species—universals in the category of substance—Abelard makes it completely clear that he is speaking in general about universals.[7] He needs, therefore, to take what are said of a subject *just* to be words in order to make his authority, Aristotle, support his nominalist views.

Not only does Abelard disagree with Boethius that there are things in all four of Aristotle's divisions. Whilst he follows him in equating what are said of a subject with universals, what are not said of a subject with particulars and what are in a subject with accidents, he does not accept that what are not in a subject include all and only substances.[8] The reason is that Abelard recognizes a kind of thing which is not an accident, and so is not in a subject, but is not a substance either.[9]

His source is Porphyry's *Isagoge,* and behind this text Aristotle himself. According to the widely used definition in the *Isagoge,* an accident is 'that which comes and leaves without the corruption of the subject.'[10] But accidental properties are not the only type of property recognized by Porphyry. The *Isagoge* also has a section on *differentiae,* what would now be called 'essential properties', such as Socrates' being alive or his rationality, which, unlike his whiteness, does not come to and leave him without his being 'corrupted'—that is to say, his ceasing to be the sort of substance, a man, which he is. Porphyry introduces these essential properties in the context of his tree of genera and species, which starts from the genus substance, of which body is a species and is itself the genus of living ('ensouled') body, and goes down to man, which is a species of the genus animal. Each species is distinguished from its genus by an essential property or, as Porphyry calls it, *differentia*—corporeal, for instance, distinguishes body from substance, ensouled distinguishes living body from body, rational differentiates man from animal. Aristotle himself explicitly declares that, like substances, *differentiae* are not in a subject, and Abelard follows him, although, of course, it is only in the case of particular *differentiae* (this rationality, for example) that there are things as well as words.[11] Although they therefore fall into different divisions of Aristotle's fourfold scheme, like his contemporaries, Abelard uses the word 'form' to refer both to particular accidents and to particular *differentiae.*

Abelard, then, recognizes three kinds of things: particular sub-stances, particular accidents and particular *differentiae*. Some inter-preters have doubted whether Abelardian forms—the particular ac-cidents and *differentiae*—should be considered as things at all (see below, pp. 184–88). But there is plenty of evidence that he does see them as things. He regularly uses the words *res* and *essentia* (in Abelard's language roughly a synonym of *res*) for them.[12] One text which supports particularly clearly the general view that Abelard re-gards all forms as things is found in his treatment of certain derived words (such as 'one', 'accident' and 'signification') which seem not to have a corresponding sort of particular form, because, if they did, there would be an infinite regress (for example, were there a particular form of unity attaching to each thing that is one, then, since that form of unity would be one, another particular form of unity would attach to it, and so on to infinity).[13] The infinite regress argument would make no sense unless the forms concerned were considered to be countable things, and Abelard here refers to the at-tached form as 'the attached thing'.[14] He solves the regress problem by saying that, for these exceptional derived words, there are no cor-responding forms—an answer that underlines his view that any par-ticular form will be a thing.[15] Abelard also revealingly explains that some composite quantities (those in time or measures of time) do *not* have a true essence, because—as he holds as a result of his presentism—each of the individuals which constitutes them ceases to exist as soon as the next comes into being.[16] Only for Where (to which When might be expected to be analogous) and posture (*situs*) are there no such indications that Abelard regards them as things.

Particular substances are the individual members of natural kinds, such as Socrates, this flower or that stone. Non-natural ob-jects, such as a house, are not substances, although they are made out of substances. Abelard makes clearer his conception of both substances and *differentiae* in his account of how they are created, which is given most fully in the *Dialectica*.[17] He distinguishes first creations from second creations. First creations are those in which 'the matters of things first began to exist—those which had no pre-existing matter.'[18] The matter of all bodies which God creates consists, Abelard says, of the four elements (fire, air, water and earth) all mixed together. The second creations are 'when he makes already created matter through the addition of substantial form enter a new existence [*novum facit ingredi esse*], as when God created man from the mud of the ground. In this there is no newness of matter, but there seems to be diversity of form alone and, so far as the form of the substance is concerned, it seems that the nature of the substance is changed.'[19] Abelard goes on to describe God's creation of the first man in more detail: 'In this second creation the matter of the earth, which already existed, could undergo the type of change called "generation" when God informed it with ensouledness, having-sense-perception, rationality, mortality and the others.'[20] Generation does not take place just during God's formation of the universe, but it is, Abelard insists, always the work of God. The turning of ashes (presumably along with sand) into glass is, for example, God's work (by contrast with the fashioning of the glass into a vessel of a particular shape); and it is God who makes the child from the matter which flows from the father—the child comes to be out of his or her father but not through him.[21] In the *Hexaemeron*, Abelard gives a vivid picture of corporeal matter being changed from on substance to another: '[Bodily substance] does not cease to be changed not just by accidental [forms] but also by substantial ones and to be made into [an individual of] various species, so that what is now inanimate now becomes a living thing, and vice versa. And what is now this, dissolved by death, goes over into another species.'[22]

Abelard, then, gives a physical reading of Porphyry's tree, with regard to creation. God does not, of course, create any bare substances. Rather—so far as bodily things are concerned—he begins by creating corporeal substance: body is, for Abelard, substance and the form corporeity,[23] but he makes it clear that the two are created together in the first creation. In the second creation, God adds to body all the differential forms needed to make each thing of each species. Although, however, body and differential forms are the elements out of which substances are made, Abelard goes on, in his discussion in the *Dialectica,* to insist that it is the whole substances which are, metaphysically speaking, primary. He declares that 'the changing of forms does not make the diversity of species and genera, but the creation of substance. For, in whatever way the forms may vary, if the identity remains, it makes no difference to the general or special essence.'[24] Abelard is not saying, contrary to what he has just written and takes as established elsewhere, that there could be a substance of such and such a sort (a man, a horse) without the appropriate differential forms. His point, rather, is that genera and species are ways of grouping substances, because of the way the *substances* are.[25] There will be different genera and species so long as things of a material nature are varied.[26] In the species which fall under the category substance, he goes on to explain, it is indeed the *differentia* which causes their diversity from one another, 'but this happens from the diversity of the substance of the things which they make. And for this reason these sorts of *differentiae,* which, coming into a substance, make both the distinction of the substance and the union of its common nature, are called "substantial".'

This passage in the *Dialectica* is not the only occasion where Abelard stresses the unity of whole substances. Although body plus the *differentiae* of being animated and having sense perception would constitute an animal that belongs to no determinate species, Abelard insists that—by contrast with body, which precedes temporally the substances formed from it—things do not exist in genera before they do in their species: we should not believe that 'animal or any genus can ever exist except in some species.'[27] Abelard is therefore adamant that there is no way in which this man is an animal plus the differential forms (mortality and rationality) that distinguish him as a human. Rather, he is an animal formed by these two forms—one thing made out of two.[28]

The other type of forms, accidental ones, is characterized by Abelard in terms of the relations between them and the substances they inform. On the one hand, the substances are not dependent on them. Abelard, like all his contemporaries, accepts Porphyry's description of an accident as 'that which comes and leaves without the corruption of the subject.' If, then, *S* is a substance and *a* is one of its accidents,

1. It is possible for S to exist without a existing.

Abelard also identifies accidents with what are in a subject and accepts Aristotle's statement that, for what is in a subject, 'when it is in something not as a part, it is impossible for it to exist without that in which it is.'[29] Abelard might then seem to be committed to holding, along with (1), its mirror image:

2. It is not possible for a to exist without S existing.

But in fact—as will be discussed in the next section—Abelard *rejects* (2).

ABELARD AND TROPES

Trope theory dates back, strictly speaking, just to 1953, when D. C. Williams published his article 'On the Elements of Being'. A trope is an abstract particular. Just as there are concrete particulars, such as the book on my desk, so there are abstract particulars, such as the shape of the book, the shade of whiteness of the page it has open, its position in relation to the twenty other books scattered on my desk, and its smell. All these tropes are particulars but are repeatable—thousands of pages, for instance, have exactly the same shade of whiteness—by different but identically similar tropes. As their exponents have been eager to point out, long before Williams devised his particular theory and gave it an inapposite name, particular properties and relations played an important, but often overlooked, role in the metaphysics of philosophers from Aristotle to Stout. Abelard has not been mentioned by the contemporary trope theorists, but there is, at the least, a prima facie similarity between Abelard's metaphysics, since his forms, all of them particular, seem to be what the contemporary theorists call tropes.[30] Over the last thirty years, three Abelard specialists have taken positions about how, more precisely, this similarity should be understood, and in doing so they have been led to consider carefully what relationship Abelard understands there to be between substances and their accidents and *differentiae*.

The first is Chris Martin's view. It was he who first noticed the likeness, remarking in a 1992 article—which, in a few bold strokes, first identified the main lines of his ontology—that Abelard 'may be characterised in contemporary terms as a transferable trope theorist.'[31] In Martin's view Abelard's tropes are the particular *accidental* forms. He adds that Abelard's ontology, unlike that of today's trope theorists, also contains particular substantial essences or natures, of an Aristotelian kind, which are the substrata for the tropes. Martin also explains what he means by saying that the tropes are transferable: 'These forms cannot exist apart from the substances to which they now adhere but before their attachment they might have gone elsewhere.'

The second view is my own, as expressed in my book on Abelard and in a more recent article on Abelard and tropes.[32] Following Martin, I drew the parallel between Abelardian forms and tropes, but I extended it to differential as well as accidental forms, and I argued that, according to Abelard, differential forms might, like accidental ones, have belonged to different subjects from those which they in fact inform. I also—here in accord with Martin—said that, in addition to tropes, Abelard's ontology includes particular substances.

The third view is Alain de Libera's.[33] He accepts my view that differential forms need to be considered along with accidental forms in thinking about Abelard's relation to trope theory. He accepts that Abelardian forms are in some ways like what are now called tropes. He points, however, to a number of underlying differences between Abelard's thinking and the Aristotelian tradition from which it derives, on the one hand, and contemporary trope theory on the other. Altogether, he concludes, Abelard comes far less close to contemporary trope theory than his realist opponent, William of Champeaux.

In order to see which of these views is the most correct, we must examine Abelard's remarks on accidental and differential forms separately in order to establish how far either can be seen as transferable tropes, and then ask (with the methodological difficulties of such a question in mind) whether they allow him usefully to be labelled as a trope theorist. Aristotle, as mentioned above, described the relationship between what is in a subject (that is to say, an accident) and its subject by saying that it is 'in something, not as a part, and not able to exist without that in which it is' (1a24–25). Boethius translates this definition as: 'I say that that is in a subject which, while it is not in something as a part, it is impossible for it to be without that in which it is' (*in subiecto autem esse dico quod, cum in aliquo sit non sicut pars, impossibile est esse sine eo in quo est*).[34] In his commentary, Boethius argues that, because Aristotle says 'without that in which it *is*' and not 'without that in which it *was*', he is not, as it might seem, insisting that accidents cannot be transferred from one substance to another—something Boethius believes happens when the smell of an apple is left on the hand of the person who touched it. According to him, Aristotle meant that an accident can change place (go from one substance to another), 'but it cannot subsist without some substance.'[35] Abelard rejects this reading entirely, tactfully suggesting that Boethius never really meant it but was speaking—as so often when, in Abelard's view, he writes something silly—'according to the opinion of others.'[36]

Yet Abelard himself also distorts Aristotle's obvious meaning. He separates the phrase 'not as a part' (*non sicut quaedam pars*) from the rest of the sentence, treating it as an interjection, and reads '*cum*' as having a temporal sense. He therefore understands the remark as saying: 'That is in a subject which, when it is in something (not as a part), it is impossible for it to be without that in which it is'. As he puts it: '[Aristotle] shows that these things [i.e. the accidents] are in Socrates in such a way that they are not there as any part of the subject substance, and also that, when they are in it, they cannot exist without it.' Read in this way, the second condition is not, Abelard says, 'that they cannot exist without it' but that 'after they are in it, they cannot exist without it', which he explains as meaning: 'Their nature will not allow that when accidents are first in something, they could subsist without it.'[37] Abelard therefore proposes

3. After *a* has become an accident of *S*, it is not possible for *a* to exist without *S* existing.

(2)—that is to say, 'It is impossible for the accident to exist without the subject in which it is now'—is perhaps false. But, as (3) makes clear, it is false not for the reason Boethius thought, that *a* might migrate from *S* to another subject, but rather because it might never have been an accident of *S* and instead have been an accident of another subject. As Abelard goes on to explain, 'It seems that the whiteness of this body, when it is innate in this body, might in the same way have come to other bodies. But when it is in this body, it cannot any longer be in another.'[38] And then, after giving some parallel examples, he concludes: 'It might perhaps happen that, although it came to this subject, it came to another subject and thus was always in the other subject, because it had never occurred [*contigisset*] to this subject. But nature cannot allow that when it is already in one, it can again be in another, that is to say, it cannot change its subject, moving from one to another.'[39]

On the face of it, Abelard's position in these two quotations (which, for ease of reference, can be called the 'Whiteness Passage') seems far less coherent than the Boethian view he rejects. Boethius's accidents are completely distinct things from the substances they inform, but they are things of a sort which can exist only so long as they are informing some substance or another. Abelard's accidents are also distinct from the substances they inform, since they might have informed different substances. But, if so, why cannot they—as Boethius believed—go from one substance to another? The parallel examples Abelard gives to (3) show that, in fact, he has a good answer to this question. He says that

4. It is not possible for a man who is blind to see

is false, whereas

5. It is not possible for him to see after he has become blind

is true.[40] The contrast between (4) and (5) is not, as it might appear from the verbal form of the sentences, between what was once possible and what is possible after a certain time. (4) does not deny the obvious truth that, before a man goes blind, it is possible for him to see. Rather, as Christopher Martin has explained in discussing another passage that treats the same contrast in more detail, (4) makes a false claim about counter-factual possibility.[41] As it happens, this person is now blind and cannot see, but—contrary to what (4) states—it might have been that he had not become blind and could see now. (5) states that, given that in fact he has become blind, he cannot see now or in the future. Abelard, as has already been explained in chapter 2 (see above, pp. 66–69), tended to think about possibilities in terms, not of alternative possible worlds, but of alternative possible life stories. The possibility falsely denied in (4) is that the person in question might have had a different life story, in which he never went blind, since it is part of human nature to be able to see. The possibility in (5) is about what can happen within a life story: if a human's life story in fact included becoming blind at time *t*, then it will have no moments after *t* in which the person in question sees (because it is in the nature of humans that, once they go blind, they cannot see again). From these parallels, it is clear that, with regard to a particular accident, such as this whiteness, Abelard does not think that there was a time when it existed independently after which it became attached to Socrates and, for some unexplained reason, cannot thereafter exist without him. Rather, he understands (3) to mean that

6. If at any moment of its existence *a* is an accident of *S*, then it is an accident of *S* at every moment of its existence.

It is part of an accident's nature to belong, not just to some subject, but to the subject to which it in fact belongs, and so it is not ad hoc to insist that, contrary to Boethius, an accident cannot move from one thing to another, and yet that it might, counter-factually, have been the case that, from the beginning of its existence, it belonged to a different subject, in the same way as it might have been the case that a blind person never became blind.

But why does Abelard not simply put forward (2), which would rule out Boethius's view even more clearly, and spare the need for interpretative legerdemain with Aristotle's wording? Although he says nothing explicitly, the explanation probably lies in his views about universals and individuation. Abelard denies that there are any really existing universals. Individuation is not, then, a matter of something universal's being made individual by a principle of individuation (such as the subject which an accident informs): accidental and differential forms are individuated essentially, in themselves.[42] If Abelard had adopted (2), however, it is hard to see how he could avoid admitting that accidents are individuated by their subjects, since it would be impossible for this whiteness, which informs Socrates, to have been anything but Socrates's whiteness. By contrast, the counter-factual possibility preserved in (3), even when interpreted as (6), that this whiteness might have belonged to a different subject, shows that the whiteness is not individuated by Socrates or any other possible subject.

Do particular *differentiae* enjoy the same definite, though very small, measure of ontological independence? Abelard's overall position suggests that they do. Since *differentiae* are considered to be particular things, the argument about individuation just made will apply to them too, and since they are not in a subject Abelard will not even have the job of explaining away Aristotle's view that it is not possible for them to exist without the substance in which they are. Chris Martin has, admittedly, argued against the independence of *differentiae*, because, he claims, to say that a man might have been rational by a different rationality implies that we can identify some man, Socrates, apart from his rationality, something Abelard believes is not possible.[43] But if the independence is taken in the same counterfactual sense analysed for accidental forms, this objection is avoided, since there could not be any moment at which Socrates lacked rationality (indeed, at which he lacked whatever particular rationality he in fact has).

One passage (the 'Rationality Passage') provides strong textual support for the view that, according to Abelard, *differentiae* have the same ontological independence as accidents. The Rationality Passage needs to be read in context.[44] Abelard begins by raising the point that, since he does not accept any real universals, every *differentia* will be this or that *differentia*, a particular. This position seems, however, to be open to the objection that there are two commonly accepted features of *differentiae* which will have to be denied, given Abelard's views. The first is that

(CAF 1) A *differentia* is predicated universally of the species, whereas it follows from Abelard's views that 'this rationality is not in many things'. The second commonly accepted feature is that

(CAF2) When its *differentia* is destroyed, the thing is necessarily destroyed.
But, Abelard explains, 'the man would not perish because of this <particular rationality>' (*neque propter eam* [sc. *hanc rationalitatem*]

homo periret). Allowing that, when Abelard says 'because of', it is short for 'because of not having', this rather gnomic comment means, it seems, that the particular man in question would not perish because of not having this particular rationality. Abelard then goes on to explain why, by his theory, this consequence (which contradicts CAF2) would come about:

[Rationality Passage] Socrates himself too, just as he is this man through it [this rationality], could also be through another <rationality>, either which exists or which never exists.

[*Ipse quoque Socrates, sicut hic homo est per eam, ita etiam posset esse per aliam, sive quae sit, sive numquam sit.*][45]

Socrates, that is to say, could do without this particular rationality and yet not perish, because he could be (presumably meant in the sense of 'might have been') rational by a different particular rationality. Abelard then goes on to explain—as he needs to do, in order to answer the criticism—how CAF1 and CAF2 can be understood so that they can, nonetheless, be retained. The claim that a *differentia* is predicated universally of its species (CAF1) applies to the words which are *differentiae*, not to the things which are *differentiae*. The claim that 'the thing' is destroyed if its *differentia* is destroyed (CAF2) should be understood 'according to the common cause of the imposition of the universal name, as if we were to say that the man cannot be anything such that it is not rational.'

The Rationality Passage, as cited above, explicitly states that a person could be rational through some other rationality than he in fact has (in the same way as something could have been white through a particular whiteness other than that by which it is in fact white). But there is a difficulty—and this is why its argumentative context has been laid out so carefully. The *posset* is in fact an emendation by the editor, Geyer, of the manuscript, which reads *possent*. It seems, though, to be a good emendation, since, with a minimum of change, it yields sense from the sentence, whereas if *possent* is left, a number of bigger changes will be needed. But there might still be a suspicion that a different meaning, requiring a different emendation, is lurking behind the passage. The plural *possent* in the manuscript raises the question of whether Abelard was talking about *men* in the plural and not, therefore, saying that an individual man, Socrates, could be rational by a different particular rationality.[46] The context, however, rules out such an interpretation. With Geyer's emendation, the whole argument makes perfect sense. The rival interpretation, in which Abelard is not talking about an individual man, would demand that '*neque propter eam* [sc. *hanc rationalitatem*] *homo periret*' be read as a statement about Man, the universal. But how could such an assertion be put by Abelard as the consequence of his own position, according to which there are no universals? Moreover, since it is plainly obvious, without further argument, that the universal *differentia* of Man would not be destroyed because a particular *differentia* of rationality perished, the Rationality Passage, instead of providing a clear explanation for what has just been asserted, would lose all point.

This long examination of Abelard's views about the ontological independence of forms was undertaken in order to throw light on the usefulness of thinking about his metaphysics in connection with trope theory. Had the question been merely whether his ontology included tropes, a positive answer could have been rapidly given, since tropes are merely particular properties and relations, as clearly are Abelardian forms. But, on careful scrutiny, Abelardian forms turn out to be, not merely tropes, but transferable tropes—though transferable only in a weak sense: counterfactually, they might have belonged to different subjects from those to which in fact they belong. Even such weak transferability brings Abelard's theory nearer to trope theory proper, such as that, for instance, expounded by D. C. Williams, inventor of the label, who regarded tropes as the elements of being, the basic constituents of everything else. By contrast, many in the long list of past philosophers who have been invoked as predecessors by trope theorists conceived tropes as non-transferable and so as very far from being basic elements in the constitution of things. Nonetheless, the fact that Abelard fully accepts Aristotle's view of substances limits his similarities with contemporary trope theorists, although these remain far more than merely coincidental. It might indeed be argued that for Abelard ultimately tropes—though tropes grouped in certain set ways—are the basis for all things, at least all material ones, since material substances can be analysed into bodies formed by tropes, their *differentiae*, to which further tropes—accidental forms—are added. Yet Abelard's insistence, discussed in the last section, that substances are in some sense primary qualifies this view. The comparison with contemporary trope theory is an illuminating one, but the reservations eloquently expressed by Alain de Libera should not be forgotten.

'A SURPRISINGLY MODERN TWIST': PETER KING'S INTERPRETATION OF ABELARD'S ONTOLOGY

A very different account of how Abelard thinks objects in the world are constituted has been given by Peter King in his lucid, dense and finely thought out chapter on Abelard's metaphysics.[47] King begins by pointing out that 'in the mundane world, i.e. everything apart from God and angels (including fallen angels), everything is made of form and matter.'[48] He describes, following Abelard's texts closely, the process of 'secondary creation', in which God, having already created primordial matter, adds successive 'substantial forms': 'to a material body he adds life, then the power of sensation, and finally rationality, thereby producing a human being. . . . But ontologically it always remains at the level of concrete individuals, from a thing to an animal to a human; at no point is there an animal that isn't a fully determinate kind of animal.'[49] It is at this point that his explanation diverges sharply from the view developed in the last two sections. King goes on to explain that, for Abelard, matter and form always exist mixed together; further,

> [Abelard] gives a surprisingly modern twist to this Aristotelian claim. The form of a physical object is just a particular configuration of its matter: 'We strictly call "form" what comes from the composition of the parts.' The form of a statue is its shape, which is no more than the arrangement of its matter—the curve of the nose, the size of the eyes, and so on. Thus forms are *su-*

pervenient on matter, and have no ontological standing independent of it (a claim to be made more precise after examining Abelard's theory of identity . . .). This is not to deny that forms exist, but to provide a particular explanation of what it is for a form to inhere in a given subject, namely for that subject to have its matter configured in a certain way. For example, the inherence of shape in the statue just is the way in which its bronze is arranged. The supervenience of form on matter in form-matter composites explains why Abelard holds that mundane things are identical with what they are made of (*Dial.* 415.26–33).[50]

But there is one exception, says King: the human soul. He refers to Abelard's explanations that human souls, unlike those of animals, are not made of primordial matter but incorporeal and capable of existence apart from their bodies and so numerically different from them. He goes on:

And since the human soul is not merely supervenient on the body, Abelard concludes that the human soul is not, strictly speaking, a form at all. Yet the human soul acts as a substantial form while it is joined to the body; if not a form, it is closely analogous to one. Abelard takes this to be the explanation of Porphyry's remark that all things come to be either from form and matter or from the likeness of form and matter (*Isag.* §4 18.9–11): human beings are only analogous to ordinary form-matter composites, whereas all other physical objects are straightforward form-matter composites (*LI Isag.* 79.19–30, and *LNPS* 564.25–565.2). Abelard therefore endorses hylomorphism for mundane objects, setting humans aside as a special case.[51]

When he comes to discuss Abelard's views on difference and identity, King keeps his promise to make his account of Abelard's views on the relation of form to matter more precise. In order to explain his point, a few words, not summarizing King, about Abelard's classification of differences and identity are needed. In the form to which it had developed by the time of the *Theologia Christiana,* and

184 ABELARD AND OUR PRESENT

had been put most clearly in the *Theologia scholarium*, Abelard held that one thing, *A*, is numerically and also essentially the same as another thing, *B*, when they have all their parts in common—for example, Socrates and that man, where that man is Socrates.[52] For *A* to be essentially different from *B* is just for it not to be essentially the same: that is to say, there is some part which *A* and *B* do not have in common. For example, my hand is essentially different from me. But for *A* to be numerically different from *B* is *not* just for it to fail to be numerically the same. *A* is numerically different from *B* if and only if *A* and *B* have no parts in common. As a result of this classification, a part is neither numerically the same as the whole to which it belongs nor numerically different from it.[53]

King draws attention to this feature of Abelard's classification, which he was the first person to notice, and claims that 'the ontological standing of forms can be clarified in terms of Abelard's theory of essential and numerical identity.' 'Putting the human soul aside as a special case', he continues, 'a mundane individual's substantial forms are essentially the same as the individual; they are also numerically the same as that individual, since neither can be destroyed without the destruction of the other, a consequence of Abelard's definition.'[54] Accidental forms, King goes on to explain, are essentially the same as the individual, but not numerically the same, because they can be created and destroyed 'without affecting the being of the individual.' He continues, 'Yet accidental forms do not differ numerically from the individual they inform, since at least each has the individual's substance as its subject of inherence, and in that sense is a metaphysical "part." Indeed, forms in general are configurations or arrangements of parts of the individual, as noted . . . above, and so merely supervene on the individual (or the individual's matter) while being neither numerically the same as it nor numerically different from it.'[55] If King is right in his interpretation, then Abelard is indeed 'surprisingly modern'. Although he would accept the existence of incorporeal things—God, the angels and human souls, all the objects in the world, human souls apart, would, on this view, consist ultimately of matter, though matter configured in various ways. But is this interpretation acceptable? There are three strong reasons for thinking that it is not:

(1) The claim that forms are merely configurations of something's matter, that they are 'supervenient on matter, and have no ontological standing independent of it', is incompatible with what Abelard says explicitly about the ontological independence of accidents and *differentiae,* in the passages discussed in the last section. According to the Whiteness Passage, for example, the whiteness by which body *A* is white might have made a different body, *B,* white. But if the whiteness were just an arrangement of the parts of *A*, then this claim would make no sense: an arrangement of *A*'s parts could not have made *B* white; only an arrangement of *B*'s parts could have done so. The Whiteness Passage makes a claim for a degree of ontological independence for accidents which rules out their merely supervening on their subjects. King does have a reason—as will shortly be explained—for regarding the Rationality Passage, about substantial forms, as not contradicting his position, but there is no obvious way in which he can reject the testimony of the Whiteness Passage.

(2) To support his view of forms as supervenient, King turns to a passage in the *Logica ingredientibus.*[56] What, exactly, is being argued in this passage? The text of the *Isagoge* being explained makes a comparison between 'things which are constituted of matter and form or have a constitution similar to matter and form' and the way in which the species man is made from its genus, animal, as its matter, and its *differentiae,* rationality and mortality, as its form.[57] According to Abelard, Porphyry is giving an analogy. Whereas, he says, a statue is properly speaking made of matter and form, a man is not. Rather, a man has a constitution *similar* to matter and form, since the relation of the bronze, the shape and the statue itself is analogous to that between animal, rationality and the man. Before showing how Porphyry makes this analogy, Abelard emphasizes the differences between the two objects being compared:

> Properly speaking, we say that matter is what came before in time and took on as subject the form [*fictum*] which the fashioner

worked in it, such as the bronze, which was bronze before it was a statue and was sculpted by the craftsman's manipulations so that it would become a statue. Properly speaking, we call a form what comes from the composition of parts, such as the form which is seen in a statue when it has a crooked nose or a straight one, big or small eyes and so on, which are matters of composition. The substance of a man, which consists of animal and rationality, is not properly speaking made up of matter and form in this way. For the animal which is the man was never an animal at a time before it was a man, nor could it ever properly have been said, 'The animal becomes the man', nor has the man been made by the manipulation of an artificer. The rationality, too, is not properly speaking said to be a form because it does not originate in the subject from the composition of parts.[58]

On King's reading, Abelard is here distinguishing between *all forms* (substantial and accidental) *but one* and their relation to matter, on the one hand, and *one exceptional form, the human soul,* and its relation to matter, on the other. The relationship of matter and form properly said to obtain between the bronze of the statue and its forms is taken to apply for all types of forms in their relation to matter except for the human soul in relation to the human body. It is this unique relationship—merely analogous to that between matter and form—which, King believes, Abelard is describing when he gives the example of the substance of a man, consisting of animal and rationality. Since, then, Abelard clearly says that the form of a statue is no more than the composition of its parts—and so, in other words, it supervenes on the matter of the statue—King feels confident in attributing to Abelard this analysis of all forms and their matter, apart from the human soul and its body.

But is Abelard really talking about the human soul and body when he uses the example of animal, man and rationality? King says, in a note, that 'Abelard follows common practice in referring to the human soul by its constituent feature *viz.* rationality',[59] but he gives no testimony to support this view. When Abelard considers explicitly whether the soul is a form (in a passage which King mentions but does not quote), he makes it absolutely clear that it is not a form but a substance.[60] It would be strange if, when he is so clear that the soul is not a form in any way, he were to say of it, as he does of rationality in this passage, that it is not *strictly speaking* a form. But King cites this comment as if it supported his interpretation and goes on to say that 'the human soul acts as a substantial form while it is joined to the body; if not a form, it is closely analogous to one'[61]—a position for which there is no evidence except his contentious interpretation of rationality as meaning the soul. A much more natural reading of Abelard's text would be to consider that, in talking about animal, rationality and man, Abelard is using his stock example of how a particular of a natural kind is constituted from a genus and *differentia*. His energies as a commentator are engaged because Porphyry has chosen a peculiarly inapposite formulation— that the genus is like matter and *differentia* like form—and has given an example—the bronze and the shape of the statue—which only underlines the inappositeness. Abelard seizes on Porphyry's 'similar to' to make clear the contrast between the case of the statue, where the matter is there already and an artificer gives it a shape, and what happens in the case of the composition of any individual of a natural kind according to the genera, species and *differentiae* of Porphyry's tree. The man and his rationality are, then, intended to provide an example of any natural thing and one of its *differentiae*.

That the passage should indeed be read in this way—as a contrast between the bronze and shape of the statue, which are properly matter and form, and the quasi-matter and quasi-form of any genus and its *differentiae* (animal and rationality being used simply as examples)—is confirmed by what Abelard gives as the criteria for proper, as opposed to quasi-, matter-form relationships. The matter must temporally precede its being informed, and the informing be done by the manipulation of an artificer. If a genus were related to its *differentia* in this way, then it would mean that, at some time, there was, for example, a living thing that was not an animal or a vegetable, or an animal that was no specific sort of animal, and, as King himself rightly observes, Abelard rejects any such possibility.[62]

If there is still doubt about the interpretation, then the closely parallel discussion in the *Logica nostrorum petitioni sociorum* can be examined. There Abelard writes:

> Matter, properly speaking, is what precedes in time the thing made of the matter, as the bronze <precedes> the bronze statue and so remains in its nature in the thing made from the matter. Properly speaking, form is what derives from some disposition of parts, as the form which is considered in the statue <comes from> the distorted eyes, the crooked nose and the other things belonging to the composition. But body is, properly speaking, the matter of a man, because it temporally precedes the man and is the subject for the forms of man—this is what matter, properly speaking, has as its characteristics. But animal is the quasi-matter, not the matter, properly speaking, because it does not temporally precede the man. . . . So a man is not, properly speaking, said to consist of animal and rationality as matter and form, as he does out of body and the composition <of the body> [*ex corpore et compositione*], or as a statue out of bronze, but the man has a likeness to the statue, which properly speaking consists of matter and form.[63]

Here Abelard makes it clear that body is *properly speaking* the matter of a human being, in the sense that humans are made from pre-existing bodily matter. The corresponding forms in the proper sense are neither the substantial forms (such as having sense perception, rationality, mortality) nor most accidental forms, but the 'composition' (*compositio*) of the body, by which Abelard probably means the particular way in which a person's bodily parts are put together.[64] Abelard would, therefore, presumably allow that these accidents are nothing more than the configuration of matter, on which they supervene, but not other accidental forms, and certainly not the substantial ones.

(3) Abelard's supposed clarification of the ontology of forms in his discussion of identity and difference is, at best, a supposition by King. Not only does Abelard say nothing in his discussion of identity

and difference to link this topic with anything he has said about forms. He also very obviously chooses as his illustrative examples integral parts (he talks about hands and bodies, and walls and houses), not metaphysical parts. But it can certainly be valuable to use one theory devised by a philosopher to clarify another, even if the philosopher himself does not make the connection. In the present case, however, it does not seem that King is really using *Abelard's* theory at all. According to King, accidental forms bear the following relationship to the individual they inform: they are (*a*) essentially the same as it, and (*b*) neither numerically the same nor numerically different from it. There is no problem, in itself, about (*b*), which is the relationship Abelard considers integral parts bear to their wholes. But, according to Abelard, if *A* is essentially the same as *B,* then it is numerically the same as *B.* According to Abelard, therefore, no things could satisfy both (*a*) and (*b*), because they would have to be both numerically the same as each other and not numerically the same as each other. Abelard's distinctions between sameness and difference do not, then, provide a good way for the theory about forms which King attributes to him to be set out— hardly surprising, since that theory seems to be far from Abelard's intentions.

King's Interpretation and the Development of Abelard's Thought

In order to support his interpretation, King refers to a passage in the manuscript of the *De intellectibus* which describes the views of Abelard and his followers.[65] The passage—hereafter *Avr*—is one of a series of notes on logical problems of the sort which exercised Abelard and his contemporaries.[66] The writer begins by distinguishing the views held by three different groups about forms (*formae*): the first group think that all forms are essences (*essentiae*—a word which in twelfth-century use means roughly 'things', 'real entities'); the second that none are, and the third that some are essences, some not. The writer is openly critical of the first group, arguing that if unity and similarity, which are forms, are considered essences, it will be impossible to avoid an infinite regress. With regard to the second group, he points out that an apparent consequence of their view is that virtues, vices and colours 'are not anything'. He does not state that this is an unacceptable consequence but leaves it to the wise to decide. He then comes to the third group, which he identifies with 'Abelard and his followers', whom he proceeds to praise by saying that 'they explain the art of logic, not obscuring it but most carefully exploring it.' He continues (the numeration is added):

> They accept as being essences only the following forms: certain qualities which [i] are in their subject in such a way that the subject does not suffice for their existence, in the way that the subject suffices for the existence of quantities; [ii] do not depend necessarily on the arrangement of the parts [of the subject] in relation to each other or to something else, in the way that the arrangement of parts in relation to each other is necessary for the bending of a figure, and for the existence of sitting there is necessary the arrangement of the parts of the subject and something else on which the subject sits; [iii] are not in [the subject] thanks to something extrinsic which is such that they cannot exist without it, in the way that some property is in someone because he possesses a horse or an ox, although it will not in any way remain when that extrinsic thing is destroyed; [iv] are not such that, when they leave their subject, a substance has to be added to it, in the way that when not-being-ensouled leaves a subject it is necessary that a substance be added to the subject, that is to say, a soul.[67]

The discussion in *Avr* does not continue beyond this point, but applying these criteria rules out (i) quantities, places and some qualities (for instance, unity); (ii) some qualities and all accidents in the category of *situs* (posture); (iii) accidents in the categories of relation, having and (probably) being-done-to and time; (iv) just the accident mentioned in the example, not-being-ensouled.[68]

It is surprising that King cites *Avr* in favour of his interpretation, since it seems, rather, to go against it. King's position is that, for Abelard, *all* forms are merely supervenient on their matter, of which they are particular configurations, and that they have no independent ontological standing. This view would be compatible with that of the second group of philosophers distinguished in *Avr*, who hold that no forms are essences. But the view that *Avr* attributes to Abelard and his followers is that some forms are essences, some are not. King ignores the fact that nothing in his previous interpretation suggests a distinction between sorts of forms, and he glides over the difficulty that *Avr* seems to say that some forms do have independent ontological standing by claiming that it says that they 'might be "things" in a loose sense, i.e. not numerically the same as their subjects.' But there is nothing in *Avr* to support this 'loose sense'. It is hard to see how, if the Abelardians say that some forms are essences, they do not hold that they are essentially distinct from their subjects. Moreover, in criterion (ii), *Avr* considers forms which consist just in the arrangement of the parts of something: this is exactly what King takes all Abelardian forms to be, but *Avr* makes it clear that Abelard and his followers thought that many sorts of forms, including those which are essences, cannot be analysed in this way.

Avr, however, is inconsistent not only with King's reading of Abelard's ontology but also with that proposed earlier in this chapter, on the basis of the *Dialectica* and the *Logica ingredientibus*. In these texts, it has been claimed, accidental forms in all categories are most probably considered to be essences or things, with the possible exception of those in the category of posture and, perhaps, of Where. The sharpness of the difference between what emerges from these works and the position attributed to Abelard in *Avr* is brought out by the fact that in the *Dialectica* and *Logica ingredientibus* Abelard clearly considers similarity as a form which, like other forms, has independent ontological standing, whereas *Avr* uses the case of similarity to attack the proponents of the first opinion, that all forms are essences.[69] It is possible, of course, that the author of *Avr* simply made a mistake and should have placed Abelard with this first group (or that he could be basing himself on what Abelard's school came to think). But another possibility is that he is correct, because Abelard's view changed after the time of the *Dialectica* and the *Logica ingredientibus*—in the years, that is to say, after about 1120. I argued in an earlier book that Abelard's views about forms did, indeed, develop.[70] Besides re-stating this evidence (which other scholars have neither criticized nor, it seems, accepted), the following section goes beyond my earlier book by trying to show—from the hints and suggestions, which are all that are found in the surviving works—how Abelard probably believed that he could fill the gap left in his metaphysics by the removal of many types of forms from his inventory of reality.

ABELARD'S LATER, SPARSER ONTOLOGY: A RE-EXAMINATION

Negatively, nothing in the writings usually dated from the mid-1120s and later states or implies that any accidents are things other than those which *Avr* says Abelard would accept. The *Logica nostrorum* and the commentary on the *Hexaemeron* both state explicitly that sitting (a particular form in the category of posture—*situs*—and excluded from thing-hood by (iii)) is not a thing.[71] But it might be argued that, by contrast with most categories of accidents, there is no direct evidence that Abelard ever thought that forms in this category were things. In the *Theologia Christiana* it is stated explicitly that both unity and 'many other forms' differ neither in essence nor in number from their subjects. This represents a change from his views in the *Logica ingredientibus* about unity and probably about some other forms, but he does not tell us which.[72] The most telling positive evidence, however, concerns the category of relation.

In the *Theologia Christiana*, Abelard asks, with regard to the relation of similarity, the rhetorical question: 'What could be more ridiculous than that, since someone is now born to whom I am similarly made, as a result of him something new is born in me which will necessarily vanish when he perishes?'[73] Abelard might here simply be ruling out just some relations—for example, those which obtain between completely unconnected substances—from being things.[74] Further on, however, Abelard argues that the relation of paternity is, similarly, not a thing. The immediate context may, at first, suggest that Abelard is talking about paternity as a relation in God, since that is the reason for the whole discussion—and, of course, relations in God are a special case because here Abelard cannot posit forms in any way independent of their subject without violating divine simplicity. But the wider context makes it clear that Abelard says clearly that fatherhood is not a thing when he is talking about creatures, not God. After having raised the question about whether the properties of the Persons of the Trinity (paternity, filiation, procession) can be predicated of God, Abelard remarks that 'just as we do not hold that *in other things* relations are different from their subjects, and yet we do not therefore join the names for them together by predication', we deny that God's paternity is God the Father or God. In the same way, he says, we do not join by predication 'the man or Socrates with the paternity he has, although the paternity is not another thing from them, nor perhaps is it the same thing, since it may not rightly be called a thing at all: it has no true essence in itself by which it might be one thing in number, essentially discrete from all other things which are not it.'[75] Abelard then breaks off this discussion. He returns to talking about Trinitarian relations and, having declared that relations *in God* are not essences or things but merely properties, then poses a hypothetical objection: if they are not things, 'they entirely do not exist [*non sint*] or are nothing, because everything that exists [*est*] is some thing [*res aliqua*].'[76] Abelard's answer is to say that the verb *esse* (to exist / to be) is equivocal. When we say 'the man exists', we mean that something is a man, but when we say 'paternity exists', we mean that 'something is a father'. Therefore, so long as something is a father, paternity exists, even though it is not a thing. Abelard then goes on to explain why, given this analysis, it does not follow from 'Whatever exists is a thing' that paternity does not exist because it is not a thing.[77] Clearly, this answer to the hypothetical objection is about, not paternity in God, but paternity in general, as the example sentences show.

Thus a considerable amount of evidence from Abelard's own *Theologia Christiana* backs up the testimony of *Avr*, at least so far as relations are concerned, and indicates that Abelard no longer regarded them, in the way he had done, as things. But how then does he explain relations (and how would he explain the other sorts of accidents which are not things)? Simply to say that a father has an accident of paternity, but that it is not a thing, does not go very far. Of course, in the *Theologia Christiana* Abelard is mainly concerned to discuss God, and any comments about accidents in mundane things are incidental illustrations. A number of comments suggest that he dealt in detail with accidents in his *Reconsideration of the 'Categories'* (*Retractatio praedicamentorum*), part of the *Grammatica*. But the *Grammatica* is lost. There is, however, one moment where, in order to avoid the criticism that, by relying on cross-references to the *Reconsideration of the 'Categories'*, he is leaving his present work incomplete, Abelard provides a brief discussion of the predication of father and paternity, which is presumably a summary of how the topic is treated in the *Grammatica*.[78] Although the passage itself is dealing with a rather narrow issue—how it can be true both that paternity is not a different thing from a father, and yet that it is false to say, 'Paternity is a father' or 'A father is paternity'—once the ideas developed by Abelard elsewhere which it uses are carefully examined, it may give the clue to how Abelard came to think about relations and the other types of accidents he no longer regarded as things. 'Paternity is a father' is easily shown to be false, since paternity is not a substance which could beget a son from itself but rather 'a property or relation of substance'.[79] His explanation for why 'A father is paternity' is much longer and, it will turn out, more revealing:

> For if a father were paternity, then a father would be a father because he participated in father [*ex participatione patris esset assignandus pater*], so that it would be entirely the same for someone to be he who is a father, and for him to have paternity in himself, that is, for him to be a father—which is entirely false. Just as it is another thing for something to be that which is prior or that which is perpetual, than for it be prior or perpetual—in the

first case, the thing which is formed is predicated; in the second case, the forms themselves are predicated—so it is other for something to be he who is a father than for it to be a father, that is, it is other to be he who has paternity than for him to have paternity, although the first cannot be without the second. Therefore when someone says about someone that he is a father, he predicates paternity, not a father. But if he were to say that he is he who is a father, that is, who has paternity, then indeed he would predicate a father himself. Therefore a father is not paternity, because something is a father, not from participation in father [*cum ex participatione patris non sit assignandus pater*], but, as has been said, from participation in paternity.[80]

The position attacked by Abelard is stronger than it might seem at first. It looks as though it is based on a simple category error and does not require the detailed refutation given. Why would anyone ever think that a father—a concrete thing—is paternity, a form which, Abelard has just argued, is not really a thing at all? But the proponent of the position has simply taken to heart this very insistence of Abelard's that fatherhood is not another thing apart from the father and is claiming that therefore non-real forms like fatherhood can be completely eliminated from the discussion.

In order to explain why this is not the case, Abelard calls on the ideas he has developed in thinking about types of differences. His discussion of this theme is not exhausted by considering the cases analysed above (see pp. 183–84) of things which are not essentially the same. He also believes that things essentially the same can differ. Yet if *A* is the same in essence as *B*, then *A* and *B* are the same thing—they have all of their parts in common: they are really not two things but just one. What Abelard has noticed, however, is that we pick out the same thing under different descriptions: for example, 'the white thing' and 'the hard thing', both of which refer to this marble bookend. In his terminology, the white thing and the hard thing are essentially the same, but they differ by definition, because being white is different from being hard. For the sake of clarity, it is useful to introduce some new terminology, which is not

Abelard's. Since two things which differ by definition are really the same thing, seen under different aspects, they can be called 'thing-aspects'. Different thing-aspects are referred to by different words or phrases ('the white thing', 'the hard thing'), but different words or phrases do not always refer to different thing-aspects. For example, 'sword' and 'blade' refer to the same thing-aspect of this weapon in front of me (in Abelard's terms: the sword and the blade do not differ by definition). They do so because 'sword' and 'blade' have the same meaning, whereas 'white' and 'hard' do not.[81] Although different thing-aspects do not entail each other, in many cases they can be predicated of one another. It is true to say, for example, when speaking of this marble bookend, that the white thing is the hard thing, and that the hard thing is the white thing. Indeed, it might seem to be a rule that different thing-aspects of the same thing are all predicable of each other, since each picks out a feature of the same thing. So, indeed, Abelard thought when he first introduced these ideas in his *Theologia Summi Boni*.[82] But, a little later, he realized that there are some cases which do not fit the rule (in parts of the *Theologia Christiana* he describes these special cases as difference 'by property', but he does not continue to use this terminology consistently).[83] Consider a statue. One of its thing-aspects is the matter of which the statue consists. Another thing-aspect is that which is made of the matter. It is not true to say that the matter is the thing made out of the matter or vice versa, because the matter existed before the thing made of the matter; indeed, the matter is something perpetual, whereas the thing made of the matter is not. There is, however, a sort of sentence that can be used to show that these mutually impredicable thing-aspects are aspects of the same thing. Whilst, in such cases, propositions of the form 'The F is the G' are false, an 'indexicalized' proposition, of the form 'That which / the thing which is F is G' will be true. Just as, pointing to the statue and using an indexical, it would be true to say 'That is the matter' and also 'That is what is made from the matter', so it is true to say: 'That which is the matter is that which is made of the matter' and vice versa.[84] To introduce another label, the indexicals ('that' or 'that which is . . .') refer not, like the nouns, to a thing-aspect but to the 'bare thing'.

With these distinctions in mind, Abelard's argument for why a father is not paternity will become clearer. The reason Abelard gives for denying that a father is paternity is that, if so, there would be no distinction between an ordinary predication ('John is a father') and an indexicalized one ('John is he who is a father'). But it is clear that there is a distinction between the two types of predication, as emerges from examples like that of the matter and the thing made from the matter—Abelard here picks a variant of this case, where the thing-aspect matter is picked out by its being perpetual, a property very evidently not shared by the thing-aspect what is made from the matter. Why does Abelard think that saying that a father is paternity has this consequence? Although his phrasing, which talks about participation in father and in fatherhood, is rather strange, his line of thought is fairly clear. The bare thing (he who is a father) is what it is just because it is this thing, the father; it is not characterized by reference to any form, such as fatherhood, precisely because it is the bare thing. The father is what it is because of fatherhood: it is fatherhood which makes John, among the other things which he is, a father. The philosopher who insists that, because fatherhood (and other such forms) are not things, the father is fatherhood renders it impossible to make this distinction. Unless fatherhood and other such forms, which are not things and cannot be said to exist, are allowed to play some explanatory role, then the whole distinction between bare things and thing-aspects will disappear. Reductionism will have gone too far, leaving insufficient metaphysical resources to explain the complexity of things revealed by Abelard's analysis of differences.

Abelard has, then, seen a problem. But has he taken steps to solve it? On the one hand, he now denies that relations such as paternity, and very probably various other sorts of accidents, are things or existents. On the other hand, he wants such unreal forms to play a part in his account of things. He seems to be open to the accusation of treating these forms like things, even whilst denying that they really exist. But there is a much more promising line of thought suggested by the framework in which this discussion takes place. It is not put forward by Abelard in any of his known writings, but it would be a plausible way for him to have treated relations and other unreal accidents in his lost *Reconsideration of the Categories*. Abelard's exploration of types of difference gives him a framework for analysing subjects and their properties, whether these properties are considered to be things (as would be the case for many forms in the category of quality, such as whiteness) or not (as in the case of fatherhood). Each property gives rise to a different thing-aspect of the thing in question—in Abelard's terminology, there are for each property things different by definition or property but essentially the same. In the case of whiteness and hardness as properties of the marble bookend, the ground for the different thing-aspects white thing and hard thing is provided by the real particular forms of whiteness and hardness attaching to the thing. In the case of the statue, the thing-aspects material and thing made from the material have their ground, not in any form, but in a history of events: the material is the material because it existed prior to the statue's being made, the thing made out of the material is what it is because it came into existence when the statue was made. Similarly—but this is conjecture, because Abelard does not discuss the case—the thing-aspect father could be grounded, not in any real form of paternity, but in a history of events: this man's having begotten a child who was then born.[85] If this were his understanding, Abelard would be right to declare, as he does, that to say that fatherhood exists is just to say that someone is a father—there is no thing that is fatherhood—and yet at the same time to insist, as he does in the passage just examined, that fatherhood cannot simply be collapsed into the father. There needs to be some ground for this bare thing having the thing-aspect father, and it would be supplied, on this account, by a history of events for which 'fatherhood' is a convenient short-hand.

This chapter has explored the relation between Abelard's metaphysics and our present by looking at his links with contemporary trope theory and scrutinizing the modern twist given to his views about how things are constituted in Peter King's interpretation. Yet much of the discussion has turned out to be oblique to these comparisons with today's thinking. It was necessary, for the sake of clarity, to start with an exposition of the basic metaphysical scheme in Abelard's earlier work, and the critique of King's interpretation has led naturally into an attempt to reconstruct how the scheme was changed by the time of the *Theologia Christiana*. This apparent change of destination does not, however, mean that the discussion here has lost its way. Rather, it has found it. To understand Abelard *as a philosopher,* his modern readers need to think about him philosophically, and in consequence they usually need to begin from ideas and questions familiar to philosophers today. But, if they are to understand what *Abelard* thought and wrote, this philosophical attention needs to be recaptured and redirected by his own lines of discussion, priorities and developing ideas.

CONCLUSION

The preceding chapters have raised questions, developed arguments and suggested conclusions on three levels. First, they aim to help readers understand better than before what Abelard thought and the place of his work in the history of philosophy. They also consider the second-order question of how philosophers and historians should go about studying Abelard. And, lastly, they have a more general methodological aspect, in which the case of Abelard becomes an example, and the four dimensions of the title mark out an approach which might be taken to any medieval philosopher, or indeed any philosopher of the past.

ABELARD'S THOUGHT AND ITS PLACE IN THE HISTORY
OF PHILOSOPHY

The most striking conclusions reached here about Abelard himself concern his semantics (chapter 5), his metaphysics of objects in the world (chapter 6) and his views about free will and determinism (chapter 2), whilst the two chapters on Abelard's past and future (chapters 3 and 4) suggest a disappointing but important conclusion about his place in the history of philosophy.

Abelard's views on how words link with things present—as Peter King rightly noticed—remarkable parallels with some late twentieth-century ideas of direct reference but at the same time—as Chris Martin rightly pointed out—are rooted in an entirely different tradition, in which the meaning of language depends on what happens in speakers' minds. This perplexing combination is the result of an approach (linked to Abelard's way of treating topical inference) which favours intensional over extensional relations between words and things.

The reading developed here of Abelard's ideas about how things are constituted is, in its main lines, not new but a much more carefully argued version of the one I proposed in my book on Abelard over fifteen years ago. Although, at least by the time of the *Logica ingredientibus,* Abelard did not think that universals (substances or accidents) existed, his ontology was anything but sparse, since it included myriads of particular accidents and particular *differentiae,* which enjoyed the sort of counter-factual independence given to tropes by some of today's theorists; but, unlike tropes, they were seen as structured into the substances which the *differentiae* helped to constitute and the accidental forms to qualify. There is strong evidence that, by the mid-1120s, Abelard had somewhat trimmed this ontology and now counted only some particular accidents as real. In my previous book, I left Abelard without any explanation to fill the gap left by this change, but here a way in which Abelard might have provided one, by using his subtle distinctions of types of difference, is sketched.

The most striking change proposed here to the accepted picture of Abelard concerns his views about freedom and determinism. Although it is widely agreed that Abelard's whole approach to ethics requires that humans can freely choose between good and evil actions, Abelard is usually thought to have emphasized the inevitability of divine providence—in a way that links him to the Stoics—especially because he argued that God cannot do other than he does. Yet this argument, it is explained here, does no more than establish that God has no alternative choices. On Abelard's view, humans *do* indeed choose between alternatives, and God must mould his best providence according to these choices which he cannot determine. Moreover, Abelard's argument that God cannot do other than he does emerges as a much stronger piece of reasoning than has been thought.

In histories of philosophy, Abelard is usually treated immediately after Anselm and shortly before the famous thirteenth-century scholastics, such as Aquinas. The examination of his links with Anselm shows that, however interesting a purely philosophical comparison between them might be, historically the relationship was one of sporadic influence, opportunistic comment and occasional misunderstanding. The images of Abelard the follower of Anselm, and Abelard the mocker of Anselm, are equally misleading: although the two men often thought in similar ways about the same problems, their lines of argument almost always originated independently and usually followed differing courses.

Similarly, historians of ideas, from Lovejoy onwards, have placed Abelard's argument that God cannot do other than he does within a stream of thought that leads from the Neoplatonists to Leibniz. The real history of this argument shows, by contrast, that it was not known in its details and was not properly confronted except by one of Abelard's immediate successors (and perhaps by Aquinas, who showed remarkable insight into its underlying point).

A METHODOLOGY FOR STUDYING ABELARD

The book as a whole makes a plea for an approach to studying Abelard that combines methods which tend, at the moment, to be used apart, by distinct groups of scholars. On the one side, Abelard's thought needs to be traced out carefully in the context of its times and, where possible, of Abelard's own chronology. Chapter 1 is intended to make such work possible by setting out a chronology that can be accepted even by the most sceptical and by indicating the difficulties to be overcome in reaching Abelard's thought through the texts which survive. Both chapters 2 and 6 give examples of this chronological and contextual study in action. On the other side, Abelard's philosophy will never be understood unless it is read philosophically. Throughout the book, Abelard's arguments are analysed and presented in a way which, it is hoped, makes them comprehensible today. A more extreme method of trying to bring Abelard's thought to life in the philosophical present is to see how closely it corresponds to positions held by philosophers today. The two chapters here (5 and 6) which examine particular instances of this method in semantics and metaphysics suggest that it can yield valuable results, but only so long as the contemporary theories are used strictly as a starting point, to provide an angle of approach which illuminates, without trying to neglect or remove, the particularities of Abelard's thinking and its rootedness in twelfth-century concerns.

FOUR DIMENSIONS AND THE HISTORY OF PHILOSOPHY

The plea to combine characteristically philosophical and characteristically historical approaches is one which could be extended to the study of any medieval philosopher, or indeed any philosopher of the past.[1] The idea of four dimensions, by which this book is structured, is a way of answering it by setting out how those writing about medieval or other past philosophers can go about being both philosophical and historical. The first three dimensions look historically at, and backwards and forwards from, the philosophers in question. The fourth connects them with philosophy today. But why attempt to be both philosophical and historical? Many who are especially interested in the fourth dimension are reluctant to give much attention to the first three historical dimensions, except as a preliminary or a sideline. And many who are interested in the first three dimensions wonder why the fourth dimension is necessary.[2] Would it not be better to leave the philosophers to pursue their philosophical interests, and the historians to do history?

An approach to philosophy of the past which confines itself to the fourth dimension is, indeed, possible. The historical text is treated as if it were a book or article just published: its value, if any, lies in how it can contribute to the discussions contemporary philosophers are now having. Past philosophy is envisaged as an abandoned, burnt-out city, from which there may be some stray items worth plundering. Their original function does not matter, so long as they can serve a purpose now. Thirty or forty years ago, when analytical philosophers first turned their attention to history, such an approach was common. Nowadays, the plunder approach is less popular, although specialists in medieval philosophy, anxious to shed their antiquarian image, tend to be more sympathetic to it than most other historians of philosophy. Treating philosophy from the past as a source of plunder can be justified, in its own terms, in so far—and just in so far—as the plunder does in fact contribute to contemporary philosophizing. Clearly, in some cases, it does (even medieval texts have been used directly in philosophy of religion and some other areas, such as modal metaphysics, by philosophers today). But these cases are not many and certainly not common enough to justify the effort of seriously studying philosophy from the past. And as soon as the question for a contemporary philosopher about a work from the past becomes broader than 'What can I get from it for my own philosophical arguments?', sticking to the fourth dimension alone becomes impossible to justify.

Many justifications, besides the inadequate one linked with the plunder approach, have been given for why contemporary philosophers should study philosophy of the past. I have proposed one which sees past philosophy as valuable for its contribution, not to first-order treatment of philosophical questions, but to second-order consideration of what sort of questions they are.[3] These questions are equally a part of philosophy as the first-order ones, although it is a characteristic fault of analytic philosophy to ignore them. And since philosophy is not a natural kind but a human practice, the evidence needed for tackling these questions is provided by the history of philosophy, which shows the various ways in which different sorts of philosophical enquiry have taken place within a wider structure of beliefs and questioning, and of intellectual and cultural life. According to my view, then, contemporary philosophers will draw the most benefit for their own work from studying the philosophy of the past if they do so in a way that is extremely sensitive to historical context. They can afford to ignore none of the first three dimensions. But even apart from my own view, once the philosophy of the past is regarded as more than booty, and so is not taken simply to mean whatever best suits its present use, questions of interpretation arise which cannot be resolved except by setting texts within an historical context and so looking at the first and probably also the second and perhaps the third dimension of the material.

Philosophers, then, should not ignore the three historical dimensions. But need historians take account of the philosophical dimension, which relates past philosophers to the philosophy of our own present? To answer the question, three different ways of understanding this dimension need to be distinguished. Past texts can be related to contemporary philosophy reflectively, or through intellectual translation, or through detailed comparison. The relation of reflection is what has just been described, when contemporary philosophers use their knowledge of past texts to think about the nature of philosophy. There is no reason why an historian need be interested in the fourth dimension, understood in this sense. Past texts are related to contemporary philosophy through intellectual translation by the effort to understand them in the terms we use now. This does not mean forcing ideas into a conceptual framework where they do not belong, replacing terms in the original with ill-matched contemporary equivalents. Rather, the intellectual translator must point out, in a clear way, which is comprehensible to us now, where and how the concepts in the original fail to match with our own. This process of intellectual translation applies not just to the detail of propositions and arguments but also to whole problems and areas of philosophy. The starting point must be one of the ways in which we now see problems and divide up philosophy (where the 'we' should be taken broadly to include a wider group of thinking people than just the members of philosophy departments), because it is we (in this broad sense) who are trying to understand. But very often the end result will be to grasp, in terms that make sense to us, how problems in the past and even the whole shape of philosophy were not the same as ours, and we might need to finish by placing our discoveries within a configuration of ideas very different from that with which we began. Intellectual translation is indispensable for any reading of past philosophy as philosophy—that is to say, for any faithful reading of it. Failure to practise it is a failure to practise not merely philosophy but also history, since the aim of the historian is not to parrot words and sentences from the past but to understand them.

A writer may go further than just providing an intellectual translation and engage in detailed comparison of some piece of past philosophy with contemporary theorizing. Such comparisons, conducted judiciously, can be valuable both as ways to increase our understanding of the text from the past and as contributions to reflection back on the nature of philosophy. But they are certainly not requisite for writing good history of philosophy, and they present some dangers: the material from the past may be distorted in order to bring it closer to contemporary discussion than it is, or the writer may be inclined to engage in tokenism, holding up an older text for admiration just because it anticipates something that is being said now. An important aim of chapters 5 and 6 of this book, which combine intellectual translation with some detailed comparison between Abelard and today's theories, is to see how far these comparisons can usefully be taken: to show what they can teach but also how they can all too easily lead us away from an accurate grasp of what someone was thinking many centuries ago.

For full citations on editions of works by Abelard, given by editor's name in the Notes, see the first section of the Bibliography, 'Editions of Works by Abelard'.

AL	Aristoteles Latinus
Apol.	Abelard's *Apologia contra Bernardum*
BGPTMA	Beiträge zur Geschichte der Philosophie und Theologie des Mittelalters
CCCM	Corpus Christianorum, Continuatio Mediaevalis
CCSL	Corpus Christianorum, Series Latina
Coll.	Abelard's *Collationes*
Comm. Cant.	Abelard's *Commentarius Cantabrigiensis in Epistolas Pauli*
Comm. Hex.	Abelard's *Commentary on the Hexaemeron*
Comm. Rom.	Abelard's *Commentary on Paul's Letter to the Romans*
Conf. fid. 'Universis'	Abelard's *Confessio fidei 'Universis'*
De int.	Abelard's *Tractatus de intellectibus*
Dial.	Abelard's *Dialectica*
GSV	*Glossae secundum vocales*
HC	Abelard's *Historia calamitatum*
LI	Abelard's *Logica ingredientibus*

LI(cat)	Abelard's *Logica ingredientibus* (*Categories*)
LI(isa)	Abelard's *Logica ingredientibus* (*Isagoge*)
LI(oi)	Abelard's *Logica ingredientibus* (*On Interpretation*)
LNPS	*Logica nostrorum petitioni sociorum*
PL	Patrologia Latina
Sc.	Abelard's *Scito teipsum*
Sent.	*Sententiae Magistri Petri Abaelardi*
Sent. Flor.	*Sententiae Florianenses*
Sent. Par.	*Sententiae Parisienses*
SN	Abelard's *Sic et non*
TChr	Abelard's *Theologia Christiana*
TSB	Abelard's *Theologia Summi Boni*
TSch	Abelard's *Theologia scholarium*

NOTES

ONE. Abelard's Developing Thought

1. See the essays now collected in Mews 2001, especially Mews 1985b, and, for a synthetic view, Mews 2005a.

2. In addition to the works cited in note 3 below, cf. Jolivet 1969, Tweedale 1976 and the various articles by Peter King and Chris Martin listed in the bibliography.

3. The *Stanford Encyclopedia* article is by Peter King (2010). The only exceptions in the *Cambridge Companion* (Brower and Guilfoy 2004) are the essays by myself and Iwakuma.

4. These antidevelopmentalist arguments with regard to Aristotle are presented most eloquently in Barnes 1995, 15–22.

5. King 2010, sec. 1.2.

6. For an example, see Marenbon 2007a, and cf. below, chapter 2, where the development of an argument between *TChr* and *TSch* is studied.

7. See Mews 1995, 55, for a list of the versions and suggestions about their dating. The editors' introduction to *SN* (ed. Boyer and McKeon) contains a full study of the recensions and their relations.

8. Take the case of *Coll.*, for instance. On the one hand, Giovanni Orlandi, after very careful scrutiny of the manuscripts, concluded, not only that Abelard had revised the work, but that the revision was unsystematic: Abelard 'came back at different times to his work, made available to him in an exemplar largely corrupted by copyists, re-reading single sections, correcting some passages, adding new materials, which in the time had occurred to him, and never revising the rest' (*Coll.*, ed. Marenbon and Orlandi, p. xcvi)—the sort of situation which, in King's view, makes dating a text impossible. On the other hand (cf. *Coll.*, pp. xxxi–xxxii), nothing of much

philosophical importance is added, and so these revisions do not in fact create difficulties for the developmentalist.

9. The following section is not, of course, intended to be a biography, even a brief one; rather, it is an attempt to establish a framework of dates that might help in ordering Abelard's writings. In Marenbon 1997a, 7–35, drawing especially on Bautier's fundamental article (1981), I give a brief but far more substantial sketch of Abelard's life, with full references to the primary and secondary sources. A very fine biography, though not chronologically arranged, has been written by Michael Clanchy (Clanchy 1997). The importance of Heloise, who is hardly mentioned in the discussion here, is brought out especially in Mews 2005a.

10. See e.g. Marenbon 1997a, 82–93; Clanchy 1997, 15–16; Mews 2005a, 16–18. But some eminent scholars still regard the issues as being complicated; see especially the essays collected in Von Moos 2005.

11. The account which follows, up until Abelard's return to Paris in the 1130s, is based on *HC*. The relevant line numbers are given parenthetically in the text, preceded by *HC*.

12. Regarding Abelard's birth date, a now lost Old French MS of the Paraclete cited by André Duchesne, Abelard's first editor, says that when Abelard died (in 1142) he was sixty-three years old; see *PL* 178:176B and cf. Clanchy 1997, 325.

13. A vituperative letter Roscelin wrote to Abelard circa 1120 (printed as an appendix to Reiners 1910) is the main source for this information; see Pagani 2004, n. 14, for full details and discussion. Mews (1995, 10–11) suggests that most of his training might have in fact been with Roscelin, but see Martin 2011, 616 n. 56.

14. These are the datings suggested in Bautier 1981, followed by, for example, myself (Marenbon 1997a), and in Clanchy 1997, as in the chronological table in Pagani 2004.

15. See Bautier 1981, 56; Mews 1985b, 97.

16. See Miramon 2011, 76.

17. Miramon 2011, 46–63. Miramon's results are linked to Grondeux 2011, which studies the events following Abelard's defeat of William over universals.

18. Mews 2011.

19. Mews 2011, 103.

20. See e.g. *Dial.*, ed. De Rijk, p. 136, line 19, p. 169, line 25, and many other passages, which show that Abelard became a close pupil of William's, who would find lines of argument to defend his master's position.

21. Mews (2011, 90–91) uses a letter from a student that can be dated to the beginning of 1112 (see Miramon 2011, 75 n. 132) to date the start of this conversion, only after which, he believes, Abelard returned to Paris from

Brittany. Miramon (2011, 59–61) sees this letter, rather, as referring to William's period of retreat away from Paris, mentioned by Abelard as having taken place after he had defeated William over universals and was teaching at Melun. Miramon's interpretation is preferable, especially because the letter seems to be written by a student who is now, at the time of writing, being taught by William in Paris but refers back to what had happened the Easter before (1111), when William had gone to a little, very poor church—events which seem to correspond to what *HC* says happened after Abelard, having defeated him over universals, was teaching in Melun (William retreated from Paris) and then moved to the Montagne Sainte-Geneviève (William returned to Paris). As a date for the dispute over universals, 1110 is preferable to Miramon's 1109, however, because *HC* suggests that the events between William's defeat and his retreat from Paris in Easter 1111 were quite quick: Abelard's victory led to the incumbent at Notre Dame offering him his job, but he had been doing it 'for only a few days' (*HC* 108) before William managed to remove him. Abelard's move to Melun followed, and 'not much later' (*non multo post*) William left Paris.

22. See Miethke 1973, 172. The text is quoted in his n. 85. Marenbon 1997a, 21 n. 49, gives a misleading cross-reference about this charter, which in fact records the restoration of a chapel to a nunnery in Angers.

23. See Lalore 1878, 1–3.

24. There is some dispute about whether the Council took place in early June 1140 or late May 1141, but recent scholars prefer 1141; see Mews 2002, 345–52.

25. On Abelard and the Council of Sens, see Marenbon 1997a, 26–32; Clanchy 1997, 307–17.

26. *Metalogicon* 2.10 (John of Salisbury 1991, p. 70, line 1, to p. 71, line 10).

27. See Marenbon 1997a, 25 n. 72.

28. Two manuscripts preserve a version of *TChr* with extra material which will be incorporated into *TSch*. Constant Mews has argued convincingly that these are copied from a working manuscript of Abelard's, which he used as he changed *TChr* into *TSch;* see Mews 1985c and his introduction to *TSch* (ed. Buytaert and Mews, pp. 210–21).

29. As Mews (1985c, 152) argues.

30. See e.g. *TChr* 2.67, and cf. Mews 1985c, 152.

31. A very balanced presentation of all the issues is given in the introduction by David Luscombe to the new edition of the *Sententie Abaelardi* (*Sent.*). The fundamental study is Mews 1986.

32. They considered that this came from a '*Liber sententiarum*', and the quotations from it found in the writings of Abelard's opponents are edited as *Lib. sent.* (see the introduction by Mews in the new edition).

33. As I observed in Marenbon (1997a, 65 n. 39), the reference in *Comm. Rom.*, ed. Buytaert, p. 70, line 816, to p. 71, line 817, to his simile of the bronze statue 'in the second book of my *Theologia*' must show that he had already adapted the five-book structure of *TChr*, in which this simile is not treated in book 2 (cf. *Comm. Rom.*, ed. Buytaert, p. 26, for the list of cross-references); Mews (in his introduction to *TSch*, ed. Buytaert and Mews, 226–27) does not see this point, but he accepts that Abelard must have 'had an idea of what his completed *Theologia* would contain' at the time he composed this commentary.

34. *Comm. Cant.*, ed. Landgraf, p. 434.

35. *Sc.*, ed. Luscombe, p. 96, line 32.

36. *Comm. Rom.*, ed. Buytaert, p. 126, lines 140–41; p. 293, lines 245–46; and p. 307, lines 348 and 352–53.

37. See *Comm. Hex.*, ed. Romig, p. 4, lines 30–35.

38. Mews (1985b, 119–20) puts forward some reasons, which he himself acknowledges to be less than conclusive, for thinking that Abelard wrote *Comm. Hex.* before *Comm. Rom.*

39. See De Santis 2002 for a thorough study of the authenticity of the sermons in the collection transmitted in the *editio princeps*. She also (135–57) discusses the dating for a number of the sermons besides those written for the Paraclete.

40. Mews (1985b, 104–26) argued for a dating to c. 1125–26, partly on grounds of (a) Abelard's developing terminology in connection with the meaning of circumcision and (b) the development of his view of sin, from 'evil will' to (by the time of *Sc.*) consent. But grounds for rejecting (a) have been given by Paola De Santis (2002, 147–53) and for rejecting (b) by Julie Allen (1998, 144–49); and in the preface to *Coll.* (ed. Marenbon and Orlandi, pp. xxix–xxx) I give reasons why neither (a) nor (b) provides conclusive arguments. Allen is wrong, however, to insist that the terms used to describe sin provide strong positive support for a late dating for *Coll.*, near the time of *Sc.*: what is distinctive in *Sc.* is not a focus on intention (which, in any case, is captured by the notion of evil will) but the idea of consent. The differences here between Mews and these other scholars shows how contestable it is to base datings on presumed development in ideas.

41. See my full discussion of this dating in *Coll.*, ed. Marenbon and Orlandi, pp. xxvii–xxxii. In her article (which I failed to consider there), Jenny Allen talks about (1998, 138) the reference in *Coll.* (sec. 4) to Abelard's *Theologia* but does not mention the explicit reference (sec. 78) to *TChr*. De Santis (2002, 152 n. 262), who supports Allen's late dating, similarly does not note the reference to this version of the *Theologia*.

42. See Mews 2008 (text, translation and arguments for the attribution; this second edition of a book first published in 1999 also includes further replies to critics); Mews 2005b (replies to critics).

43. Sylvain Piron, who translated the letters into French, has also provided some of the best arguments for their authenticity (Piron 2005 [in the introduction to his French translation of the letters], 2009, 2011). Michael Clanchy, Abelard's best biographer, has accepted the attribution. But many scholars are hostile to it: my own attack (Marenbon 2008b) gives full bibliography. The weightiest study of *Epistolae duorum amantium* and its authorship is Von Moos 2003.

44. See Marenbon 2008a, 65–66; 2011a, 182–85.

45. See Marenbon 2008a, 68–70; for a fuller discussion and Working Catalogue, Marenbon 2000b; for a considerably revised and improved version of the Catalogue for *Categories* commentaries, Marenbon, forthcoming-b.

46. One possible ancient model for literal exegesis might have been the *prior editio* of Boethius's commentary on *De interpretatione*, which was designed deliberately to provide a straightforward introduction to the text, avoiding the long digressions and explanations of the longer commentary on the work he also wrote. The twelfth-century literal commentaries were, however, often much more literal and pedantic than Boethius is here.

47. See Marenbon 2008a, 66–68.

48. See Marenbon 2011a, 197; and, on layering and anonymity in twelfth-century commentaries more generally, Marenbon 2012, 415–17. An example of a commentary where differences between versions in various manuscripts show up the existence of different layers is C8 (and C14, which is really a version of C8). The letters P (for Porphyry's *Isagoge*), C (for the *Categories*) and H (for *On Interpretation*) followed by an arabic numeral refer to the catalogue in Marenbon 2000 (and, for the *Categories*, Marenbon 2013).

49. Rosier-Catach (Grondeux and Rosier-Catach 2011, 146–47) shows how Abelard took what he read in the *Glosulae* on Priscian (or perhaps rather, had heard from William's own lips) as the teaching of William of Champeaux, his master: this material includes what can now be seen as glosses inherited by William as well as William's own distinctive additions.

50. The method of taking a copy of oral teaching to the master to be corrected is described at first-hand in a work (discussed in detail in chapter 2, below, pp. 57–59) that gives Hugh of St Victor's teaching, the *Sententiae de divinitate* (see edition in Piazzoni 1982, p. 912, line 5, to p. 913, line 40). Bernhard Bischoff discusses this evidence in a famous article (1935).

51. In one MS (Paris BNFr 13368), commentaries on the *Isagoge* (P3) and *On Interpretation* (H11) are attributed to 'Rhabanus'—very probably Hrabanus Maurus, a ninth-century theologian of the ninth century. The attribution in Marenbon 2001 of P19 to 'Guarinus Cantaber' is wrong: Guarinus Cantaber is mentioned in this fragment of a commentary (Oxford, Bodleian Laud. lat. 67, fols. 6rb, 7ra), and the commentary may well derive from this (otherwise unknown) master's teaching, but it is not attributed to him as a literary work.

52. William's *Introductiones* are edited and discussed in Iwakuma 1993. On the identity of Garlandus and the date of *Dial.*, see Marenbon 2011a, 194–96.

53. For example, *Quoniam de generali* (linked to Walter of Mortagne), edited in Dijs 1990, and *De generibus et speciebus*, edited in Peter Abelard 1836, 507–50, and King 1982, 2:143–85 (this treatise also discusses mereology; it may well not be an integral work).

54. The title '*Introductiones parvulorum*' depends on identifying these *Literal Glosses* with an earlier work of his which Abelard mentions in *Dial.* and calls by this name (for a list of references, see Martin 2011, 608 n. 16). It is debatable whether Abelard could have meant to refer to commentaries by the word 'Introductiones' (see Mews 1985b, 75, critically discussed at Martin 2011, 608–11), but since it will be argued (see below) that the *Literal Glosses* are not by Abelard, the matter is of little importance.

55. In fact, in the case of the *Isagoge* (fol. 156ra) this *incipit* is put in abbreviated form, but it is written out at the head of *De divisione* (fol. 146ra), and it is damaged at the beginning of *On Interpretation* (fol. 128ra). There are photographs of the three folios in Rosier-Catach 2011, 808–10. Cousin (Peter Abelard 1836, xii–xiv) describes all four commentaries accurately, but in place of the commentary on *On Interpretation* attributed to Abelard, he prints (Peter Abelard 1836, 597–601) a short extract from a different commentary on this text (H12), from elsewhere in the same manuscript.

56. See below, pp. 30–31.

57. As noted in Green-Pedersen 1984, 424–25.

58. *Dial.*, ed. De Rijk, p. 114, line 30, and p. 566, line 26.

59. Much of this material was discovered and first presented in De Rijk 1966. I gave a list of it at Marenbon 1997a, 51 n. 60. Since then Professor Yukio Iwakuma has kindly let me have his transcriptions of all the passages he knows from twelfth-century manuscripts which mention individual masters, and from these I have been able to add to my original list. Iwakuma discusses this material in Iwakuma 2013, and he has now made this list publicly available on the web as an appendix (www.s.fpu.ac.jp /iwakuma/papers/MastersII.pdf).

60. An edition of the commentary in Paris BNF lat 15015 (H15) by Peter King (forming a companion volume in the CCCM to the Jacobi and Strub edition of Abelard's *LI(oi)* commentary) is in press; and see *LI(oi)*, ed. Jacobi and Strub, pp. liv–lv, and Jacobi, Strub and King 1996. The *Introductiones montane minores* is edited in De Rijk 1967, 7–71. For the *Summa dialecticae artis*, see William of Lucca 1975. The *Tractatus de dissimilitudine argumentorum* is edited in De Rijk 1962, 459–89. On the note following the text of *De int.*, see below, chapter 6, pp. 189–92.

61. Cousin's introduction to Peter Abelard 1836, xiv, followed by e.g. Geyer 1933, 502–7, and Dal Pra's introduction to Peter Abelard 1969, xxiii–xxvi.

62. Cameron 2011a; Martin 2011.

63. Cameron 2011a, 649–50.

64. Cameron 2011a, 658–61.

65. Martin 2011, 623–41.

66. See Minio-Paluello's introduction to his edition of *LI(oi)*, xxxix–lxi, where he notes other features that link the piece to Abelard. Minio-Paluello also observes that there are cross-references which suggest the piece is a fragment from a longer work. De Rijk (1962, 109–10) has suggested that the work in question might be the *Fantasiae* to which Abelard refers in *Dial.* (ed. De Rijk, p. 448, lines 3–4). I argue against this identification in Marenbon, forthcoming-b.

67. We can assume that Abelard did not normally repeat himself in his teaching from his explanation, in *HC* 351–54, that an effect of his love affair with Heloise was to make him lose interest in his teaching, so that instead of using his *ingenium* he simply followed the routines he knew, reciting over again what he had previously invented. This comment would lose its point unless Abelard were making a contrast with what had previously been his approach to teaching.

68. For two different challenges to this view, see below, pp. 40–41.

69. *Dial.*, ed. De Rijk, p. 535, lines 7–8; for Abelard's references to Dagobert, see p. 142, line 15, and p. 146, line 23.

70. See e.g. *LI(oi)* 3.92 (ed. Jacobi and Strub, p. 121, lines 672–73; ed. Geyer, p. 360, line 5).

71. Geyer 1933, 598.

72. See his introduction to Peter Abelard 1969. A complete list of cross-references in *LI* is given in Mews 1985b, 76 n. 15.

73. Geyer does not pause to justify its authenticity. On the strange story of its discovery and subsequent loss, see Geyer's introduction to his edition of *LI*, x–xii.

74. Grabmann 1911; Geyer 1933, 610–12.

75. Ottaviano, introduction to *GSV*, pp. 96–103.

76. Mews 1984, 55.

77. This edition is already at an advanced stage. I am enormously grateful to Peter King and Chris Martin for having discussed with me their problems and hypotheses. I had previously accepted, like everyone, the authenticity of *LNPS* and had even been persuaded by Mews that *GSV* should be considered a work of Abelard's. King and Martin easily convinced me to abandon these over-confident positions. I then, however, continued with my own investigations, and so it may well be that their final conclusions, based on a much more thorough study of the material, are different from mine.

78. The lemma is 'Quod enim describentes' (Porphyry 1966, 6:26), *GSV* 4.2 (ed. Ottaviano, p. 147), MS fol. 76rb. (Ottaviano's edition of *GSV* is untrustworthy, but I have fortunately had at my disposal both a transcription of the MS by Yukio Iwakuma, collated with *LI* and *LNPS*, and, thanks to Chris Martin, digital images of the folios of the MS. Folio citations are to MS Milan Ambrosiana M63 sup.)

79. There is one exception. At *GSV* 5.3 (ed. Ottaviano, p. 154), MS fol. 76vb, there is the lemma 'Nosse autem oportet' (Porphyry 1966, p. 9, line 1). The comment attached to this lemma accepts the idea that the words 'genus' and 'species' are relatives, because it is impossible for there to be a genus without there being at some time a species. But it goes on to give an alternative gloss, which follows exactly the line of *LNPS* (ed. Geyer, p. 542, lines 9–31), that they are not relatives but quasi-relatives, and then to take this as if it were the commentator's view ('Since, however, as we have said, they are not relatives, since a genus [i.e. a genus word] can exist without species, that is, be instituted in such a way as to predicable of many things differing in species in what they are').

80. The first lemma in *GSV* after the gap is PLANUM AUTEM ERIT (Porphyry 1966, p. 9, line 10), at 5.7 (ed. Ottaviano, p. 164), MS fol. 77vb. In *LNPS* it is EXTREMA VERO (Porphyry 1966, p. 10, line 18), ed. Geyer, p. 550, line 37.

81. For further discussion, see below, pp. 183–85, 195–96.

82. *GSV* 5.1 (ed. Ottaviano, p. 152), MS fol. 76vb.

83. *LNPS*, ed. Geyer, p. 509, lines 36–37.

84. *LNPS*, ed. Geyer, p. 534, lines 2–3.

85. *LI(isa)*, ed. Geyer, p. 3, lines 4–6: 'Utilitas autem, ut ipse Boethius docet, cum principaliter ad Praedicamenta dirigatur. Quadrifariam tamen spargitur, quod postmodum,ubi ipse id dicet, diligentius aperiemus.' Abelard then explains this usefulness in detail from p. 5, line 1, to p. 7, line 19. It was Chris Martin who first drew my attention to the fact that the *glosule* referred to are *LI(isa)* or something like it.

86. *GSV* 4.1 (ed. Ottaviano, p. 145), MS fol. 76ra.

87. Mews 1984, 40.

88. Catarina Tarlazzi has suggested to me that, on the contrary, the master in question may have been a realist, since some exponents of material essence realism, popular early in the twelfth century, took their ideas from the section of Boethius's commentary where he is arguing that universals do not exist. The master may have been pointing out the value of this section, by contrast with the solution Boethius then gives, where, he considers, Boethius is merely talking about words. Ingenious though this interpretation is, I find it forced, but it is attractive, since it would allow the master to be identified with William of Champeaux.

89. *LI*(*isa*), ed. Geyer, p. 30, line 34, to p. 32, line 12.

90. *GSV* 4.1 (ed. Ottaviano, p. 145), MS fol. 76ra. In *LNPS*, ed. Geyer, p. 528, line 28, to p. 530, line 19, it is not made clear that Boethius is supposedly taking genera and species as designating words, but there is no suggestion that there is a change between how they are taken in posing the problem and in giving the solution.

91. For Abelard's explicit naming of his teacher Roscelin, see *Dial.*, ed. De Rijk, p. 554, line 37, to p. 555, line 1: 'Fuit autem, memini, magistri nostri Roscellini tam insana sententia ut'. In *Dial.* Abelard frequently refers to 'magister noster' (without any name)—see e.g. p. 57, lines 2–3; p. 59, line 6; p. 60, lines 12, 17; p. 64, line 16; p. 67, line 5; p. 82, line 7. All these references are very plausibly to William of Champeaux. On Abelard's interpretation of Porphyry's questions, see *LNPS*, ed. Geyer, p. 526, line 35, to p. 527, line 29; cf. *GSV* 3.5 (ed. Ottaviano, pp. 129–30), MS fol. 74va.

92. *LNPS*, ed. Geyer, p. 534, line 36.

93. *LNPS*, ed. Geyer, p. 540, lines 10–12. From the corresponding passage in *GSV* 4.2 (ed. Ottaviano, p. 148), MS fol. 76rb, where it is explained how the definition of 'genus' must be understood so as to ensure it excludes 'possible' and 'necessary', it seems likely that this comment was an incidental comment attached to the point made there—although 'possible' and 'necessary' are not—of course—genera, they are, in the Master's view, universal words.

94. *LNPS*, ed. Geyer, p. 525.

95. *LNPS*, ed. Geyer, p. 526, lines 4–7 (MS Lunel 6, fol. 17va): '<N>ota (MS; Geyer *ita*) tamen quod magister hanc propositionem, "Genera et species subsistunt", falsam esse concedit, quia talis est sensus "Genera et species subsistunt": aliqua subsistentia sunt genera et species' (my punctuation).

96. *LNPS*, ed. Geyer, p. 529, lines 38–40 (MS Lunel 6, fol. 19rb): 'quod aliqua [MS; Geyer *aliquae*] substantia [MS, Geyer *substantiae*] sit [MS; Geyer

sint] genus, penitus denegamus, cum nulla essentia sit universalis, sicut superius ostensum est.'

97. For these parallels, see below, pp. 39–40.

98. Mews 1985b, 80–81.

99. See Wilks 1998, on what he calls 'essential predication' and its use in *LNPS* and *TChr.*

100. *GSV* 5.7 (ed. Ottaviano, pp. 161–64), MS fol. 77va–b.

101. Here are two examples. In the discussion of whether the phoenix is a species, there is a moment (*GSV* 5.7, ed. Ottaviano, p. 163, MS fol. 77vb) when *GSV* talks about what is, from the evidence of *LI*, Abelard's own view as something 'they' (not 'we') say ('They say that those who want the phoenix to be a species are in this following the opinion of others. . . . For they say that Porphyry did not want the phoenix or the sun to be in any way species but only individuals'). *GSV* goes on, however, to put this Abelardian line as its own. In the discussion of *ens*, *GSV* seems to put forward (5.8, ed. Ottaviano, pp. 166–67, MS fols. 78ra–b) as one of the views it advocates that *ens* is predicated equivocally, so that its meaning is changed by the word attached to it. This is not the view in *LI*, and in *LNPS* (ed. Geyer, p. 551, lines 22–34) it is rejected, in a discussion often close to that found (garbled) in *GSV.*

102. Both Morin (in his introduction to *De int.*, pp. 14–16) and I (Marenbon 1997a, 50–51) suggest that it might be a piece from the *Grammatica* to which Abelard refers in *TChr* (see below, p. 194).

103. On its authenticity, see Morin's introduction to *De int.*, pp. 8–13.

104. In Marenbon 1997a, 52, I concluded (on the basis of limited published material and some manuscript material I had seen) that there was little new to be found about Abelard's logic from these testimonies. Since then, I have had the benefit of reading a large collection of transcriptions by Yukio Iwakuma of all the passages in anonymous commentaries which mention Abelard, and I think that this very considerable body of texts should be properly analysed before we draw any conclusions. In any case, however, one could not be sure about when Abelard formulated the doctrines concerned: Do the manuscripts, for instance, which pit Abelard's views against Alberic's base themselves on lectures given by Abelard in the 1130 (as I assumed), or could Alberic be discussing written reports of Abelard's views, which might relate to an earlier period?

105. Geyer 1933, 600–603. In this section I shall not consider the *Literal Commentaries*, which are probably inauthentic—they have usually been thought to be from early in Abelard's career (see above, pp. 301–31), except by Clanchy (1997, 103–4), who associates them with his Parisian teaching in the 1130s; nor shall I consider the *Secundum Magistrum Petrum*

sententie, which seem to date from the same period as the new material found in *LNPS* (see Marenbon, forthcoming-b).

106. Compare *TSB* 2.83 with *TChr* 3.138.

107. See Marenbon 2007a, 243, for a fuller discussion. There is also further discussion of Abelard's theory about differences in chapter 6 below, pp. 183–85, 195–96.

108. Cf. *GSV* 6.1 (ed. Ottaviano, p. 178, MS fol. 79rb) with *LNPS*, ed. Geyer, p. 558, lines 17–21. This section of *GSV* is edited by Geyer in the same volume as *LI* and *LNPS*, p. 588 (see line 11).

109. As noted by Constant Mews; see above, note 98.

110. This view is set out in Jacobi and Strub 1995, an important discussion for anyone thinking about the structure of Abelard's logical commentaries.

111. Jacobi, Strub and King 1996.

112. The arguments of Jacobi, Strub and King are scrutinized in detail, and reasons given to reject them, in Marenbon 2004.

113. Constant Mews (1985b, 74–104) attacked earlier views, which placed *Dial.,* or at least its final revision, in the 1130s or later. He placed the work before *LI* but after Abelard became a monk. Most scholars accepted his arguments, at least in so far as they established that *Dial.* should not be dated after *LI.* I argued (Marenbon 1997a, 40–43) that Mews's dating should be pushed back even a little further, to before 1117, and Mews now (2005a, 259 n. 2 to ch. 3) accepts my view, at least for most of the work, proposing a dating between 1112 and 1117/18 (2005, 43); Chris Martin suggests an even earlier dating, in which he is 'beginning work on the final sections of *Dial.* around 1112' (2011, 622). For the historiography of dating *Dial.,* see Marenbon 1997a, 40 n. 16.

114. *Dial.,* ed. De Rijk, p. 151, line 15 (cf. p. 152, line 21); p. 319, lines 1–6.

115. Nicolau d'Olwer (1945, 378–79) drew attention to these passages; Mews (1985b, 97) dismissed the point; I (Marenbon 1997a, 42) re-stated it; and Mews (2005a, 43) now makes it himself.

116. *Dial.,* ed. De Rijk, pp. 469–71.

117. See Marenbon 1997a, 41–42; Mews (2005a, 43), however, feels that 'we cannot be sure' whether this passage was not added after 1117.

118. *Dial.,* ed. De Rijk, pp. 210–22; *LI(oi)* 9.19–99 (ed. Jacobi and Strub, pp. 248–68; ed. Geyer, pp. 420–31).

119. See Marenbon 1997a, 42–43.

120. See *LI(oi)* 6.47 (ed. Jacobi and Strub, p. 200, lines 449–51; ed. Geyer, p. 400, lines 2–4) (and contrast the whole passage in which this reference is made with *Dial.,* ed. De Rijk, p. 181, line 17, to p. 183, line 17); cf. Marenbon 1997a, 41; and also see *LI(oi)* 12.18 (ed. Jacobi and Strub, p. 401, lines 250–64; ed. Minio-Paluello, p. 13, line 15, to p. 14, line 4).

121. Cf. *Dial.*, ed. De Rijk, p. 62, lines 17–31, with *LI(cat)*, ed. Geyer, p. 184, line 38, to p. 186, line 14, and cf. Marenbon 1997a, 41 and 146–47.

122. For semantics of propositions, see Guilfoy 2004 (though here the difference between *Dial.* and *LI* is exaggerated); for topical reasoning, Martin 2010; for the meaning of the substantive verb, Marenbon 1999.

TWO.   An Unpopular Argument (I)

1. Abelard very often puts the problem as being whether God can do more or fewer things than he does, or simply whether he can do more than he does, but the question he has in mind, as his discussion shows, is best captured by 'otherwise'.

2. Some parallel cases with regard to his logic emerge even from a quick scrutiny of the discussions of his views in anonymous commentaries and treatises (cf. above, pp. 29–30) from the 1140s and later.

3. Islamic thinkers had thought about a very similar problem before Abelard (see Ormsby 1984), but there is no real possibility that he knew about their speculations.

4. *SN* 35.1 (ed. Boyer and McKeon, p. 184, lines 2–10). This passage is not, however, in the earliest version of *SN* (that in MSS *TCEB*) which contains the question (the very earliest version, *Z*, does not). The previous question in *SN* is whether God has free choice (*liberum arbitrium*), but the passages chosen, and the issues raised, are very different from those related to NAG.

5. *Timaeus* 29E (Plato 1975, ed. Waszink, p. 22, lines 18–20): 'Optimus erat, ab optimo porro inuidia longe relegata est. Itaque consequenter cuncta sui similia, prout cuiusque natura capax beatitudinis esse poterat, effici uoluit'. Abelard quoted this in *SN TCEB*, q. 35 (ed. Boyer and McKeon, p. 588), but not in his later versions of *SN*, as well as at *TChr* 5.35 and *TSch* 3.30. In *TChr* he rejects this view (see below, p. 54), whereas in *TSch* he calls it 'a most true piece of reasoning'. A reason for this change is suggested in Marenbon 1997b, 120–22. On when Abelard began to study Plato, see Marenbon 1997b, 118–19.

6. *Timaeus* 28A (Plato 1975, ed. Waszink, p. 20, lines 20–22); quoted in *TSch* 3.32 and (in a different context) in *TChr* 1.2.

7. *Quaestiones lxxxiii*, q. 50 (Augustine 1975, p. 77), quoted in *TSch* 3.31 (ed. Buytaert and Mews, p. 513, lines 419–22) and in *SN TCEB* (ed. Boyer and McKeon, p. 588) along with the one from *Timaeus* 29E.

8. *Quaestiones lxxxiii*, q. 24 (Augustine 1975, p. 29), quoted in *TSch* 3.31 (ed. Buytaert and Mews, p. 513, line 442, to p. 514, line 445).

9. *Coll.*, sec. 225.

10. For example, Passage 5 affirms that God could have chosen another way than through the death of Christ to redeem us (see below, pp. 101–8); passage 6 affirms that he could have become incarnate in someone other than a descendant of Adam; passage 7 states that he could have made all things at once; passage 8 states openly that 'he can do many things that he neither does nor wishes.'

11. *TSch* 3.48: the argument of this passage is discussed below, p. 65. On Augustine's general tendency to open up a range of non-actualized providential possibilities for God (almost the direct opposite, it will be argued, of Abelard's approach), see Knuuttila 1993, 69–70.

12. See *TSch* 3.37–38, referring to Jerome, *Epistula* 22.5. Peter Damian denied Jerome's claim. The interpretation of his position is not clear (see Knuuttila 1993, 64–67).

13. *TChr* 5.29–32.

14. *Sent.* 163.

15. For further discussion of the difference between epistemic and realist/metaphysical interpretations of Boethius, only the latter of which imply that God is timelessly eternal, see Marenbon 2005, 50–51, and Marenbon 2013.

16. *Sent.* 163 (ed. Luscombe, p. 83, lines 1857–59): 'Deus igitur cum sit cui nulla mutatio temporis obsistat—quippe nichil est inter eius eternitatem et ultimum temporis momentum'. Although this comment is not very clear, it is striking that Abelard asserts a simultaneity, not between divine eternity and every moment of time, but rather between it and one moment of time, the last.

17. *Sent.* 162 (ed. Luscombe, p. 82, lines 1841–42): 'ab eterno quippe sciuit me lecturum hodie; in eternum sciet me legisse hodie.'

18. *LI(oi)* 9.77–78 (Jacobi and Strub, p. 262, lines 459–62 and 465–67): 'sed more humano loquentes simplicem eius essentiam et in se omnino inuariabilem pro his, que per eum inuariabilem fieri contingunt et uarie a nobis excogitantur, uariis designamus nominibus'; 'Similiter cum modo me sedentem modo non sedente dicitur scire uel intelligere me sedentem et non intellegere uel scire me sedentem, nulla est in ipso uariatio'.

19. The same is true when, later in the book (5.57, ed. Buytaert, p. 371, lines 791–96), Abelard returns to the idea that God does everything of necessity: 'Natura uero diuina sicut omnino incommutabilis est atque inuariabilis, ita et in omni suo statu eo modo quo permanet incommutabiliter persistit, atque ex ipsa sua incomparabili bonitate ad omnia quae uelle eum et facere oportet, necessario, ut ita dicam, inuitatur ut et sic uelit et perficiat.' The idea here is that there is just one way that God can be, the best way, and being that best way means always willing, and so doing, the best.

20. When he rewrites exactly the same argument in *TSch*, he makes it clear (3.39, ed. Buytaert, p. 517, line 537) that the person concerned *numquam saluandus est*.

21. The link between (13) and (14) is expressed as that of a premise and conclusion, rather than that of an 'if . . . then . . .' statement, but Abelard goes on to treat it as if it had been an 'if . . . then . . .' statement. Abelard is usually sensitive to this difference, but here it is not important.

22. Abelard explains (*TChr* 5.33 (ed. Buytaert, p. 360, lines 466–76)) that, supposing it were true that if *p*, then *q*, but false that if possibly *p*, then possibly *q*, then an impossibility would follow from a possibility, and this, he says on Boethius's authority, would be 'entirely false'.

23. The whole passage, *TChr* 5.33 (ed. Buytaert, p. 360, line 459, to p. 361, line 487, abbreviated), runs: 'Quis enim negare audeat quod non possit Deus eum qui damnandus est saluare, aut meliorem illum qui saluandus est facere, quam ipse futurus sit collatione suorum donorum, aut omnino dimisisse ne eum umquam crearet? Quippe si non potest Deus hunc saluare, utique nec ipse saluari a Deo potest. Necessaria quippe est haec reciprocationis consecutio, quod si iste saluatur a Deo, Deus hunc saluat. Vnde si possibile est hunc saluari a Deo, possibile est Deum hunc saluare. . . . Et si non sit possibile Deum hunc saluare, non est possibile hunc a Deo saluari, hoc est, ut supra posuimus, si non potest Deus hunc saluare, utique nec ipse saluari a Deo potest, ac per hoc nec omnino saluari quem nonnisi per Deum saluari posse constat. Quod si saluari iste non potest, profecto liberum iam perit arbitrium frustra que homini illi ea quae ad saluationem pertinent iniunguntur, qui saluari omnino non potest nec ea facere quibus saluari possit.'

24. This conclusion, obviously implied in *TChr*, is brought out clearly in *TSch* 3.40, where Abelard says, 'God can therefore do what he will never do'.

25. *TChr* 5.34 (ed. Buytaert, p. 361, lines 488–92): 'Similiter etsi illum Deus meliorem facere non potest, utique nec ipse ab eo melior fieri potest atque ita nec ullo modo melior fieri. . . . Absit autem ut aliquem nostrum adeo bonum esse concedamus ac perfectum, ut ulterius crescere non possit.'

26. In *Comm. Rom.* 1.20 (ed. Buytaert, p. 69, lines 772–76), Abelard also mentions as Plato's view 'that God could not have made the world better than he made it.'

27. *TChr* 5.37 (ed. Buytaert, p. 361, lines 512–16): 'Quomodo etiam, inquam, diceremus non posse dimittere quin ea quandoque faciat quae facit, nisi necessario ea quandoque faciat? Si enim non potest illa non facere, utique haec eum necesse est facere, ac per hoc ea necesse est fieri.'

28. *TChr* 5.57 (ed. Buytaert, p. 371, lines 782–91). For the continuation of the passage, see above, p. 221, note 19.

29. On Hugh and Abelard, see Luscombe 1970, 183–97; Poirel 2002, 345–420.

30 For the date, see Van den Eynde 1960, 100–103. For discussion of *De sacramentis*, see below, pp. 75–76.

31. Van den Eynde 1960, 74–77 and Tableau Synoptique.

32. Piazzoni 1982, 940 (Hugh of St Victor, *Sententiae de divinitate* [*Sent. divinit.*] 4.4.146–48). I have changed Piazzoni's punctuation where necessary.

33. Piazzoni 1982, 940 (*Sent. divinit.* 4.148–50): 'Asserunt enim potestatem equalem esse cum eiusdem uoluntate, ita quod neutrum aliud excedat, sic dicentes quia quicquid Deus potest facere, illud uult facere.'

34. Piazzoni 1982, 940 (*Sent. divinit.* 4.156–58): 'Nituntur qui superiorem tenent sententiam, immo falsitatem, probare quod Deus nec aliud aliquid possit facere quam faciat, nec aliter, nec melius, quam faciat.'

35. Piazzoni 1982, 940 (*Sent. divinit.* 4.160–62).

36. Piazzoni 1982, 940 (*Sent. divinit.* 4.166–72): 'Per rationem asserunt Deum nihil posse aliter facere quam faciat. Dicunt enim quia si ratio est quare hoc modo faciat, non est ratio quare hoc modo non faciat. Non enim ad duo opposita sic equaliter sic habebit ratio: non utrumlibet eorum fiat rationabiliter. Si enim unum eorum ratio est fieri, et aliud ratio est non fieri, quia contraria contrariis conueniunt. Si autem non est ratio quare hoc modo Deus aliquid non faciat, ut potest igitur Deus non hoc modo facere, non igitur potest aliter facere.'

37. Piazzoni 1982, 940–41 (*Sent. divinit.* 4.173–89): 'Cogens ratio est illa que ad duo opposita sic se habet quod si unum eorum fiat, necessario rationabiliter [Piazzoni inserts here *et aliud*, which was added in one MS; this phrase destroys the sense of the sentence] fit. Si uero alterum, nullo modo rationabiliter fit, ut diligere proximum uel non. . . . Patiens ratio est illa que sic se habet, quod ad duo utrumque rationabiliter potest fieri secundum arbitrium facientis, et si unum eorum fit, rationabiliter fit; si uero alterum, nec illud quidem irrationabiliter fit—ut me sedere uel me non sedere: si sedeam, bene fit, si non sedeam, et hoc etiam bene fit. . . . In Deo respectu creaturarum nulla cogens ratio est sed tantum permittens. Quicquid enim Deus facit, si sic faciat, rationabiliter facit; si sic non faciat, et hoc etiam rationabiliter fit.'

38. Piazzoni 1982, 941 (*Sent. divinit.* 4.199–202): 'Dicunt enim quia si aliquam rem meliorem possit facere quam faciat, et non uelit, inuidia uideretur esse. Sed in summe bono inuidia esse non potest, ut ait Plato: "Ab optimo porro inuidia longe relegata est."'

39. Piazzoni 1982, 942 (*Sent. divinit.* 4.234–39): 'Dicunt etiam illi superiores quod uniuersitas melius posset fieri quam facta sit, quia eius natura non repugnat ad hoc quod melior fieret, sed Deus non potuit eam meliorem facere quam fecerit uel facturus sit, premissis de causis, sicut uox audibilis est licet non sit qui eam posset audire, et ager excoli potest etsi nemo sit qui eum excolere possit. Nullo enim animali existente, et ager excoli potest et uox audiri.'

40. Piazzoni 1982, 942–43 (*Sent. divinit.* 4.240–69).

41. See points [8] and [15] in the translation and analysis above, pp. 49–50.

42. *TSch* 3.35.

43. *TSch* 3.32 (ed. Buytaert and Mews, p. 513, lines 435–36); cf. 3.37.

44. Abelard does indeed consider that God is the highest reason, but this simply means that he must follow the reason for acting in each case (*TSch* 3.37): 'Nor can he, who is the highest reason, either will anything or perform any act against what is fitting to reason. For nothing which diverges from reason can be reasonably willed or acted.' This, in fact, constitutes another, briefer argument for the conclusion that God cannot do other than he does: there is a reason why *x*, and not anything else, should be done by God at *t*; God as highest reason cannot go against what it is reasonable to do; God cannot not do *x* at *t*.

45. *TSch* 3.33.

46. *TSch* 3.36.

47. But see chapter 4, pp. 122–23, for a criticism which finds a way in which God could act for a reason although two courses of action are equally good in themselves.

48. *TSch* 3.48.

49. Cf. the discussion above (pp. 54–55) of Abelard's relation to Augustine on the question of God's freedom of choice.

50. *TSch* 3.40 (ed. Buytaert and Mews, p. 512, lines 512–14): 'cum ea quae dimittere non potest, necessitas magis quadam propriae naturae compulsus quam gratuita uoluntate ad haec facienda inductus agat.'

51. *TSch* 3.54 (ed. Buytaert and Mews, p. 543, lines 748–49): 'nec coactio dicenda est qua etiam *uolens* id facere cogatur'. But the MSS and editions read, not *uolens* here, but *nolens*, which reduces the sentence to nonsense.

52. On the way in which Abelard retains the idea that God acts in some sense freely, although he lacks alternative possibilities, see Perkams 2003.

53. The central ideas in this section are already found, though not always formulated very well, in Marenbon 1991. Fine, nuanced accounts of Abelard's modal theory are given in Knuuttila 1993, 82–96, and in Martin 2001.

54. *LI*(*oi*) 12.18 (ed. Jacobi and Strub, p. 401, lines 250–64; ed. Minio-Paluello, p. 13, line 15, to p. 14, line 4).

55. See above, chapter 1, p. 43.

56. *Dial.*, ed. De Rijk, p. 195, line 12, to p. 198, line 7.

57. *LI*(*oi*) 12.20 (ed. Jacobi and Strub, p. 402, lines 273–78; ed. Minio-Paluello, p. 14, lines 14–20).

58. *Dial.*, ed. De Rijk, p. 193, line 31, to p. 194, line 3.

59. Cf. Knuuttila 1993, 94–95. Knuuttila's discussion as a whole is particularly valuable for showing that Abelard's various remarks on modality can probably not be fitted into a single, coherent theory.

60. See e.g. *Dial.*, ed. De Rijk, p. 219, lines 19–21: 'Posset enim aliter evenire quam evenit, et secundum Dei providentia contingere, pro eo scilicet quod aliam providentiam habuisse posset quam istam quam habuit secundum alium eventum'; *LI*(*oi*) 9.95 (ed. Jacobi and Strub, p. 266, line 558, to p. 267, line 564; ed. Geyer, p. 430, lines 21–27).

61. See *Dial.*, ed. De Rijk, p. 209, line 23, to p. 210, line 18 (where the activity in question is reading).

62. See also below, chapter 6, pp. 177–78.

63. *TSch* 3.39–40. I leave *damnandus* untranslated, because no English word conveys the dual sense of 'ought to be damned' and 'will in fact be damned.'

64. *TSch* 3.49.

65. *TSch* 3.53 (ed. Buytaert and Mews, p. 523, lines 227–31).

66. See Marenbon 2005, 55–91, for a detailed discussion.

67. *Sent. Flor.* 23 (ed. Ostlender, p. 11, lines 7–9): 'Nihil potest facere sine ratione, ergo nulla pratermittit facienda sine ratione, ergo non potest facere quae non facit. Nam ratio est quare praetermittat facere quam non facit.' In order to go through, this argument needs at least the additional premise: If there is a reason for God to omit to do *x* at time *t*, then there is not a reason for God to do *x* at *t*. Even granting that by 'a reason' is meant a conclusive reason, such a premise rules out moral dilemmas; but perhaps even those who believe that humans face moral dilemmas would agree that God does not face them. Abelard backs up his point in the following lines by the consideration that God's will must be the best, so that any other than what it actually is would be worse; and it is eternal, and so fixed.

68. *Sent.* 146; *Sent. Par.*, ed. Landgraf, p. 20, lines 15–19.

69. *Sent.* 150.

70. *Sent. Par.*, ed. Landgraf, p. 21, lines 9–13.

71. *Sent.* 151 and *Sent. Par.*, ed. Landgraf, p. 23, lines 7–23 (on whether Peter could have been juster than he was); *Sent. Flor.* 23 (ed. Ostlender, p. 11, lines 15–20) (on salvation, but rather garbled).

72. *Sent.* 149; *Sent. Par.*, ed. Landgraf, p. 20, line 29, to p. 21, line 7, and p. 22, lines 17–25.

73. This distinction is made explicitly in the account in *Sent. Par.* (ed. Landgraf, p. 22, lines 17–25): 'And so it should be understood that God does all things in the way in which all things can happen better. He does not say "better" as a noun but "better" as an adverb. As if I were to say, he gave to someone that he should make two vases, one of clay and the other of bronze. He did not make one better than another, because he made the clay vase as well according to its material as the bronze one, but he did make a better vase (i.e. the bronze one): "better" is a noun/adjective.'

74. See *Sententiae* 1.44, cap. 1.4: 'Si modus operationis ad sapientiam opificis referatur, nec alius, nec melior esse potest. . . . Si vero referatur modus ad rem ipsam quam facit Deus, dicimus quia et alius et melior potest esse modus' (Peter the Lombard 1971, p. 304, line 30, to p. 305, line 1).

75. They have not been edited, but there are substantial extracts published in the footnotes to the edition of Master Roland's *Sentences* (Roland 1891) by Gietl, and in Luscombe 1970, 253–60. Gietl considered that Omnebene used Roland's *Sentences*, but Luscombe (1970, 258) queries this judgement. It is most probable that Omnebene wrote before Abelard's condemnation. For the date of Roland's *Sentences*, see below, p. 119.

76. Luscombe 1970, 255.

77. *De sacramentis* 1.2.22 (*PL* 176:214–16). The first scholar to notice this and other uses by Hugh in *De sacramentis* of material from or close to this earlier *reportatio* was Ludwig Ott (1937, 518 n. 59). Van den Eynde (1960, 120) refers to Ott (but to the wrong footnote), saying that Ott drew 'attention sur le fait que la réfutation de la thèse abélardienne figure déjà dans les *Sententiae de divinitate*, mais sous une forme moins soignée.' Ott had not in fact made any such comparison of the two discussions, and what Van den Eynde says is here the reverse of the truth. In his authoritative discussion of relations between Abelard and Hugh, Luscombe (1970, 189 n. 6) follows Van den Eynde in considering the argument against Abelard 'similar, but less finished' in *De divinitate* (which he does not discuss further), as compared to the version in *De sacramentis*. The passage in *De sacramentis* is found word for word in Hugh's *Explanatio in Canticum Beatae Mariae*, *PL* 175:425A–427A (cf. Van den Eynde 1960, 119–20; Luscombe (1970, 189 n. 6); Poirel 2002, 374), which—because of this and another parallel—has been dated to before *De sacramentis*. But both these passages read as unexpected digressions in the *Explanatio*. It seems very strange that Hugh should have gone to trouble in reformulating and condensing his discussion in order to insert it, irrelevantly, into this work, whereas it is natural that he would want to cover the topic in his systematic *De sacramentis*. Per-

haps the dating is wrong, or perhaps this and the other passage were inter-
polated into the *Explanatio*.

   78. *De sacramentis* 1.8.9 (*PL* 176:311).

   79. Luscombe 1970, 191; Poirel 2002, 374.

   80. The work is printed in *PL* 176:41–174. For the date, see Van den
Eynde 1960, 101–3, and for the relationship to Abelard, see Luscombe 1970,
198–213.

   81. *Summa sententiarum* 1.14 (*PL* 176:69B–C): 'Non est praemittendum
hic quosdam scientia inflatos dicere Deum non posse facere aliud quam
facit, vel dimittere de his quae facit aliquid. Quod ita volunt assignare.
Quidquid Deus facit bonum est fieri et justum (non enim potest facere nisi
quod est justum), et quod bonum est fieri, non debet non fieri; igitur non
debet Deus dimittere quae facit, et quod non debet non potest; ergo non potest non facere quae facit. Similiter probant quod non potest aliud facere
quam facit, hoc modo. Quod non facit non debet fieri, quia si deberet fieri
illud faceret; et quod non debet fieri a Deo non potest fieri ab eo: ergo non
potest facere ea quae dimittit facere.'

   82. *Summa sententiarum* 1.14 (*PL* 176:69C): 'Sed ut mihi videtur, sub
hoc verbo latet venenum. Si enim dicimus non debet Deus illa facere; in-
ferunt ergo non potest facere. Si dicimus debet illa facere; ergo non potest
dimittere quin faciat, sed neutrum de Deo concedendum est.'

   83. *PL* 176:69C–D: 'nihil ipse ex debito sed sola bonitate facit.'

   84. See above, p. 63.

   85. In Landgraf 1934, 61–285. On the authorship and date, see Landgraf 1934, xliv–xlvi, liii–liv; Luscombe 1968; Evans 1991, 1. The early date
suggested here is that argued by Evans.

   86. Indeed, the comment is almost identical verbally (Landgraf 1934,
p. 267, lines 28–29: 'Sola enim bonitate, et non ex aliquo debito, omnia
facit'). Its editor thought that the *Ysagoge* used the *Summa sententiarum* as a
source (Landgraf 1934, li), and this passage bears out that idea, although it
has become uncertain, in the light of the new, earlier dating of the *Ysagoge*
(cf. Evans 1991, 2). The closeness in the texts, but the greater detail in the
Summa sententiarum, mean that the *Ysagoge* could have derived the material
from the *Summa* here, but not vice versa. Joint dependence on a third text,
or on oral teaching, closely transcribed, is also possible.

   87. Abelard sets out his theory of grace most fully in his *Comm. Rom.*
240–42. Abelard leaves it rather unclear whether some people might not
be given grace at all (for example, pagans), though the tendency of his
thinking as a whole is to suggest that it would be available to them. But, at
least so far as those who receive it initially, there is no need for an extra gift
of grace, which God might give or withhold, to go on acting well. God offers

his grace freely to them all. See Marenbon 1997a, 326–27, and Marenbon 2011b.

88. *Sent.* 151 (ed. Luscombe, p. 75, lines 1671–72).

89. *Sent.* 151 (ed. Luscombe, p. 75, lines 1668–69).

90. *Sent.* 151 (ed. Luscombe, p. 75, lines 1673–76). *Sent. Par.*, ed. Landgraf, p. 23, lines 16–17, makes the *solidi* example clearer: 'I could receive more pennies from you, who are poor, than you could give me.'

91. *Sent. Par.*, ed. Landgraf, p. 23, lines 3–10.

92. *Coll.*, sec. 210. Abelard also touches on the same view in the discussion in *TSch* (3.44).

93. *Comm. Hex.*, secs. 451–55.

94. *Coll.*, sec. 219 (my translation, ed. Marenbon and Orlandi).

95. As the Christian goes on to say (*Coll.*, sec. 220): 'Cum itaque nichil nisi Deo permittente fieri constet—nihil quippe ipso inuito uel resistente fieri posse—certumque insuper sit nequaquam Deum aliquid sine causa permittere nichilque omnino nisi rationabiliter facere, ut tam permissio eius quam actio rationabilis sit profecto, cum uideat cur singula que fiunt fieri permittat; cur et ipsa facienda sint non ignorat, etiamsi mala sint uel male fiant. Non enim bonum esset ea permitti, nisi bonum esset et fieri, nec perfecte bonus esset qui, cum posset, non disturbaret id quod fieri bonum non esset, immo patenter arguendus in eo quod non sit bonum fieri consentiendo ut fiat.'

96. See e.g. Marenbon 1997a, 251–81.

97. *Coll.*, sec. 221.

98. *Coll.*, sec. 220 (the Latin is quoted in note 95 above).

99. Faust 1932, 193 (cited in Knuuttila 1993, 86) considers Abelard's argument a theological version of Diodorus Cronus's Master Argument (for the origin of this comparison, see below, chapter 4, p. 139); Lovejoy (1936) 1970, 72, says that Abelard 'made manifest both the deterministic and antinomian implications of principles which nearly everyone accepted'; Oakley 1984, 45, describes Abelard as subscribing to 'necessitarian optimism'; according to Mews 2005a, 214, the implication of the NAG argument is that 'the world cannot be made differently from the way it is.' Knuuttila 1993, 86, has a very subtle view of the matter: the created order is 'the only one God can create, although it is not the only possible world.' Knuuttila would thus bring Abelard very close to Leibniz, one of whose tactics for preventing his conviction that God must create the best possible world from implying that all things happen of necessity was to distinguish between what is logically possible and what God, given his nature, can bring about (cf. below, chapter 4, pp. 14–44). But Abelard gives no indication of having made such a distinction, and the passage cited by Knuuttila ((*LI(oi)* 9.560–63, ed. Jacobi and Strub, p. 430, lines 23–26): 'Nec tamen

falleretur deus, quia sicut res aliter posset euenire, ita et ipse aliter posset prouidisse, ut, sicut hoc modo tantum prouidit, ita et alio tantum prouidisset, qui similiter cum euentu alio rei concordasset sicut iste modus prouidentiae cum isto euentu') is better taken as evidence that Abelard accepted that all sorts of events are genuinely open and might, even given God's power and goodness, have happened otherwise (in which case God would have foreknown that they would happen otherwise).

100. Normore (2004, 2006) has written interestingly on Abelard's closeness to Stoic thought. He seems, though it is not entirely clear, to take NAG to have deterministic consequences.

Introduction to Part II

1. See Moonan 1989 (on his use of Plato's *Timaeus*) and Mews 1988 (on his use of Jerome).

2. Some connections, however, have been made with the Stoics—see Normore 2004.

THREE.   Abelard and Anselm

1. Vanni Rovighi 1965, 51.

2. The second part of Gasper and Kohlenberger 2006 is given over entirely to essays comparing Anselm and Abelard, but it is only those by Mews, Perkams and (rather negatively) Ernst which look at the question of influence. The essays by Colman, Kohlenberger, Yamazaki and Shimizu make philosophical comparisons, without asserting a direct link.

3. Robson (1996, 336–38) provides a wide-ranging survey of use of this work in the twelfth century. He is wrong, however, to say that 'aspects of the treatise were criticized by Peter Abelard' (336) and to refer to Abelard's letter 15, as printed in *PL* 178. That letter, as the edition makes clear, is a letter *to* Abelard, not by him. The author is Roscelin—cf. the following note, and also below, pp. 101–7.

4. For Roscelin's letter, see Reiners 1910, 62–80.

5. See Rivière 1936.

6. Robson 1996, 336 n. 11, and Mews 2006, 216–19.

7. Mews 2006, 204–13, makes an extended comparison, although he does not produce any undeniable cases of influence.

8. See Hugh of St Victor, *De sacramentis, PL* 176:291B–D. Here he summarizes Anselm's idea that there are two wills in rational creatures,

one for rightness, the other for the convenient (*commodum*), which Anselm developed in *De casu diaboli*, chs. 12–13, and repeated, with some changes, in *De concordia* 3.11–13; cf. Vanni Rovighi 1965, 52, esp. nn. 116 and 117.

9. The work's editor notes possible use of *De libertate arbitrii* and *De conceptu virginali*, as well as perhaps knowledge of *Cur Deus homo* (Landgraf 1934, pp. 93–95, 117, 189).

10. Sharpe 2009.

11. *Ep.* 14, ed. Smits, p. 280, lines 28–30: 'contra illum magnificum ecclesie doctorem Anselmum Cantuariensum archiepiscopum adeo per contumelias exarsit'.

12. *TChr* 4.83: 'Fuit et quidam nouissimis temporibus nostris, Anselmus uidelicet Cantuariensis metropolitanus, qui, seruata substantiae unitate, ualidiorem uisus est similitudinem ad haec quae diximus induxisse. . . . Ponit itaque praedictus archiepiscopus quasi tria eiusdem substantiae, fontem uidelicet, riuum et stagnum: fontem quidem ex quo est riuus quasi Patrem ex quo Filius, stagnum uero quod ex fonte et riuo prouenit quasi Spiritum qui ex Patre et Filio procedit.'

13. *De incarnatione Verbi* (2a recensio) 13 (Anselm 1946b, p. 31, lines 19–23): 'Tres igitur sunt fons, rivus, lacus, et unus Nilus, unus fluvius, una natura, una aqua; et dici non potest quid tres. Nam neque tres aut Nili aut fluvii aut aquee aut naturae sunt, neque tres aut fontes aut rivi aut lacus. Unum igitur dicitur hic de tribus et tria de uno, nec tamen tria de invicem.'

14. Abelard, *TChr* 4.83 (ed. Buytaert, p. 304, lines 1218–20): 'Posuit etiam riuum in fistula quasi Filium in carne humana, ac si riuum infistulatum dicamus Verbum incarnatum'. Cf. *De incarnatione Verbi* (2a recensio) 14 (Anselm 1946b, p. 33, lines 4–8): 'Si enim rivus per fistulam currat a fonte usque ad lacum: nonne solus riuus, quamvis non alius Nilus quam fons et lacus, ut ita dicam infistulatus est, sicut solus filius incarnatus est, licet non alius deus quam pater et spiritus sanctus?'

15. *TChr* 4.83 (ed. Buytaert, p. 304, lines 1221–33).

16. Clanchy 1990.

17. Luscombe 2002; cf. Mews 2006, 197–98.

18. *De incarnatione Verbi* (2a recensio) 13 (Anselm 1946b, p. 31, line 24, to p. 32, line 1): 'Quod si obicit non esse singulum quemque aut fontem aut rivum aut lacum, aut binos perfectum Nilum sed partes Nili: cogitet totum hunc Nilum, ex quo incepit usque dum desinet, esse in tota quasi aetate sua; quia nec ipse totus est simul aut loco aut tempore sed per partes, nec perfectus erit donec desinat esse. Habet enim quandam in hoc cum oratione similitudinem, quae quamdiu quasi ex oris fonte procedit perfecta non est; et cum perfecta est iam non est.' The comparison with speech is clearly influenced by Boethius's *Commentary on the Categories* 208A–C. I

am grateful to Alisa Kunitz-Dick for her comments on this passage in Anselm and its relationship to Boethius.

19. Perkams 2006, 148.

20. Compare Anselm 1946a, p. 105, line 9, and *TChr* 5.18 (= *TSch* 3.18).

21. Anselm 1946a, p. 105, lines 12–13.

22. *TChr* 5.18 (= *TSch* 3.18).

23. *TChr* 5.20; *TSch* 3.20.

24. *TChr* 5.20; *TSch* 3.20.

25. *TChr* 5.21; *TSch* 3.21.

26. *TChr* 5.19; *TSch* 3.19.

27. For the reasons suggested above, Perkams (2006, 148) is, at the least, exaggerating when he says that Abelard explains divine omnipotence 'in exactly the same way as Anselm in the *Proslogion*'.

28. *Comm. Rom.* 2.3.26 (ed. Buytaert, p. 113, line 124, to p. 118, line 274).

29. *Comm. Rom.* 2.3.26 (ed. Buytaert, p. 114, line 135, to p. 116, line 202).

30. *Comm. Rom.* 2.3.26 (ed. Buytaert, p. 116, line 216, to p. 117, line 225).

31. Peppermüller 1972, 86–91.

32. Luscombe 1983, at 215.

33. Reiners 1910, p. 67, line 31, to p. 68, line 3: 'Sed de donno Anselmo archiepiscopo, quem et vitae sanctitas honorat et doctrinae singularitas ultra communem hominum mensuram extollit, quid dicam? Ait enim in libro, quem 'Cur deus homo?' intitulat, aliter deum non posse hominem salvare nisi sicut fecit, id est nisi homo fieret et omnia illa quae passus est pateretur. Eius sententiam sanctorum doctorum, quorum doctrina fulget ecclesia, vehementer impugnant.'

34. Cf. Luscombe 1983, 208–9.

35. Luscombe 1983, 217.

36. Weingart 1970, 91–93.

37. Luscombe (1983, 216–17) provides a tactful but convincing critique of Weingart's position. It is in fact true, however, that Abelard finds a way in which humans could have been redeemed otherwise than they were, but not of the sort Weingart thought; see below, pp. 105–7.

38. *TChr* 5.13 = *TSch* 3.15.

39. Weingart 1970, 91–92.

40. Perkams 2006, 148.

41. See *Cur Deus homo* 1.25. Anselm considers that he has shown that it is not possible that humans should not have been saved, or should have been saved by some other way than by Christ, and that it therefore follows that 'it is necessary that it happened through Christ'; Anselm 1946b, p. 95, lines 15–21.

42. Rogers 2008, 73–76, gives a clear account of Anselm's libertarianism with respect to created, rational agents.

43. Rogers 2008, 195.

44. Abelard, *TSch* 3.54 (cf. above, chapter 2, p. 66); Anselm, *Cur Deus homo* 2.17; cf. Leftow 1995, 170. (Strangely, Rogers takes no account of this article.) Taken literally, this statement implies a complete dependence of all necessities on God, of the sort held, centuries later, by Descartes, who argued that '3 + 4 = 7' is true as a result of the divine will. But, as will become clear from his discussion of the Incarnation, Anselm holds that many necessities are independent of God's will and in some sense constrain it. (I am grateful to one of the anonymous readers of my MS for pointing this out.)

45. Leftow 1995, 169.

46. *Cur Deus homo* 1.10 (Anselm 1946b, p. 67, lines 2–6): 'volo tecum pacisci, ut nullum vel minimum inconveniens in Deo a nobis accipiatur, et nulla vel minima ratio, si maior non repugnat, reiiciatur. Sicut enim in Deo quamlibet parvum inconveniens sequitur impossibilitas, ita quamlibet parvam rationem, si maiori non vincitur, comitatur necessitas.' Anselm repeats the first part of his principle in the *De incarnatione Verbi* (2a recensio) 10 (Anselm 1946b, p. 26, line 4): 'quamlibet parvum inconveniens in deo est impossibile.'

47. *Tchr* 5.38 = Reiners 1910, p. 68, lines 6–21.

48. Compare Augustine, *De trinitate* 13.10, 'non alium modum possibilem deo defuisse cuius potestati cuncta aequaliter subiacent, sed sanandae nostrae miseriae convenientiorem modum alium non fuisse nec esse oportuisse', and Abelard, *Sent.* 172 (ed. Luscombe, p. 88, lines 1980–81), 'Hoc multis denique aliis modi sed nullo tam convenienti facere potuit.'

49. *Sent.* 172 (ed. Luscombe, p. 88, line 1980, to p. 89, line 1987).

50. *Sent.* 151 (ed. Luscombe, p. 75, line 1674, to p. 76, line 1684). For analysis of the discussion about whether Peter could have been juster than he was, see above, chapter 2, pp. 83–84.

51. *Sent. Par.*, ed. Landgraf, p. 23, line 24, to p. 24, line 2: 'Contra hoc videtur, quod Augustinus dicit: "Fuit et alius modus possibilis Deo." Sed et iste modus potentie refertur ad rem subiectam, sicut cum dico: chimera est opinabilis, opinionem refero ad rem subiectam, non ad chimeram, quia, cum dico: chimera est opinabilis, non dico, quod chimera possit opinari, sed dico, quod aliquis potest opinari chimeram. Similiter cum dico: fuit et alius modus possibilis Deo, id est, ratio in rebus fuit, quod modus redemptionis aliter fieret.'

52. *TSch* 3.46.

53. Recent extended treatments of Abelard's ethics include King 1995; Marenbon 1997a, 213–331; Perkams 2001.

54. See e.g. Enders 1999; Goebel 2001; Trego 2010.

55. See above, p. 99.

56. Abelard has a technical vocabulary to express this point, and it changes, with his introduction of the term 'consent'. For a summary, see Marenbon 1997a, 251–64.

57. *Coll.*, sec. 206.

58. See e.g. Wilks 2012, as discussed below.

59. *De conceptu virginali* 4 (Anselm 1946b, p. 144, lines 22–23): 'dixi nullam actionem per se iniustam dici, sed propter iniustam voluntatem.'

60. *De conceptu virginali* 4 (Anselm 1946b, p. 144, line 27 to p. 145, line 8): 'Sed si aliqua actio qua fit aliquid, quae non est nisi dum fit aliquid, et eo peracto transit ut iam non sit, aut opus quod fit et remanet— verbi gratia cum in scribendo quod scribi non debet transit scriptio, qua fiunt figurae quae remanent—esset peccatum: transeunte actione ut iam non sit, transiret similiter peccatum nec iam esset; aut quamdiu remaneret quod fit, numquam deleretur peccatum. Sed videmus peccata saepe et non deleri actione deleta, et deleri opere non deleto. Quare nec actio quae transit nec opus quod remanet est aliquando peccatum.'

61. Wilks 2012, 592.

62. *De libertate arbitrii* 5 (Anselm 1946a, p. 214, line 24).

63. *De libertate arbitrii* 5 Anselm 1946a, p. 214, line 19–23): 'Ligari enim potest homo invitus, quia nolens potest ligari; torqueri potest invitus, quia nolens potest torqueri; occidi potest invitus, quia nolens potest occidi; velle autem non potest invitus, quia velle non potest nolens velle. Nam omnis volens ipsum suum velle vult.'

64. *De libertate arbitrii* 5 (Anselm 1946a, p. 214, line 27, to p. 215, line 32).

65. *Sc.*, ed. Luscombe, p. 6, line 24, to p. 8, line 20.

66. *Sc.*, ed. Luscombe, p. 8, line 26, to p. 10, line 2.

67. See *Sc.*, ed. Luscombe, p. 4, lines 27–30, and p. 14, lines 17–19; cf. Marenbon 1997a, 258–61.

68. The question of Abelard's and Anselm's relation to Augustine, especially on the question of intention in ethics, is a complicated one, and though a comparison would be fascinating, it is beyond the scope of this chapter. A beginning to the task is made in Wilks 2012, but to be complete the comparison needs to be more than three-way, since Abelard both read Augustine directly and was influenced by—and reacted to—him as mediated through the theologians of his time and just before, such as Anselm of Laon, William of Champeaux and their pupils. Some of the groundwork for this comparison was done in Blomme 1958; further important discussion is found in Knuuttila 2004, 168–72, 178–81.

69. *De veritate* 12; Anselm 1946a, p. 194, line 26.

70. Kantian readings of Anselm have been a speciality of German interpreters, although most have pointed out the differences as well as the

similarities. See e.g. Recktenwald (1998, 26), who, talking of the distinction Anselm makes within his notion of goodness between happiness and rightness, remarks that 'die Radikalität dieser Scheidung kehrt in der Philosophiegeschichte erst bei Kant wieder'; Goebel 2001, esp. 404–8; cf. Ernst 2006, 156 n. 2.

71. See Perkams 2001, 334–38; I follow his assessment (335) of the main point in common found by them.

72. King 1995, 213.

73. Ernst 2006.

FOUR.   An Unpopular Argument (II)

1. This analysis is repeated from chapter 2, (18) to (24), for the reader's convenience.

2. 'Quod ea solummodo possit Deus facere vel dimittere vel eo modo tantum vel eo tempore quo facit, non alio' (7) (Mews 1985a, 109).

3. See frags. 13, 14 and 15 (*Apol.*, ed. Buytaert, p. 368, lines 65–86).

4. *Conf. fid.* '*Universis*' 6.1 (ed. Burnett, p. 135): 'Deum ea solummodo facere posse credo que ipsum facere convenit, et quod multa facere posset que numquam facit.'

5. Burnett's introduction to *Conf. fid.* '*Universis*', p. 113.

6. See above, chapter 2.

7. This Roland used to be identified with Rolandus Bandinelli, who became Pope Alexander III, but no longer; cf. Noonan (1977). See Luscombe 1970, 244–53, for a general assessment of Roland's relationship to Abelard.

8. There are a number of other texts from the mid- and late twelfth century, besides Roland's *Sentences* and those of Peter the Lombard, which discuss Abelard's views about God and alternative possibilities. They include works by Robert of Melun (cf. Luscombe 1970, 291–92; Colish 1994, 1:296), Robert Pullen (*Sententiae* 1.15; *PL* 186:709C–714B; cf. Colish 1994, 1:293), the *Summa sententiarum* 1.14 (*PL* 176:68C–70B; cf. Colish 1994, 1:293–94) and Peter of Poitiers (*Sententiae* 1.7; Peter of Poitiers 1943, 48–61). Colish (1994, 1:290–302) gives a learned survey of the various discussions as a background to her presentation of Peter the Lombard's view, although her analyses are often different from mine. She also claims (1:292) that the school of Gilbert of Poitiers tackled Abelard's view in a particularly effective way, hoisting him, as she puts it, by his own petard, by showing the 'intrinsic limits of the logic he taught'. But in the *Sentences* from Gilbert's school (2.38–39; see also Häring 1978, 119), only the position of whether God could

have done better than he does is tackled, and the lines along which it is considered are close to those in Abelard's *Sententiae*. (In the other redaction of Gilbert's *Sententie*, also cited by Colish, there is no significant discussion of the problem.)

9. Luscombe (1970, 247) discusses Roland's treatment briefly; Colish (1:295 n. 131) is under the strange misapprehension that Roland 'rushed to [Abelard's] support' on this question. There is an extended discussion of this passage in Boh 1985, 186–93. Boh shows very clearly that Roland does not accept Abelard's position. He gives a detailed logical analysis of how Roland presents the Abelardian reading of Augustine's remarks on divine omnipotence (Boh 1985, 187–90; cf. above, p. 65), and he summarizes the rest of Roland's formulation of the Abelardian view, but he passes very quickly over Roland's own solution.

10. He discusses (Roland 1891, p. 53, lines 4–5, and p. 55, lines 22–24) the example of God making it rain today, given at *TSch* 3.45 but not found in *TChr*), and the quotations used as authorities for the position that God cannot do more than he does are in part the same as those in *TSch* (and not parallelled at this point in *TChr*) (see below, note 12). Among the authoritative texts cited to show that God *can* do more than he does are one that is found in both *TChr* and *TSch* and two that are found in *TChr* but not *TSch* (see below, note 16), but the analysis of the text found in both occurs only in *TSch* (see below, note 19).

11. See *Sent.* 147 (ed. Luscombe, p. 73, line 1630) for Esau and Jacob and 151 (ed. Luscombe, p. 76, line 1681) for Judas.

12. Roland 1891 begins (p. 49, line 31, to p. 50, line 3) with a passage alluding to the Book of Wisdom (xii, 18), which is very close in wording and argument to *TSch* 3.38; he goes on (p. 50, lines 5–10) to quote Augustine on God's power being limited to what he wills, as Abelard does at *TSch* 3.48 and *TChr* 5.23; then (p. 50, lines 13–17) he cites Augustine's *De diversis quaestionibus lxxxiii* on God not having been able to generate a better Son than he did—exactly the quotation used in *TSch* 3.31 as an authority for God's not being able to do more than he does; the final citation (p. 50, line 18, to p. 51, line 3) is also attributed to Augustine, but in fact, although it bears a vague relation to a passage in *De Genesi ad litteram* (4.16), is much closer to Abelard's commentary on the *Hexaemeron*, sec. 306 (cf. also *TChr* 1.3). In *TChr*, Abelard does not give authorities in direct support of his view. In *TSch*, besides the citation from Augustine on John, he gives other authorities not used by Roland.

13. Roland 1891, p. 51, lines 7–11: 'Si ideo non potest currere vel peccare, quia non convenit eum facere: ergo eadem ratione lapidem aliquem de loco suo non potest movere, quia non convenit, ut moveat, quod exinde apparet, quod dimittit. Si enim conveniret, ut moveret, et moveret.'

14. The text at Roland 1891, p. 51, line 18, which reads, 'Creare animam et non creare eadem sunt duo', should almost certainly be emended by replacing *eadem* with *eandem*.

15. Roland 1891, p. 51, line 17, to p. 52, line 7.

16. Roland 1891, p. 52, line 14, to p. 54, line 2. One quotation, drawn from Matt. 26:53 (p. 52, lines 14–17), is given in *TChr* 5.39 and *TSch* 3.41 (where Abelard goes on to give an analysis, summarized by Roland, explaining why this text is an authority for the position; two others, from Augustine (Roland 1891, p. 52, lines 17–18—God could have raised up Judas just as he did Lazarus; p. 52, line 21, to p. 53, line 2—God could have made man by mixing his soul with the earth (attributed to Jerome by Roland)), are found in *TChr* 5.40 and 5.39 respectively.

17. Roland 1891, p. 54, lines 3–4: 'Rationibus et auctoritatibus supra sufficienter probatum videtur, Deum non posse plura quam faciat, et contra.'

18. Roland 1891, p. 54, line 9, to p. 55, line 2.

19. At *TSch* 3.42 he explains why Christ's remark (Matt. 26:53) that he could call on his Father and he would send more than twelve legions of angels does not imply that God could do other than he does. Roland (1891, p. 52, lines 14–16) had cited this argument against Abelard's position but does not return to it.

20. Roland 1891, p. 54, line 9, to p. 55, line 22. The most strikingly Abelardian is the use of the distinction between passive and active possibility (Roland 1891, p. 55, lines 3–7): 'Quod autem dicitur: "qui suscitavit Lazarum in corpore, potuit suscitare Judam in mente", sic intelligitur: "potuit suscitare Judam", si voluisset, *vel aliter: "potuit suscitare Judam", id est, nature Jude non repugnabat, quin posset eum suscitaret.*' (This point is then illustrated with a comparison to a stone at the bottom of the sea, which is visible although I cannot see it.) Boh (1985, 192) rightly notes the interest of this passage but then claims that Abelard's analysis of the case is 'more subtle', citing *TSch* 3.49 but substituting for the 'he' (referring back to the *damnandus*) of Abelard's text Judas. Rather, the Abelardian view discussed by Roland uses a shorthand version of the approach put forward in *TSch* to deal with the specific example of Judas, which is not raised there, although it was discussed in the *Sententie*.

21. Roland 1891, p. 53, lines 4–5, and p. 55, lines 22–24; cf. *TSch* 3.45.

22. Roland 1891, p. 53, lines 5–8, and p. 55, line 24, to p. 56, line 9.

23. Roland 1891, p. 56, lines 14–20.

24. Roland 1891, p. 56, lines 13–14.

25. Roland 1891, p. 56, lines 20–28. The answer to the objection about divine necessity is different from, but not incompatible with, that in *TSch*

3.54 (see above, p. 66). The answer to the second objection is rather feeble.

26. The printed text in Gietl's edition of Roland begins this section: 'Nobis autem asserentibus Deum plura posse facere quam faciat, obviare quodammodo videntur predicte auctoritates et rationes, quas ita determinamus dicentes' (Roland 1891, p. 56, lines 29–31). But Gietl himself, in his introduction (xvii n. 1), explains that this is a printing error and that the MS reads *Vobis autem asserentibus*. Yet the sense shows that, whatever the manuscript reading, Roland must originally have said or written *Nobis*. His point is that, for those who, like him, reject Abelard's thesis (that God *cannot* do more than he does), the authoritative citations produced by the Abelardians to support their case *appear* to cause problems but need not, because they can be read, as he goes on to explain, in a way that does not support Abelard's position.

27. Roland 1891, p. 56, line 32, to p. 57, line 16.

28. Roland 1891, p. 57, line 27, to p. 58, line 1.

29. Roland 1891, p. 52, lines 7–13.

30. Roland 1891, p. 58, lines 7–21.

31. See Luscombe 1970, 261–80, and Colish 1994 for general assessments of the relationship between Abelard and the Lombard. Marenbon 2007c looks (227–31) at aspects of moral theory on which the Lombard may have been influenced by Abelard, but it is mostly devoted to a longer, but worse, discussion of the matter considered here—the treatment in the *Sentences* of the argument that God cannot do other than he does.

32. Peter the Lombard, *Sent.*, bk. 1, d. 43 (Peter the Lombard 1971, p. 298, line 7, to p. 299, line 3).

33. A confirmation that Abelard's own presentation was in terms of doing or desisting from a particular action is given in a text published (wrongly—see Brady 1966) among the *quaestiones* of Odo of Soissons. It comes from someone who claims himself to have heard Abelard saying it: 'Magister Petrus Abaelardus dicebat, quod Deus non potest facere, nisi quod facit; nec dimittere, nisi quod dimittit. . . . Si faceret quid quod modo dimittit, jam ageret contra illam rationem qua modo illud dimittit; et si dimitteret quod modo facit, contra illam ageret qua se facturum illud proposuit. Sic audivi illum docentem' (Pitra 1888, 113).

34. Peter the Lombard 1971, p. 299, lines 9–14: 'His autem respondemus, duplicem verborum intelligentiam aperientes et ab eis involuta evolventes, sic: "Non potest Deus facere quod bonum est et iustum", id est non potest facere nisi illud quod, si faceret, bonum esset et iustum, verum est; sed multa potest facere quae nec bona sunt nec iusta, quia nec sunt nec erunt, nec bene fiunt, quia nunquam fient.'

35. See Marenbon 2005, 58–60.

36. The Lombard does not, however, like talking about God's right-ness—what God 'ought' to do—at all, since it makes it seem as though he lies under an obligation, when God lies under no sort of obligation at all.

37. *Summa aurea*, bk. 1, tr. xi, cap. 7; William of Auxerre 1980, p. 216, lines 13–34: 'Sed queritur utrum possit aliud facere quam facit. Videtur quod non, quia non potest facere nisi quod bonum et iustum est; sed omne quod bonum est et iustum fieri ipse facit; ergo non potest aliud facere quam facit. . . . Alie obiectiones solvuntur per distinctionem huius verbi "est", quod potest significare actualem inherentiam vel naturalem coheren-tiam. Utrum [?: *leg.* unde?] dicimus quod hec est duplex: "Deus non potest facere nisi quod bonum et iustum est fieri." Si hoc verbum "est" significet actualem inherentiam, falsa est. Si naturalem coherentiam, vera est. Sed in hac significatione falsa est, nec omne quod bonum et iustum est ipse facit, et sic non procedit argumentatio' (punctuation slightly adjusted).

The discussion of whether God can do other than he does takes place within a treatment of whether God could make things better than he did—a theme which is handled in Abelard's *Sententiae* and which tends to be treated separately in the thirteenth- and fourteenth-century tradition: see above, p. 74.

38. Pars 1, inq. 1, tr. iv, qu. 2, membr. 2, cap. 2 (Alexander of Hales 1924, 219–20).

39. Pars 1, inq. 1, tr. iv, qu. 2, membr. 2, cap. 2, arguunt 2.2 (Alexander of Hales 1924, 219b): 'Item, si potest aliquid de potentia quod non potest de iustitia: exeat illa potentia in actum, illud ergo aut est iustum aut iniustum. Si est iniustum: ergo potest Deus facere non-iustum; si iustum: ergo solum potest quod iustum est.'

40. Pars 1, inq. 1, tr. iv, qu. 2, membr. 2, cap. 2, resp. 2 (Alexander of Hales 1924, 220b).

41. Bonaventure, *Commentary on the Sentences of Peter Lombard*, bk. 1, d. 43, dubia 1 and 2 (Bonaventure 1882, 776–77).

42. Albert the Great, *Commentary on the Sentences of Peter Lombard*, bk. 1, d. 43 (Albert the Great 1893, 376–77, 380–81, 383–84).

43. William of Ockham 1979, p. 623, lines 12–14.

44. William of Ockham 1979, p. 640, lines 7–12.

45. *Summa logicae* 3.1.34 (William of Ockham 1974, p. 452, lines 4–7).

46. For an account of the distinction between ordained and absolute power, and how Scotus and later medieval thinkers changed it, see Courte-nay 1990 and Gelber 2004, 309–49. Courtenay (see esp. 45–55) sees a link between Abelard and the origins of the distinction, principally because of a view of his not discussed in this book, the position that sentences express contents which are timelessly true.

47. Aquinas, *Commentary on the Sentences of Peter Lombard*, bk. 1, d. 43, qu.2, a.2 (Aquinas 1929, 1010): 'Nihil enim potest facere, quod si fieret, non esset justum. Aut potest intelligi quod ex justitia sua determinetur ad aliquod unum faciendum, ita quod aliud facere non possit: et sic falsum est.'

48. Aquinas, *Commentary on the Sentences of Peter Lombard*, bk. 1, d. 43, qu.2, a.2, ad 4 (Aquinas 1929, 1011–12).

49. Aquinas's way of tackling the problem in his *Sentences* commentary is followed closely by Durandus of St Pourçain in his own *Sentences* commentary, bk. 1, d. 43, q. 5 (digital transcription with corrections of Venice 1571 edition by Thomas Institute, Cologne, http://durandus.phil-fak.uni-koeln.de/12823.html, 1193–96).

50. Aquinas, *Quaestiones disputatae de potentia Dei*, q. 1, a. 5: 'hic error, scilicet Deum non posse facere nisi quae facit . . . fuit quorumdam theologorum considerantium ordinem divinae iustitiae et sapientiae, secundum quem res fiunt a Deo, quem Deum praeterire non posse dicebant; et incidebant in hoc, ut dicerent, quod Deus non potest facere nisi quae facit. Et imponitur hic error magistro Petro Almalareo.' (The edition used is Thomas Aquinas 1965—as available at CorpusThomisticum.org; there is no Leonine edition of this work yet.) Already in the mid-seventeenth century, John of St Thomas (John Poinsot), in his course of Thomistic theology (q. 25; disp. 11, art. 1), had seen a possible connection between this passage and Abelard (he says that that he does not know whether the Almalareus mentioned by Aquinas is the same as 'Abaylardus'), though he was prevented from seeing how exactly Almalareus's doctrine corresponds to Abelard's, because he still had relied on reports of Abelard's views by those who attacked him as a heretic; see John of St Thomas 1643, 427. Maurer (1976) 293 n. 8, assumes, without argument, that the Almalareus mentioned by Aquinas is Abelard.

51. On this information, see below, p. 138.

52. Aquinas, *Summa theologiae*, pt. 1, q. 25, a. 5. The question itself poses a different problem: that God cannot act in a way other than he has foreknown and foreordained that he will act. This point is answered in the reply to the first objection, by using the powers distinction. What God has foreordained is what he does according to his ordained power, but he can, by his absolute power, do otherwise. The body of the question, however, is devoted to giving an answer to the Abelardian problem, which is evoked, not in the question itself, but especially in the first of the initial arguments.

53. *Doctrinale* 1.10 (Thomas Netter 1532, fol. 20vb).

54. Bernard's letter-treatise against Abelard is letter 190 in Bernard of Clairvaux 1977. It survives in 117 manuscripts from the twelfth to the fifteenth centuries.

55. *Capitula haeresum* 1969, p. 474, lines 36–57.

56. *Doctrinale* 1.10 (Thomas Netter 1532, fol. 20vb). He quotes (in order), nos. 3, 5 and 1 of group 3: *TSch* 3.39 (Peter Abelard 1969, p. 474, lines 46–48), *TSch* 3.56 (Peter Abelard 1969, p. 474, lines 54–57), and *TSch* 3.32 (Peter Abelard 1969, p. 474, lines 38–42).

57. Thomas Netter 1532, fol. 21ra; Hugh of St Victor, *De sacramentis* 1.2.22 (*PL* 176:214B–215A): see above, chapter 2, pp. 75–76.

58. *Doctrinale* 2.107 (Thomas Netter 1557, fol. 187va). Jerome talks about the dispute between Diodorus and Chrysippus in his *Dialogus adversos Pelagianos* 1.9.

59. *De controversiis* 3.15 (Bellarmine 1862, 351a).

60. *De controversiis* 3.17 (Bellarmine 1862, 354a).

61. On contemporary interpreters misreading Abelard's position, see above, chapter 2, notes 99 and 100.

62. Leibniz 1999, p. 2575, line 29: 'Hoc falsum, alioquin nihil esset possibile, nisi quod actu educeretur.'

63. The *Dictionnaire* is available on the Web in various scanned versions, mostly of the 1820 edition of Beuchot. A selection of the most important philosophical articles is found in Bayle 1982 (reproduced photographically from the fifth edition of 1740, which preserves the carefully planned original layout of the pages).

64. Leibniz, *Théodicée*, sec. 171 (Leibniz 1885, 215–16).

65. He repeats the same idea in sec. 235 (Leibniz 1885, 257).

66. Rateau 2008, 534: 'Nous arrivons alors à cet étonnant paradoxe: Leibniz conteste la position d'Abélard soutenant que Dieu ne peut pas faire ce qu'il ne fait pas, alors que cette thèse ne contredit pas (à condition de préciser que ce qui n'est pas crée reste en soi possible) l'idée qu'il se fait lui-même de l'omnipotence.'

67. See Adams 1994, 9–52, esp. 12–15.

68. For the distinction between this sense and the attributive one, see above, chapter 2, pp. 78–79.

69. Cf. Adams 1994, 13.

Introduction to Part III

1. For a more detailed study of this re-discovery, see Marenbon 2006.

2. Jolivet 1969. Nuchelmans (1973) was the first person to show the originality and importance of Abelard's views on the semantics of propositions. De Rijk contributed to the understanding of Abelard, not only by putting it into a context (1962, 1967), but also in studies of aspects of his logic and metaphysics (e.g. 1986). Irène Rosier-Catach has taken this tradition forward, reaching new levels of technical grasp and historical precision

through her detailed knowledge of the contemporary grammatical literature and her work on unpublished manuscripts; see Rosier-Catach 1999,
2003a, 2003b, 2004, 2007, 2012.

3. See Tweedale 1976; Jacobi 1981, 1985; Jacobi, Strub and King 1996;
Knuuttila 1981, 178–87, and Knuuttila 1993, 82–96; Libera 1981; 1999, 281–
498; 2002a; 2002b, 122–26, 269–97. (Libera 1999 provides the closest
and most sustained analysis of Abelard's famous theory of universals yet to
have been written; because it is in French, and part of a long book, those
in the anglophone analytic camp have entirely ignored it—there is, for instance, no reference to it in the *Cambridge Companion to Abelard*.)

FIVE.   Abelard and the 'New' Theory of Meaning

1. King 1982.
2. King 2010. This part of King's entry is without substantive changes
from his original 2004 version.
3. For the distinction between the question of what terms mean and
the question of how their meaning is determined, see e.g. Braun 2006,
502–3; Stalnaker 1997, 535–36. In principle, a causal theory of reference
need not be tied to an identification of meaning with reference.
4. This account of the theory is based especially on Kripke 1980;
Putnam 1975, 1988; Searle 1983, esp. 197–230; Wiggins 1994. It is supposed
simply to provide a sketch of the views King had in mind when he made
the link between Abelard and the 'new theorists'; although Kripke and
Putnam, for this purpose, can be taken together, their views on the area differ in many ways.
5. Cf. Kripke 1980, 135.
6. The quotation is from *LI(isa)*, ed. Geyer, p. 23, lines 22–24; for the
text of the complete passage, see n. 36 below.
7. Martin 2009.
8. Martin 2009, 193–95.
9. Rosier-Catach 2004, 19–23.
10. King 1982, 464–67. King's interpretation is followed by Kevin
Guilfoy (2004, 210–11); see Martin's detailed criticisms: 2010, 201–2.
11. Martin 2010, 203–6.
12. King 2007. Martin does not mention this article, because he did
not see it before his own article was ready.
13. King 2007, 174.
14. King 2007, 175.
15. King 2007, 175.

16. *LI*(*cat*), ed. Geyer, p. 112, lines 37–40: 'Quantum tamen ad causam impositionis nominis prima et principalis significatio intellectus dicitur, quia scilicet ideo tantum vocabulum rei datum est, ut intellectum constituat.'

17. See Spade 1980 and Marenbon 1997a, 182.

18. *Dial.*, ed. De Rijk, p. 222, lines 28–31: 'Sunt enim, quemadmodum dictiones, alie une in sensu, ut que unam habent impositionem, sicut univoce et singulares, alie vero multiplices, que scilicet diversas habent impositionis causas, sicut equivoce.'

19. *Dial.*, ed. De Rijk, p. 588, lines 20–23: 'Sed harum alie ex una impositione et eadem causa pluribus date sunt, ut que univoce dicuntur, alie diversas habent impositionis causas, ut que equivoce ac proprie multiplices appellantur. Univoca quidem est, ut "homo", cuius unam impositionis causam in omnibus veris hominibus una eius definitio quam secundum illam habet, firma est probatio, que est "animal rationale mortale".'

20. *LI*(*isa*), ed. Geyer, p. 19, line 19, to p. 20, line 14.

21. On *status*, see e.g. Marenbon 1997a, 191–95; Jacobi 2004, 136.

22. *LI*(*oi*) 9.77 (ed. Jacobi and Strub, p. 262, lines 448–54; ed. Geyer, p. 428, lines 1–7): 'quia uero homines . . . recte secundum diuersas uocabulorum causas diuersa fatum et prouidentiam dixit, sicut aliud risibile esse, aliud nauigabile esse dicimus, cum tamen idem sit penitus nauigabile et risibile, ac est tale, ac si quod aliud sonat "risibile", aliud "nauigabile" secundum diuersas impositionis causas.'

23. Other words also do the same job for Abelard, such as *sonare* in the passage quoted in the previous note: for a passage that brings *sonare* and *sententia* together, see *Dial.*, ed. De Rijk, p. 595, lines 4–10.

24. *Dial.*, ed. De Rijk, p. 582, lines 16–20: 'Una autem vox dicitur quae unam sententiam secundum unam impositionis causam tenet, velut "homo", "album" [In his edition, De Rijk wrongly in my view emends *album* here to *albus* and punctuates '*homo albus*'] aut "Socrates"; licet enim "homo" et "album" diversis imposita sint, idem tamen de singulis enuntiata notant et secundum eamdem naturam aut proprietatem omnibus imposita sunt.'

25. The word has a related but different sense, in which it is used elsewhere by Abelard, of 'opinion', 'view' or 'position': there are different *sententiae* on universals, or there is the *sententia* of such and such a master.

26. *Dial.*, ed. De Rijk, p. 99, lines 7–9; p. 125, lines 19–21.

27. *LI*(*isa*), ed. Geyer, p. 54, lines 23–27: 'Nam fortasse substantia sensibilis et corpus sensibile quodammodo diversa sunt genera et aequalia sicut animal rationale mortale et animal gressibile bipes diversae sunt quantum ad significationem speciei, sed non oppositae et cum sint aequales in nominatione, sunt in sententia diversae.'

28. *Dial.,* ed. De Rijk, p. 593, lines 29–34: 'Sed cum his quandoque non habundemus, sufficit qualiscumque rei demonstratio propter rem subiectam declarandam potius quam propter sententiam nominis aperiendam. Veluti si "coloratum esse" determinamus "substantiam corpoream", hec quidem assignatio secundum sententiam nominis non est; non enim in "colorato" vel substantie vel corporis significatio tenetur.'

29. *LI(cat)*, ed. Geyer, p. 118, lines 23–27: 'Si quis autem hominem determinans dicat: animal risibile, rerum subiectarum vocabulo hominis continentiam determinat, sed sententiam nominis non aperit per "risibile", cuius sensus in sententia hominis non tenetur. Potest itaque haec descriptio hominis esse quantum ad rerum continentiam, non quantum ad nominis sententiam.' The same point is made in *LI(oi)* 11.49 (ed. Jacobi and Strub, p. 379, lines 446–50; ed. Geyer, p. 477, lines 35–40): 'Nota autem quod si dicatur "coruus niger" uel "homo risibilis", non est huiusmodi superfluitas quantum ad uim uocum, cum uidelicet praemissum non contineat sententiam sequentis. Sed quantum ad determinationem non ualet, cum uel omnis coruus sit niger uel omnis homo risibilis.' The example is less clear, however, because Abelard does not point out explicitly that, while there are many black things that are not crows, it is not just that all men are capable of laughter but that only men are capable of laughter.

30. In *Dial.* (ed. De Rijk, p. 593, lines 31–33, quoted in note 28 above) he will not even use the word 'define' in its connection: he says, rather, that we 'determine' bodily substance as 'to be coloured'. But in *TSB* (2.85) and *TChr* (3.143), making the same point though shifting the example verbally, Abelard describes 'coloured substance' as a definition of body but explains that it is not the sort of definition he has in mind.

31. On *differentiae,* see below, chapter 6, pp. 170–71.

32. *Dial.,* ed. De Rijk, p. 593, lines 34–36: 'At vero si sic diceretur: "coloratum est quod colore formatum est", hec diffinitio secundum nominis sententiam consisteret. Nihil enim aliud "coloratum" notare videtur quam illa oratio.'

33. *Dial.,* ed. De Rijk, p. 594, lines 7–9.

34. *Dial.,* ed. De Rijk, p. 594, lines 11–29: 'Si enim plures alie sint ipsius differentie constitutive, que omnes in nomine "corporis" intelligi dicantur, non totam "corporis" sententiam hec diffinitio tenet, sicut enim nec hominis diffinitio "animal rationale mortale" vel "animal gressibile bipes". . . . Cum autem et bipes et gressibilis et perceptibilis disciplinae ac multe quoque forme fortasse alie hominis sint differentie, que omnes in nomine "hominis" determinari dicuntur . . . apparet "hominis" sententiam in diffinitione ipsius totam non claudi sed secundum quamdam partem constitutionis sue ipsum diffiniri. Sufficiunt itaque ad diffiniendum que non sufficiunt ad constituendum. Sicut enim homo preter rationalitatem

vel mortalitatem non potest subsistere, ita nec preter ceteras differentias, quibus eque substantia ipsius perficitur, ullo modo potest permanere.'

35. *Dial.*, ed. De Rijk, p. 595, lines 13–31: 'Erit autem fortassis questio utrum in nomine speciei omnes ipsius differentie intelligantur, sicut dictum est. Si enim imponentis intellectum respiciamus, non videtur verum, cum ipse fortasse omnes ipsius differentias <non> nominaverit, sicut nec accidentia. . . . Sed ad hec dico . . . licet autem impositor non distincte omnes intellexerit hominis differentias, secundum omnes tamen quecumque esse<n>t, tamquam ipsas confuse conciperet, vocabulum accipi voluit. Aut si secundum quasdam tantum differentias "hominis" nomen imposuit, secundum eas tantum nominis sententia consistere debet ac secundum eas tantum diffinitio sententie assignari potest.'

36. *LI(isa)*, ed. Geyer, p. 23, lines 6–24: 'Inde etiam bene divinae menti, non humanae huiusmodi per abstractionem conceptiones adscribuntur, quia homines, qui per sensus tantum res cognoscunt, vix aut numquam ad huiusmodi simplicem intelligentiam conscendunt et ne pure rerum naturas concipiant, accidentium exterior sensualitas impedit. . . . Unde homines in his quae sensu non attractaverunt, magis opinionem quam intelligentiam habere contingit, quod ipso experimento discimus. Cogitantes enim de aliqua civitate non visa, cum advenerimus, eam nos aliter quam sit excogitasse invenimus. Ita etiam credo de intrinsecis formis quae ad sensus non veniunt, qualis est rationalitas et mortalitas, paternitas, sessio, magis nos opinionem habere. Quaelibet tamen quorumlibet existentium nomina quantum in ipsis est intellectum magis quam opinionem generant, quia secundum aliquas rerum naturas vel proprietates inventor ea imponere intendit, etsi nec ipse bene excogitare sciret rei naturam aut proprietatem.' On Abelard's view of Plato's theory, as expressed here, see Marenbon 1997b, 112–16.

37. Martin 2010, 176.

six.   Abelard and Contemporary Metaphysics

1. See below, p. 174, for a brief explanation of tropes and trope theory.

2. Aristotle, *Categories* 1a25–26. For Boethius's translation, see below, p. 176.

3. Aristotle, *Categories* 1a16–1b6; in Boethius's Latin translation, Aristotle 1961, p. 5, line 18, to p. 6, line 10.

4. Boethius, Commentary on *Categories*, *PL* 64:169C–D.

5. *LI(cat)*, ed. Geyer, p. 127, lines 17–20.

6. Abelard may well not have been a nominalist in this sense earlier, when he was writing *Dial*. Comments in that work which seem to suggest that there are in some sense universal things have been noted by some writers (e.g. Marenbon 1997a, 129; Mews 2011, 103–4). I am grateful to Chris Martin for pointing out to me how pervasive this realist language is in *Dial*. Since the section in which he would have discussed the *Isagoge* is missing from the only MS of the work, and his discussions in the text as it survives point in various different directions, there are no definite conclusions to be drawn about his view of universals at this stage. That, as reported in *HC* (see above, chapter 1, p. 16), Abelard convincingly attacked William's material essence realism c. 1109–10, very probably before *Dial*. was finished, does not show that, at this stage, Abelard had rejected every version of realism, as he would certainly do later.

7. See Marenbon 1997a, 180–81.

8. *LI(cat)*, ed. Geyer, p. 132, lines 17–18.

9. It is also worth noting that Abelard's ontology includes accidents of accidents. To explain different shades of colour, Abelard has to posit additional particular accidents of brightness which attach to particular accidents of a colour, such as whiteness, which are themselves identically similar; see e.g. *LI(cat)*, ed. Geyer, p. 160, lines 39–40; p. 163, lines 12–15; and p. 145, lines 15–19.

10. Porphyry 1966, p. 20, lines 7–8.

11. Aristotle, *Categories* 3a21–3a26 (Aristotle 1961, p. 10, lines 5–9). Cf. *LI(cat)*, ed. Geyer, p. 128, lines 10, 27.

12. See e.g. *Dial.*, ed. De Rijk, p. 56, line 23; *LI(cat)*, ed. Geyer, p. 195, lines 4–5 and line 11, and p. 252, lines 1–5.

13. See *LI(cat)*, ed. Geyer, p. 124, line 13, to p. 125, line 7.

14. *LI(cat)*, ed. Geyer, p. 124, lines 16–17: 'rem tamen adiacentem non habent propter infinitatis inconveniens.' It is true (see below, note 71) that a later text suggests that Abelard thought that forms might be countable without being things (*res*), but the wording here makes it clear that he is talking about things. Moreover, it is hard to see why an infinity of forms that are not things would present a problem.

15. 'One' is a slight exception. Abelard *does* think that substances have an attached form of unity; he thinks, however, that the unity of this attached form is explained, not by another form, but by the mere fact of its being personally discrete—that it is not any other thing; see *LI(cat)*, ed. Geyer, p. 124, lines 17–29.

16. *LI(cat)*, ed. Geyer, p. 192, lines 26–28.

17. *Dial.*, ed. De Rijk, p. 418, line 5, to p. 421, line 8. Cf. *Comm. Hex.*, ed. Romig, p. 9, lines 151–61.

18. *Dial.*, ed. De Rijk, p. 419, lines 1–2.

19. *Dial.*, ed. De Rijk, p. 419, lines 13–17.

20. *Dial.*, ed. De Rijk, p. 419, lines 31–33.

21. *Dial.*, ed. De Rijk, p. 419, line 37, to p. 420, line 12. Abelard does not mention the sand, but it is needed.

22. *Comm. Hex.* 21 (on Gen. 1:1) (ed. Romig, p. 10, lines 181–85). Although this passage appears in only one manuscript, its presence in the *Abbreviatio* of *Comm. Hex.* strongly supports its authenticity.

23. See e.g. *LI(isa)*, ed. Geyer, p. 25, lines 10–11; *LNPS*, ed. Geyer, p. 510, lines 12–15.

24. The whole of this passage is *Dial.*, ed. De Rijk, p. 420, line 29, to p. 421, line 8: 'Hic igitur substantie motus quem generationem dicimus, soli Deo ascribendus est tam in primis quam in postremis creationibus. In quibus quidem nature creationibus generales ac speciales constitute sunt substantie. Neque enim forme mutatio diversitatem specierum aut generum facit, sed substantie creatio. Quocumque enim modo varientur forme, si identitas manserit, nihil ad essentiam generalem vel specialem agitur. Cum autem et forme nulle diverse sint, diversa tamen poterunt esse genera, ut sunt generalissima in sue discretione substantie, aut fortasse quedam species, ut de speciebus accidentium infinitatem vitantes concedimus. Quamdiu itaque essentia materialis nature in se diversa atque aliud ab alia fuerit, diversa contingit esse genera vel species. Diversitas itaque substantie diversitatem generum ac specierum facit, non forme mutatio. Nam etsi in speciebus substantie specierum diversitatis causa sit differentia, hoc tamen ex rerum diversitate substantie quam faciunt, contingit. Unde etiam substantiales sunt appellate huiusmodi differentie, que in substantiam venientes et discretionem substantie faciunt et unionem communis nature; neque enim alia in speciali aut generali natura concludimus nisi ea que natura substantie divina univit operatio.' In Marenbon (1997a, 128–30), I wrongly suggested that this passage fitted awkwardly with Abelard's view of body and differential forms. In Marenbon (2008c, 98–100), I corrected this interpretation and gave a complete, commented translation of the passage. It might even be that when Abelard talks about forms here he has in mind accidental forms alone. That certainly seems to be the case in a passage from *LI(isa)* (ed. Geyer, p. 13, lines 18–33) about individuation, which has some parallels with this passage from *Dial.*

25. Some of the language Abelard uses here could easily be read as if he accepted that species and genera really exist; cf. above, note 6.

26. Abelard remarks (*Cum autem et forme nulle diverse sint* . . .) that there can be diversity without difference in form—for example, the ten categories are diverse, simply in themselves, and the same is, it seems, may be true of the species of accidents. But this is rather beside the point, since Abelard is concerned with substances, and they, he agrees, are made di-

verse by differential forms. Perhaps he is simply trying to emphasize that we should attend to what is diverse, however it is made so, rather than to what makes it diverse.

27. *Comm. Hex.* 21 (on Gen. 1:1) (ed. Romig, p. 9, line 166, to p. 10, line 172): 'omne genus tamquam materiam speciei preponunt, ut animal homini, licet in ipsa hominis conditione, per existentie actum, natura animalis humanam minime precederet naturam; cum id uidelicet quod homo est non ante animal quam hominem esse credamus, nec umquam animal aut aliquod genus nisi in aliqua sua specie fas sit existere'. (I have modified the punctuation from the edition.)

28. See *LI(isa)*, ed. Geyer, p. 80, line 22, to p. 81, line 12. *Dial.*, ed. De Rijk, p. 415, lines 24–34, suggests that even with regard to matter that precedes what is made from it—as body does a human being—it is true to say that the thing made from the matter is the matter. The passage, though, is hard to interpret, because Abelard is not saying, as this assertion might seem to imply, that the forms count for nothing: his point is that the whole is nothing but all of the parts taken together, so that the wood and stones in a house are nothing but the house and, as in the *LI* passage discussed, a man is nothing but an animal informed by rationality and mortality.

29. See above, note 2.

30. See Marenbon 2008c for a more detailed account of contemporary trope theory from the perspective of its possible relation to Abelard. As will become obvious, my comments in the following paragraphs take up and continue the argument beyond the point I reached in that article and correct what I say there in some respects.

31. Martin 1992, 112. This article is an abridgement of a longer, unpublished piece, on which Martin has since worked further. His main position has remained the same, despite a doubt (discussed below) about how it can be that accidental forms become fixed to their subjects.

32. Marenbon, 1997a, esp. 114, 120–23, and Marenbon 2008c.

33. Libera 2002a; Libera 2002b, 122–26, 269–97. I reply to his detailed objections in Marenbon 2008c, 93–95.

34. Aristotle 1961, p. 6, lines 1–2. Boethius almost certainly intends the 'cum', not temporally, but in the sense of 'while' or 'whereas', adding a condition, rendering Aristotle's '*ho en tini mê hôs meros huparchon*'—a locution which cannot be rendered into Latin with equal neatness.

35. Boethius 1847, 173B.

36. *LI(cat)*, ed. Geyer, p. 130, line 28, to p. 131, line 9.

37. *LI(cat)*, ed. Geyer, p. 129, lines 27–33.

38. *LI(cat)*, ed. Geyer, p. 129, lines 34–36: 'Videtur enim, ut huius corporis albedo, quando huic corpori innata est, aliis similiter posset advenire. Sed cum in isto sit, nullo modo amplius in alio potest esse.'

39. *LI*(*cat*), ed. Geyer, p. 130, lines 6–9: 'Posset fortasse contingere, ut cum huic subiecto advenerit, alii advenisset, et ita semper in alio esset, quod nunquam huic contigisset. Sed non potest natura pati, ut cum iam alii insit, in alio iterum sit, hoc est subiectum mutare non potest de uno transeundo ad aliud.' Abelard repeats exactly the same idea a little later (*LI*(*cat*), ed. Geyer, p. 147, lines 33–35), this time using 'knowledge of grammar' as his example of a particular accident.

40. *LI*(*cat*), ed. Geyer, p. 129, line 37, to p. 130, line 2: 'Veluti si dicamus: "eum qui caecus est, non est possibile videre" falsum est. Si vero cum determinatione dicamus: "non est possibile videre, postquam caecus est" . . . verum est.'

41. Martin 2001.

42. See *LI*(*isa*), ed. Geyer, p. 13, lines 18–27, and cf. Gracia 1984, 204–12. Gracia's account is not, however, correct so far as substances are concerned. Abelard believes that substances are each individuated by a particular form of unity, which is itself essentially individuated; see above, note 15. But these accidents of unity would be required, not to distinguish individuals from universals (which do not exist in reality), but to tie together a complex entity as one thing, separate from others. By contrast, forms are not complex and so simply come as individuals.

43. Martin bases his (justified) view that, for Abelard, an individual such as Socrates could not be individuated apart from his rationality especially on *LI*(*isa*), ed. Geyer, p. 65, lines 5–11, where it is argued that 'Socrates' and 'this man' stand for exactly the same thing, the substance of the man, which is a discrete thing from everything else. I am grateful to Chris Martin for discussing this issue with me in detail and allowing me to read an unpublished article of his on the subject.

44. The whole passage reads as follows in Geyer's edition (the Rationality Passage is italicized) (*LI*(*isa*), ed. Geyer, p. 84, lines 14–26): 'Cum autem rationalitatem differentiam dicamus, ea autem non sit nisi haec vel illa rationalitas, oportet hanc vel illam esse differentiam. Sed profecto omnis differentia de specie universaliter dicitur praedicari et destructa ea necessario destrui res. *At vero haec rationalitas pluribus non inest neque propter eam homo periret. Ipse quoque Socrates, sicut hic homo est per eam, ita etiam posset esse per aliam, sive quae sit,sive numquam sit.* Quod ergo dicitur differentiam de specie universaliter praedicari, hoc ad vocem universalem quae differentia dicitur, referendum est, et quod res speciei non posset esse sine differentia, hoc secundum communem causam impositionis nominis universalis accipiendum est, ac si ita dicamus hominem non posse esse aliquid ita, quod non sit rationalis.' I am very grateful to Caterina Tarlazzi, who showed me the structure of the argument in this passage, which I had

not properly grasped. I have followed her in explaining it here. Her own reading of the content of the argument is, however, quite different from mine.

45. *LI(isa)*, ed. Geyer, p. 84, lines 19–21. This passage is cited in Marenbon 1997a, 120 n. 10; Libera 2002a, n. 27; Libera 2002b, 284–85; Marenbon 2008c, 90.

46. This possibility was put to me by Chris Martin in discussion.

47. King 2004, 75–77, 87–88.

48. King 2004, 75.

49. King 2004, 75–76.

50. King 2004, 76.

51. King 2004, 77.

52. In *TChr* (3.153), Abelard talks about numerical and essential identity separately but states that they are equivalent (ed. Buytaert, p. 252, lines 1862–63): 'cum omne idem essentialiter cum aliquo sit idem numero cum ipso, et e conuerso'. In *TSch* (2.95) he simply treats the two sorts of identity together (ed. Buytaert and Mews, p. 454, lines 1415–16): 'Tam numero autem quam essentialiter idem sunt.' By contrast, in *TSB* (2.83; ed. Buytaert and Mews, p. 143, lines 760–66), Abelard held that, if *A* and *B* are essentially the same, they are numerically the same, but not vice versa. Parts, he argued, are the same in number with their whole, but they are not essentially the same. In his later expositions, he avoids this argument by denying that parts are numerically the same as their whole: they are merely not numerically different.

53. *TChr* 3.153, ed. Buytaert, p. 252, lines 1866–68: 'Pars quippe quaelibet diuersa est essentialiter a suo toto, sed non diuersa numero; nec fortassis eadem numero, nisi quis forte numero idem negatiue dicat, hoc est non diuerso numero'; *TSch* 2.97.

54. King 2004, 87.

55. King 2004, 88.

56. *LI(isa)*, ed. Geyer, p. 78, line 34, to p. 79, line 30. King (see quotation above, p. 183) gives the reference just to the last part of this text, but one needs the whole text to understand the discussion. King also cites a parallel text in *LNPS*, which I discuss below, p. 188.

57. For Boethius's translation (as used by Abelard and his contemporaries), see Porphyry 1966, p. 198, lines 9–15.

58. *LI(isa)*, ed. Geyer, p. 79, lines 5–18: 'Proprie quidem materiam dicimus eam, quae tempore quoque praecessit et subiecta fictum operantis in se suscepit, sicut aes, quod ante aes fuit quam statua et attractione artificis sculptum est, ut statua fieret. Formam vero proprie dicimus eam quae ex compositione partium venit, sicut illam quae in statua consideratur ex curvo naso vel directo, ex parvis et magnis oculis et ceteris, quae pertinent

ad compositionem. Unde statua proprie ex materia et forma constare dicitur. Substantia vero hominis quae ex animali et rationalitate consistit, non [ea] ita proprie ex materia et forma componitur. Animal namque quod est homo, numquam prius tempore animal fuit quam homo nec proprie umquam dici potuit: "Animal fit homo" nec artificis attractione homo factus est. Rationalitas quoque proprie forma non dicitur, quia secundum dispositionem partium subiecto non innascitur.'

59. King 2004, 114 n. 44.

60. *LI(cat)*, ed. Geyer, p. 212, line 38, to p. 213, line 5: 'Iuxta quod fortasse Chalcidius asserit Aristotelem non putare animam substantiam esse, sed formam. Sed si forma esset anima, qua ratione diceret in Qualitate dementiam vel iram qualitates esse animae? Numquid forma aut insanit aut irascitur? Praeterea ipse superius scientiam vel grammaticam in subiecto esse in anima dixit. Quomodo autem si forma esset, scientiam haberet?'

61. King 2004, 77.

62. See the quotation from King 2004 on p. 182 n. 49 above. An exception might be thought to be provided by the relationship between the genus 'bodily substance' and its *differentiae*. But it is more plausible to think that Abelard distinguished between his historical account of how things are made, from body to which forms are added, at some point in time after the body has started to exist, and his metaphysical, as the adding of successive *differentiae* to substance—in an order of natural but not chronological priority—to reach a particular substance of a fully determinate kind.

63. *LNPS*, ed. Geyer, p. 564, lines 14–29: 'Proprie materia est quae materiatum tempore praecedit, sicut aes statuam aeream et in materiato ideo in sua natura remanet. Proprie forma est, quae ex aliqua dispositione partium innascitur, sicuti forma, quae in statua consideratur, ex pravis scilicet oculis, ex curvo naso et ex aliis quae pertinent ad compositionem. Corpus autem proprie est materia hominis, quia tempore praecedit hominem et subiectum formas hominis praecedit, quod habet proprie materia. Sed animal quasi materia hominis est, non proprie materia, quia animal tempore non praecedit hominem. . . . Unde homo proprie ex materia et forma constare non dicitur ex animale [so correctly MS; Geyer: animalitate] et rationalitate, sicut ex corpore et compositione, vel sicut statua ex aere, sed similitudinem tenet homo cum statua, quae constat ex proprie materia et forma.'

64. Cf. *LI(isa)*, ed. Geyer, p. 42, lines 6–9: 'Compositionem autem possumus accipere sive ex conventu partium in quantitate, sicut ex membris coniungentibus Priamum, sive ex informatione apparentium accidentium'.

65. King 2004, 118–19 n. 79. King translates just the last sentence of the passage, as transcribed by Cousin.

66. MS Avranches, Bibliothèque municipale 232, fols. 68v–71v. *Tr. de int.* and these passages (named by Iwakuma *Quaestiones Abrincenses*) form a separate book from the rest of the MS. I am very grateful to Yukio Iwakuma for letting me have his transcription of this whole set of logical notes. For my own transcription of the text of the passage concerning Abelard and his followers (fol. 69r), see Marenbon 1997a, 159 n. 45; I use this as the basis for my translation here.

67. The writer then recapitulates: 'For they say that no form is an essence about which any of the following are the case: (i) it is sufficient for the subject to be present; (ii) or the arrangement of the parts in relation to each other or to something else [is sufficient]; (iii) or it is in [the subject] thanks to something extrinsic, without which it could not exist; (iv) or a substance needs to be added when it leaves.' Although in the main statement he had talked about 'qualities' which are not of types (i) to (iv) whilst here it is 'forms' not of these types, he may be using 'qualities' to mean forms in general (a usage Abelard recognizes as current—see *LI(cat)*, ed. Geyer, p. 223, line 37, to p. 224, line 2).

68. King takes (iv) to mean that the accidents must be positive. As given, the criterion is much narrower.

69. *Dial.*, ed. De Rijk, p. 105, line 9, to p. 106, line 12; *LI(cat)*, ed. Geyer, p. 249, lines 1–36; cf. Marenbon 1997a, 146.

70. See Marenbon 1997a, 155–60.

71. See *LNPS,* ed. Geyer, p. 535, lines 8–10: 'haec sessio et haec sessio, de quibus praedicatur sessio, non sunt vocabula rerum numero differentium, cum haec sessio et haec sessio non sint res'; and *Comm. Hex.*, ed. Romig, p. 73, lines 1937–39: 'Non enim cum aliquem sedere accidit, quandam rem tunc dicimus esse que prius non fuerit, uel quandam rem perisse que prius in stante fuisset.'

72. *TChr* 4.46: 'Nemo quippe recte intelligens unitatem aut plerasque alias formas ita a subiectis substantiis diuidit, ut eas ab eis numero uel essentialiter diuersas existimet.' Abelard's previous view (see above, note 15) was that substances each have an accident of unity but that the accidents of unity do not each have their own accident of unity, or else there would be an infinite regress. The danger of this regress shows that Abelard must have regarded the form of unity as numerically distinct from its subject.

73. *TChr* 3.170. Martin Tweedale (1976, 188–204) discusses this comment and the passages which are examined here below. My understanding of this very difficult material is different from his, partly because he considers it to be an elaboration of the theories put forward in *Dial.* and *LI*, whereas I believe that it shows Abelard has changed his views.

74. In his extended, so far unpublished discussion of Abelard's meta-physics, this is the view taken by Chris Martin. He says that Abelard leaves it unclear which sorts of relations are things and which not.

75. *TChr* 4.155 (ed. Buytaert, p. 343, lines 2465–70).

76. *TChr* 4.157 (ed. Buytaert, p. 343, lines 2481–83).

77. *TChr* 4.157 (ed. Buytaert, p. 343, line 2483–p. 344, line 2504).

78. *TChr* 4.158 (ed. Buytaert, p. 344, lines 2505–12).

79. *TChr* 4.158 (ed. Buytaert, p. 344, lines 2528–31).

80. *TChr* 4.158 (ed. Buytaert, p. 344, lines 2512–28).

81. Abelard puts having the same or different meaning in logical terms of mutual entailment. 'It is a sword' entails and is entailed by 'It is a blade', whereas 'It is hard' neither entails nor is entailed by 'It is white', or 'It is animal' entails but is not entailed by 'It is a man'. (In contemporary classical logic, the equivalence or failure of equivalence between such propositions would only establish the identity or non-identity of the extensions of the terms concerned. But Abelard regarded entailment intentionally, so that the antecedent has to require the consequent, which is to say that it contains the meaning of the consequent.) See *TSB* 2.84, 96–97.

82. *TSB* 2.83: 'et omnia eadem essentialiter dicuntur quecumque predicatione essentie inuicem coniungi possunt, quod tale est ac si diceremus idem predicatione'—a comment that is simply omitted when Abelard re-uses this passage in *TChr* 3.139. Identifying sameness by predication with sameness by essence, as the last phrase does, would mean that only thing-aspects which can be predicated of each other are aspects of the same thing, a position which the example of the material and the thing made of the material shows to be wrong.

83. See Marenbon 2007a, 246–47.

84. See *TChr* 4.86–90. Wilks (1998) provides an acute discussion of Abelard's use of these sorts of propositions (he calls them 'essential predication locutions'), though cf. Marenbon 2007a, 240 n. 25.

85. In the examples given by Abelard, the cases of difference by definition, where the thing-aspects are predicable of each other, are ones where, it seems, a really existing form acts as their ground; whereas the cases where there is no really existing form are those of difference by definition, where the thing-aspects are not predicable of each other. The view sketched here as possibly what Abelard would have thought allows thing-aspects not grounded on real forms but predicable of each other ('The father is the sitting man'). This extension is not implausible, since Abelard does not maintain the distinction between difference by definition and by property which he establishes in book 3 of *TChr*, preferring to talk more generally of difference by definition or property (cf. above, note 83).

CONCLUSION

1. My general book (Marenbon 2007b) could be seen, indeed, as an attempt to make this plea more generally for medieval philosophy: witness the title *Medieval Philosophy: An Historical and Philosophical Introduction.* For some further thoughts on methodology, see Marenbon 2011c and 2011d.

2. One of the anonymous readers of my completed MS posed exactly this question: 'If we can understand Abelard's philosophy on its own, why consider contemporary discussions at all?' It is at this reader's suggestion that I have extended my methodological discussion here.

3. I develop these ideas in Marenbon 2011c, 2011d.

BIBLIOGRAPHY

Editions of Works by Abelard

The following list of Abelard's works is arranged alphabetically by title. It includes reports of Abelard's teaching and aims to be complete, including even texts not discussed in this book. Only the best edition and, where it exists, English translation are usually cited. Below, *"Opera theologica"* refers to *Petri Abaelardi opera theologica,* CCCM 11–14 (Turnhout: Brepols) (vols. 1 and 2, 1969; vol. 3, 1987; vol. 4, 2001; vol. 5, 2004; vol. 6, 2006–). *"Philosophische Schriften"* refers to *Peter Abaelards philosophische Schriften,* ed. B. Geyer, BGPTMA 21 (Münster: Aschendorff, 1919–31).

Abbreviatio commentariorum Petri Abaelardi in Epistolam ad Romanos (1130s or later). Edited by A. M. Landgraf, 'Petri Abaelardi Expositionis in Epistolam S. Pauli ad Romanos Abbreviatio', *Bohoslavia* 31 (1936): 7–45.

Abbreviatio Petri Abaelardi expositionis in Hexaemeron (1130s?). Edited by C. S. F. Burnett in *Opera theologica,* 5:135–50.

Apologia contra Bernardum (1140–41). Edited by E. M. Buytaert, in *Opera theologica,* 1:357–68. English translation by J. M. Ziolkowski in *The Letters of Peter Abelard: Beyond the Personal* (Washington, DC: Catholic University of America Press, 2008), 116–29.

Carmen ad Astralabium (probably c. 1141). Edited by J. M. A. Rubingh-Bosscher, *Peter Abelard: Carmen ad Astralabium. A Critical Edition* (Groningen: [J. M. A. Rubingh-Bosscher], 1987).

Collationes (also called *Dialogus inter Philosophum, Iudaeum et Christianum;* most probably c. 1130). Edited by J. Marenbon and G. Orlandi, *Peter Abelard: Collationes* (Oxford: Oxford University Press, 2001), with English translation.

Commentarius Cantabrigiensis in Epistolas Pauli (mid-twelfth century). Edited by A. M. Landgraf, *Commentarius Cantabrigiensis in epistolas Pauli e schola Petri Abaelardi* (Notre Dame: University of Notre Dame Press, 1937–45).

Commentary on the Hexaemeron (probably 1130s). Edited by J. Romig, in *Opera theologica*, vol. 5.

Commentary on Paul's Letter to the Romans (probably mid-1130s). Edited by E. M. Buytaert, *Opera theologica*, vol. 1. English translation of prologue and extract in *Medieval Literary Theory and Criticism, c. 1100 – c. 1375: The Commentary Tradition*, rev. ed., ed. A. Minnis, A. B. Scott and D. Wallace (Oxford: Oxford University Press, 1991), 100–105.

Confessio fidei ad Heloisam (1140–41). Edited by C. S. F. Burnett, '"Confessio fidei ad Heloisam": Abelard's Last Letter to Heloise? A Discussion and Critical Edition of the Latin and Medieval French Versions', *Mittellateinisches Jahrbuch* 21 (1986): 147–55.

Confessio fidei 'Universis' (1140–41). Edited by C. S. F. Burnett, 'Peter Abelard, *Confessio fidei "Universis"*: A Critical Edition of Abelard's Reply to Accusations of Heresy', *Mediaeval Studies* 48 (1986): 111–38.

De intellectibus (probably c. 1122–25). Edited by P. Morin, *Abélard: Des Intellections* (Paris: Vrin, 1994) (with French translation).

Dialectica (probably begun by 1110 or earlier and finished before 1117). Edited by L. M. De Rijk, *Petrus Abaelardus: Dialectica*, rev. ed., Wijsgerige Teksten en Studies 1 (Assen: Van Gorcum, 1970).

Epistolae 2–8 (c. 1132–35). Edited by (2–5) J. T. Muckle, 'The Letter of Héloïse on the Religious Life and Abelard's First Reply', *Mediaeval Studies* 15 (1953): 47–94; (6–7) J. T. Muckle, 'The Personal Letters between Abelard and Héloïse', *Mediaeval Studies* 17 (1955): 240–81; (8) T. McLaughlin, 'Abelard's Rule for Religious Women', *Mediaeval Studies* 18 (1956): 241–92. Slightly improved Latin texts, with extensive commentary and Italian translation, of the *Historia calamitatum* and *Epistolae* 2–8 are given in I. Pagani, *Epistolario di Abelardo e Eloisa* (Turin: Unione tipografico-editrice Torinese, 2004). English translation (of the *Historia calamitatum* and *Epistolae* 2–8) by B. Radice, revised by M. T. Clanchy, in *The Letters of Abelard and Heloise* (London: Penguin, 2003).

Epistolae 9–14 (various dates). Edited by E. R. Smits, *Peter Abelard: Letters IX–XIV. An Edition with an Introduction* (Groningen: privately printed, 1983). English translation by J. M. Ziolkowski in *The Letters of Peter Abelard: Beyond the Personal* (Washington, DC: Catholic University of America Press, 2008).

Epistola 15 (*'Letter to His Socii'*) (1140–41). Edited in R. Klibansky, 'Peter Abailard and Bernard of Clairvaux', *Mediaeval and Renaissance Studies*

5 (1961): 1–27 at 6–7. English translation by J. M. Ziolkowski in *The Letters of Peter Abelard: Beyond the Personal* (Washington, DC: Catholic University of America Press, 2008), 108–10.

Exposition of the Lord's Prayer (probably 1130s). Edited by C. S. F. Burnett, 'The Expositio Orationis Dominicae "Multorum legimus orationes": Abelard's Exposition of the Lord's Prayer', *Revue bénédictine* 95 (1985): 60–72.

Glossae secundum vocales. Based in part on the *Logica ingredientibus* and in part on other reports of Abelard's teaching, close to those used in the *Logica nostrorum petitioni sociorum*. Edited by C. Ottaviano, *Testi medieval inediti* (Florence: L. S. Olschki, 1933), 105–207 (an edition full of errors); extracts in *Philosophische Schriften*, 583–88.

Historia calamitatum (Epistola 1) (c. 1132). Edited by J. Monfrin, *Abélard: Historia Calamitatum. Texte critique avec une introduction* (Paris: Vrin, 1959). For translation, see *Epistolae 2–8*.

Liber sententiarum Magistri Petri (late 1130s). A *reportatio* of Abelard's theological teaching, quoted by his critics but repudiated by him. Reconstructed from works attacking Abelard. Edited by C. J. Mews in *Opera theologica*, 6:162–71.

Logica ingredientibus (c. 1119, though some scholars believe that the sections on *On Interpretation* and *De topicis differentiis* might be later). Edited by B. Geyer in *Philosophische Schriften*, fasc. 1–3 (*Isagoge, Categories, On Interpretation* from *M* only); the authentic ending of *On Interpretation* was first edited in L. Minio-Paluello, *Twelfth-Century Logic*, vol. 2, *Abaelardiana inedita* (Rome: Edizioni di storia e letteratura, 1958), 3–108, but now there is an edition of the whole commentary on *On Interpretation* from both manuscripts by K. Jacobi and C. Strub: *Petri Abaelardi Glossae super peri hermeneias*, CCCM 206 (Turnhout: Brepols, 2010). The commentary on *De topicis differentiis* is edited by M. Dal Pra in *Pietro Abelardo: Scritti di logica*, 2nd ed. (Florence: Nuova Italia, 1969), 205–330. The discussion of universals from the commentary on the *Isagoge* is translated by P. V. Spade in *Five Texts on the Mediaeval Problem of Universals* (Indianapolis: Hackett, 1994), 26–56. There is an abbreviated translation of part of the *De interpretatione* commentary in H. Arens, *Aristotle's Theory of Language and Its Tradition: Texts from 500 to 1750* (Amsterdam: John Benjamins, 1984), 231–302.

Logica nostrorum petitioni sociorum (probably not entirely authentic, but uses authentic material from later than *LI* [c. 1125?]). Edited by B. Geyer in *Philosophische Schriften*, fasc. 4; a new edition is being prepared by P. King and C. J. Martin.

Problemata Heloissae (probably later 1130s). *PL* 178:677–730. English translation by E. M. McNamer, *The Education of Heloise: Methods, Content and*

Purpose of Education in the Twelfth Century, Mediaeval Studies 8 (Lewiston, NY: Mellen, 1991), 111–83.

Reportatio of ethical and thelogical lectures, closely related to *Scito teipsum* (late 1130s). Marginalia. Edited by C. S. F. Burnett and D. E. Luscombe, 'A New Student for Peter Abelard: The Marginalia in British Library MS Cotton Faustina A. X', in *Itinéraires de la raison: Études de philosophie médiévale offertes à Maria Candida Pacheco,* edited by J. F. Meirinhos (Turnhout: Brepols, 2005), 169–92.

Scito teipsum (also called *Ethica,* probably late 1130s). Edited by D. E. Luscombe, *Peter Abelard's Ethics* (Oxford: Oxford University Press, 1971), with English translation. There is a more recent edition by R. M. Ilgner (*Opera theologica,* vol. 4), but Luscombe's text remains preferable.

Secundum Magistrum Petrum sententie (probably mid-1120s). Edited in L. Minio-Paluello, *Twelfth-Century Logic,* vol. 2, *Abaelardiana inedita* (Rome: Edizioni di storia e letteratura, 1958), 111–21.

Sententiae Florianenses (mid-1130s). Critical edition, edited by H. Ostlender, Florilegium patristicum 19 (Bonn, 1929).

Sententiae Magistri Petri Abaelardi (mid-1130s). Edited by D. E. Luscombe, in *Opera theologica,* 6:5–152.

Sententiae Parisienses (mid-1130s). Edited by A. Landgraf, *Écrits théologiques de l'école d'Abélard* (Louvain: Spicilegium sacrum lovaniense, 1934), 1–60.

Sermones (various dates). A set of sermons (nos. 2, 4, 14, 25, 32), definitely intended for the Paraclete, is edited in P. De Santis, *I sermoni di Abelard per le monache del Paracleto,* Medievalia Lovaniensia, ser. 1.31 (Louvain: Louvain University Press, 2002), 173–246. *PL* 178:379–610 reprints a much larger collection, including twenty-eight further sermons, some of which may not be authentic, from the *editio princeps* (and an extra sermon, no. 34). Sermon 30 is edited in A. Granata, 'La dottrina dell'elemosina nel sermone "Pro sanctimonialibus de Paraclito"', *Aevum* 47 (1973): 32–59 at 54–59. Another sermon (35) is edited by L. J. Engel, '*Adtendite a falsis prophetis* (MS Colmar, H. 152v–153v): Un texte de Pierre Abélard contre les Cisterciens retrouvé', in *Corona gratiarum: Miscellanea patristica, historica et liturgica, Eligio Dekkers O. S. B. II lustra complenti oblata,* Instrumenta Patristica 9 (Bruges: S. Pietersabdij, 1975), 2:195–228. This sermon is translated in C. Waddell, '*Adtendite a falsis prophetis:* Abaelard's Earliest Known Anti-Cistercian Diatribe', *Cistercian Studies Quarterly* 39 (2004): 371–98.

Sic et non (probably first made c. 1121 and then revised and extended up to early 1130s). Edited by B. B. Boyer and R. McKeon, *Peter Abailard: Sic et Non. A Critical Edition* (Chicago: University of Chicago Press, 1976–77). English translation of prologue in *Medieval Literary Theory and Criticism, c. 1100 – c. 1375: The Commentary Tradition,* rev. ed., ed. A. Minnis, A. B. Scott and D. Wallace (Oxford: Oxford University Press, 1991), 87–100.

Soliloquium (probably written shortly before *TChr*). Edited in C. S. F. Burnett, 'Peter Abelard, "Soliloquium": A Critical Edition', *Studi medievali,* 3rd ser., 25 (1984): 857–94 (with English translation).

Theologia Christiana (c. 1122–26). Edited E. M. Buytaert in *Opera theologica,* 2:71–372. There is an abbreviated English translation by J. R. McCallum, *Abelard's Christian Theology* (1948; repr., Merrick, NY: Richwood, 1976). Book 3, lines 138–64 (on sameness and difference) have been translated by P. King and are available at http://individual.utoronto.ca /pking/translations/ABELARD.TC.3.138-164.pdf.

Theologia scholarium (later 1130s). Edited by E. M. Buytaert and C. Mews, in *Opera theologica,* 3:309–549. (There is also a short version of the work, not cited here, edited by Buytaert, in *Opera theologica,* 2:399–451.)

Theologia Summi Boni (c. 1120). Edited by E. M. Buytaert and C. J. Mews, in *Opera theologica,* 3:83–201.

Other Works

Adams, R. M. 1994. *Leibniz: Determinist, Theist, Idealist.* New York: Oxford University Press.

Albert the Great. 1893. *Opera omnia.* Vol. 26. Edited by A. Borgnet. Paris: Vivès.

Alexander of Hales. 1924. *Summa theologica I.* Edited by B. Klumper and Patres Collegii S. Bonaventurae. Quaracchi: Collegium S. Bonaventurae.

Allen, J. A. 1998. 'On the Dating of Abailard's *Dialogus:* A Reply to Mews'. *Vivarium* 36:135–51.

Anselm of Canterbury. 1946a. *Opera omnia.* Vol. 1. Edited by F. S. Schmitt. Edinburgh: Nelson.

———. 1946b. *Opera omnia.* Vol. 2. Edited by F. S. Schmitt. Edinburgh: Nelson.

Aristotle. 1961. *Categoriae vel praedicamenta.* Edited by L. Minio-Paluello. AL 1.1–5. Bruges: Desclée de Brouwer.

Augustine. 1975. *De diversis quaestionibus octoginta tribus liber I.* Edited by A. Mutzenbecher. CCSL 44A. Turnhout: Brepols.

Barnes, J. 1995. Introduction to *The Cambridge Companion to Aristotle,* edited by J. Barnes. Cambridge: Cambridge University Press.

Bautier, R. H. 1981. 'Paris au temps d'Abélard'. In *Abélard en son temps: Actes du 9ᵉ centenaire de la naissance de Pierre Abélard (14–19 mai 1979),* edited by J. Jolivet, 1–77. Paris: Les Belles Lettres.

Bayle, P. 1982. *Oeuvres diverses: Volumes supplémentaires*. Vol. 1. *Choix d'articles tirés du Dictionnaire historique etcritique*. Edited by E. Labrousse. Hildesheim: Olms.

Bellarmine, Robert. 1862. *De controversiis*. Vol. 4. Opera omnia Roberti Bellarmini 4. Milan: Battezzati.

Bernard of Clairvaux. 1977. *Sancti Bernardi opera*. Vol. 8. Edited by J. Leclercq and H. Rochais. Rome: Editiones cistercienses.

Biard, J. ed. 1999. *Langage, sciences, philosophie au XIIe siècle*. Paris: Vrin.

Bischoff, B. 1935. 'Aus der Schule Hugos von St Viktor'. In *Aus der Geisteswelt des Mittelalters*, 246–50. BGPTMA Supplement vol. 3. Münster: Aschendorff. Reprinted in B. Bischoff, *Mittelalterliche Studien*, 2:182–87 (Stuttgart: Hiersemann, 1967).

Blomme, R. 1958. *La doctrine du péché dans les écoles théologiques de la première moitié du XII siècle*. Universitas Catholica Lovaniensis. Dissertationes ad gradum magistri in Facultate Theologica vel in Facultate Iuris Canonici consequendum conscriptae, series 3, 6. Louvain: Publications universitaires de Louvain.

Boethius. 1847. 'Commentary on Aristotle's *Categories*'. In *PL* 64:159–294.

Boh, I. 1985. 'Divine Omnipotence in the Early *Sentences*'. In *Divine Omniscience and Omnipotence in Medieval Philosophy: Islamic, Jewish and Christian Perspectives*, edited by T. Rudavsky, 185–211. Synthese Historical Library 25. Dordrecht: Reidel.

Bonaventure. 1882. *Opera omnia*. Vol. 1. Quaracchi: Collegium S. Bonaventurae.

Brady, I. 1966. 'Peter Manducator and the Oral Teachings of Peter Lombard'. *Antonianum* 41:461–65.

Braun, D. 2006. 'Names and Natural Kind Terms'. In *The Oxford Handbook of Philosophy of Language*, edited by E. Lepore and B. C. Smith, 490–515. New York: Oxford University Press.

Brower, J. 2006. 'Anselm on Ethics'. In *The Cambridge Companion to Anselm*, edited by B. Davies and B. Leftow, 222–56. Cambridge: Cambridge University Press.

Brower, J., and K. Guilfoy, eds. 2004. *The Cambridge Companion to Abelard*. Cambridge: Cambridge University Press.

Cameron, M. 2011a. 'Abelard's Early Glosses: Some Questions'. In Rosier-Catach 2011, 647–62.

———. 2011b. 'The Development of Early Twelfth-Century Logic: A Reconsideration'. In Rosier-Catach 2011, 677–94.

Capitula haeresum. 1969. *Anonymi capitula haeresum Petri Abaelardi*. In *Petri Abaelardi opera theologica*, vol. 2, edited by E. M. Buytaert, 473–80. CCCM 12. Turnhout: Brepols.

Clanchy, M. T. 1990. 'Abelard's Mockery of St Anselm'. *Journal of Ecclesiastical History* 41:1–23.

———. 1997. *Abelard: A Medieval Life*. Oxford: Blackwell.

Colish, M. L. 1994. *Peter Lombard*. 2 vols. Leiden: Brill.

Courtenay, W. M. 1990. *Capacity and Volition: A History of the Distinction of Absolute and Ordained Power*. Quodlibet: Ricerche e strumenti di filosofia medievale 8. Bergamo: Lubrina.

De Rijk, L. M. 1962. *Logica modernorum: A Contribution to the History of Early Terminist Logic*. Vol. 1. Assen: Van Gorcum.

———. 1966. 'Some New Evidence on Twelfth Century Logic: Alberic and the School of Mont Ste Geneviève (Montani)'. *Vivarium* 4:1–57.

———. 1967. *Logica modernorum: A Contribution to the History of Early Terminist Logic*. Vol. 2, pt. 2. Assen: Van Gorcum.

———. 1986. 'Peter Abelard's Semantics and His Doctrine of Being'. *Vivarium* 24:85–128.

De Santis, P. 2002. *I sermoni di Abelard per le monache del Paracleto*. Medievalia Lovaniensia, ser. 1, 31. Louvain: Leuven University Press.

Dijs, J. 1990. 'Two Anonymous 12th-Century Tracts on Universals'. *Vivarium* 28:85–117.

Enders, M. 1999. 'Abälards "intentionalistische" Ethik'. *Philosophisches Jahrbuch* 106:135–58.

Ernst, S. 2006. 'Grundlegung der Ethik bei Anselm von Canterbury und Peter Abaelard'. In Gasper and Kohlenberger 2006, 155–71.

Evans, M. 1991. 'The *Ysagoge in Theologiam* and the Commentaries Attributed to Bernard Silvestris'. *Journal of the Warburg and Courtauld Institutes* 54:1–42.

Faust, A. 1932. *Der möglichkeitsgedanke: Systemgeschichtliche Untersuchungen*. Vol. 2. Heidelberg: Winter.

Gasper, G. E. M., and H. Kohlenberger, eds. 2006. *Anselm and Abelard: Investigations and Juxtapositions*. Toronto: Pontifical Institute of Mediaeval Studies.

Gelber, H. G. 2004. *It Could Have Been Otherwise: Contingency and Necessity in Dominican Theology at Oxford, 1300–1350*. Studien und Texte zur Geistesgeschichte des Mittelalters 81. Leiden: Brill.

Geyer, B. 1933. 'Untersuchungen'. In *Peter Abaelards philosophische Schriften*, ed. B. Geyer, 589–633. BGPTMA 21. Münster: Aschendorff.

Goebel, B. 2001. *Rectitudo: Wahrheit und Freiheit bei Anselm von Canterbury. Eine philosophische Untersuchung seines Denkansatzes*. BGPTMA n.f. 56. Münster: Aschendorff.

Grabmann, Martin. 1911. 'Mitteilungen über scholastischen Funden in der Bibliotheca Ambrosiana zu Mailand'. *Tübinger theologische Quartalschrift* 93:538–44.

Gracia, J. J. E. 1984. *Introduction to the Problem of Individuation in the Early Middle Ages.* Washington, DC: Catholic University of America Press.

Green-Pedersen, N. J. 1984. *The Tradition of the Topics in the Middle Ages.* Munich: Philosophia Verlag.

Grondeux, A. 2011. 'Guillaume de Champeaux, Joscelin de Soissons, Abélard et Gosvin d'Anchin: Étude d'un milieu intellectuel'. In Rosier-Catach 2011, 3–43.

Grondeux, A., and I. Rosier-Catach. 2011. 'Les Glosulae super Priscianum et leur tradition'. In Rosier-Catach 2011, 107–79.

Guilfoy, K. 2004. 'Mind and Cognition'. In Brower and Guilfoy 2004, 200–222.

Häring, N. 1978. 'Die Sententie Magistri Gisleberti Pictavensis Episcopi'. *Archives d'histoire doctrinale et littéraire du Moyen Âge* 45:83–180.

Hugh of St Victor. 1854. *De sacramentis.* In PL 176:173–618.

Iwakuma, Y. 1993. 'The Introductiones dialecticae secundum Wilgelmum and secundum G. Paganellum'. *Cahiers de l'Institut du Moyen-Âge grec et latin* 63:45–114.

———. 2013. 'Alberic of Paris on Mont Ste Geneviève against Peter Abelard'. In *Logic and Language in the Middle Ages: A Volume in Honour of Sten Ebbesen,* edited by J. L. Fink, H. Hansen and A. M. Mora-Márquez, 27–47. Investigating Medieval Philosophy 4. Leiden: Brill.

Jacobi, K. 1981. 'Die Semantik sprachlicher Ausdrücke, Ausdrucksfolgen und Aussagen in Abailards Kommentar zu Peri hermeneias'. *Medioevo* 7:41–89.

———. 1985. 'Diskussionen über unpersönliche Aussagen in Peter Abaelards Kommentar zu Peri Hermeneias'. In *Mediaeval Semantics and Metaphysics,* edited by E. P. Bos, 1–63. Artistarium, supplementa 2. Nijmegen: Ingenium.

———. 2004. 'Philosophy of Language'. In Brower and Guilfoy 2004, 126–57.

Jacobi, K., and C. Strub 1995. 'Peter Abaelard als Kommentator'. In *Aristotelica et Lulliana magistro doctissimo Charles H. Lohr septuagesimum annum feliciter agenti dedicata,* edited by F. Dominguez Reboiras, R. Imbach, T. Pindl and P. Walter, 11–34. Instrumenta Patristica 26. The Hague: Nijhoff.

Jacobi, K., C. Strub and P. King. 1996. 'From *intellectus verus/falsus* to the *dictum propositionis:* The Semantics of Peter Abelard and His Circle'. *Vivarium* 34:15–40.

John of Salisbury. 1991. *Metalogicon.* Edited by J. B. Hall. CCCM 98. Turnhout: Brepols.

John of St Thomas. 1643. *Cursus theologici in primam partem Divi Thomi. II.* Lyons: Prost.

Jolivet, J. 1969. *Arts du langage et théologie chez Abélard*. Études de philosophie médiévale 57. Paris: Vrin.

———. 1981. *Abélard en son temps: Actes du 9ᵉ centenaire de la naissance de Pierre Abélard (14–19 mai 1979)*. Paris: Les Belles Lettres.

King, P. 1982. *Peter Abailard and the Problem of Universals*. No. 8220415. Ann Arbor, Mich.: University Microfilms International.

———. 1995. 'Abelard's Intentionalist Ethics'. *Modern Schoolman* 72:213–31.

———. 2004. 'Metaphysics'. In Brower and Guilfoy 2004, 65–125.

———. 2007. 'Abelard on Mental Language'. *American Catholic Philosophical Quarterly* 81:169–88.

———. 2010. 'Peter Abelard'. In *The Stanford Encyclopedia of Philosophy (Winter 2010 Edition)*, edited by E. N. Zalta, http://plato.stanford.edu/archives/win2010/entries/abelard/.

Knuuttila, S. 1981. 'Time and Modality in Scholasticism'. In *Reforging the Great Chain of Being*, edited by S. Knuuttila, 163–257. Dordrecht: Reidel.

———. 1993. *Modalities in Medieval Philosophy*. London: Routledge.

———. 2004. *Emotions in Ancient and Medieval Philosophy*. Oxford: Oxford University Press.

Kripke, S. A. 1980. *Naming and Necessity*. Cambridge, Mass.: Harvard University Press.

Lalore, C. 1878. *Collection des principaux cartulaires du diocèse de Troyes*. Vol. 2. Paris: Thorin and Lacroix.

Landgraf, A. 1934. *Écrits théologiques de l'école d'Abélard: Textes inédits*. Spicilegium Sacrum Lovaniense. Études et documents 14. Louvain: Spicilegium Sacrum Lovaniense.

Leftow, B. 1995. 'Anselm on the Necessity of the Incarnation'. *Religious Studies* 31:167–85.

Leibniz, G. W. F. 1885. *Die philosophischen Schriften von Gottfried Wilhelm Leibniz*. Vol. 6. Edited by C. I. Gerhardt. Berlin: Weidmann. Reprint, Hildesheim: Olms, 1961.

———. 1999. *Philosophische Schriften*. Ser. 6, vol. 4, pt. C. Berlin: Akademie Verlag.

Libera, A. de. 1981. 'Abélard et le dictisme'. In *Abélard: Le 'Dialogus', la philosophie de la logique*. Geneva: Cahiers de la revue de théologie et de philosophie = *Cahiers de la revue de théologie et de philosophie* 8:59–92.

———. 1999. *L'art des généralités: Théories de l'abstraction*. Paris: Aubier.

———. 2002a. 'Des accidents aux tropes: Pierre Abélard'. *Revue de métaphysique et de morale* 4:509–30.

———. 2002b. *La référence vide: Théories de la proposition*. Paris: PUF.

Lovejoy, A. O. 1970. *The Great Chain of Being: A Study of the History of an Idea*. Cambridge, Mass.: Harvard University Press.

Luscombe, D. E. 1968. 'The Authorship of the *Ysagoge in Theologiam*'. *Archives d'histoire doctrinale et littéraire du Moyen Âge* 35:7–16.

———. 1970. *The School of Peter Abelard: The Influence of Abelard's Thought in the Early Scholastic Period*. Cambridge Studies in Medieval Life and Thought, n.s. 14. Cambridge: Cambridge University Press.

———. 1983. 'Saint Anselm and Abelard'. *Anselm Studies* 1:207–29.

———. 2002. 'St Anselm and Abelard: A Restatement'. In *Saint Anselm: A Thinker for Yesterday and Today*, edited by C. Viola and F. Van Fleteren, 445–60. Lewiston, N.Y.: Edwin Mellen.

Maierù, A., and L. Valente, eds. 2004. *Medieval Theories on Assertive and Non-assertive Language*. Florence: Olschki.

Marenbon, J. 1991. 'Abelard's Concept of Possibility'. In *Historia Philosophiae Medii Aevi: Studien zur Geschichte der Philosophie des Mittelalters*, edited by B. Mojsisch and O. Puta, 595–609. Amsterdam: Grüner. Reprinted in Marenbon 2000a.

———. 1997a. *The Philosophy of Peter Abelard*. Cambridge: Cambridge University Press.

———. 1997b. 'The Platonisms of Peter Abelard'. In *Néoplatonisme et philosophie médiévale*, edited by L. Benakis, 109–29. Rencontres de philosophie médiévale 6. Turnhout: Brepols. Reprinted in Marenbon 2000a.

———. 1999. 'Abélard, le verbe 'être' et la prédication'. In Biard 1999, 199–215.

———. 2000a. *Aristotelian Logic, Platonism and the Context of Early Medieval Philosophy in the West*. Variorum Collected Studies Series 696. Aldershot: Ashgate.

———. 2000b. 'Medieval Latin Commentaries and Glosses on Aristotelian Logical Texts, before c. 1150 AD'. In Marenbon 2000a. (Revision of a work originally published in 1992.)

———. 2004. '*Dicta*, Assertion and Speech Acts: Abelard and Some Modern Interpreters'. In Maierù and Valente 2004, 59–80.

———. 2005. *Le temps, l'éternité et la prescience de Boèce à Thomas d'Aquin*. Paris: Vrin.

———. 2006. 'The Rediscovery of Peter Abelard's Philosophy'. *Journal of the History of Philosophy* 44:331–51.

———. 2007a. 'Abelard's Changing Thoughts on Sameness and Difference in Logic and Theology'. *American Catholic Philosophical Quarterly* 81:229–50.

———. 2007b. *Medieval Philosophy: An Historical and Philosophical Introduction*. London: Routledge.

———. 2007c. 'Peter Abelard and Peter the Lombard'. In *Pietro Lombardo*, 225–39. Spoleto: Centro italiano di studi sull'alto medioevo.

————. 2008a. 'Logic at the Turn of the Twelfth Century'. In *Medieval and Renaissance Logic,* vol. 2 of *Handbook of the History of Logic,* edited by D. M. Gabbay and J. Woods, 65–81. Mediaeval and Renaissance Logic. Amsterdam: North Holland.

————. 2008b. 'Lost Love Letters? A Controversy in Retrospect'. *International Journal of the Classical Tradition* 15:267–80.

————. 2008c. 'Was Abelard a Trope Theorist?' In *Compléments de substance: Études sur les propriétés accidentelles offertes à Alain de Libera,* edited by C. Erismann and A. Schneewind, 85–101. Paris: Vrin.

————. 2011a. 'Logic at the Turn of the Twelfth Century: A Synthesis'. In Rosier-Catach 2011, 181–217.

————. 2011b. 'Peter Abelard's Theory of Virtues and Its Context'. In *Knowledge, Discipline and Power in the Middle Ages: Essays in Honour of David Luscombe,* edited by J. Canning, E. King and M. Staub, 231–42. Studien und Texte zur Geistesgeschichte des Mittelalters 106. Leiden: Brill.

————. 2011c. 'When Was Medieval Philosophy?' Inaugural lecture, University of Cambridge, November 2011, www.dspace.cam.ac.uk/handle /1810/240658; podcast, www.sms.cam.ac.uk/media/1191806.

————. 2011d. 'Why Study Medieval Philosophy'. In *Warum noch Philosophie: Historische, systematische und gesellschaftliche Positionen,* edited by M. van Ackeren, T. Kobusch and J. Müller. Berlin: De Gruyter, 2011.

————. 2012. 'Theology and Philosophy'. In *European Transformations: The Long Twelfth Century,* edited by T. F. X. Noble and J. Van Engen, 403–25. Notre Dame: Notre Dame University Press, 2012.

————. 2013. 'Divine Prescience and Contingency in Boethius's *Consolation of Philosophy*'. *Rivista di storia della filosofia* 68:9–21.

————. Forthcoming-a. 'Glosses and Commentaries on the *Categories* before 1200: A Revised Working Catalogue'. In *Aristotle's Categories in the Byzantine, Arabic and Latin Traditions,* edited by S. Ebbesen, J. Marenbon and P. Thom. Copenhagen: Royal Danish Academy.

————. Forthcoming-b. 'Les *sophismata* à l'époque de la *logica vetus*'.

Martin, C. J. 1992. 'The Logic of the Nominales, or, The Rise and Fall of Impossible *Positio*'. *Vivarium* 30: 110–26.

————. 2001. 'Abaelard on Modality: Some Possibilities and Some Puzzles'. In *Potentialität und Possibilität: Modalaussagen in der Geschichte der Metaphysik,* 97–125. Stuttgart: Fromman-Holzboog.

————. 2009. 'Imposition and Essence: What's New in Abaelard's Theory of Meaning?' In *The Word in Medieval Logic, Theology and Psychology,* edited by T. Shimizu and C. S. F. Burnett, 173–214. Turnhout: Brepols.

————. 2010. 'The Development of Abaelard's Theory of Topical Inference'. In *Les lieux de l'argumentation: Histoire du syllogisme topique d'Aristote à Leibniz,* edited by J. Biard and F. Mariani Zini, 249–70. Studia Artistarum 22. Turnhout: Brepols.

———. 2011. 'A Note on the Attribution of the *Literal Glosses* in Paris, BNF, lat. 13368 to Peter Abelard'. In Rosier-Catach 2011, 605–46.

Maurer, A. 1976. 'Ockham on the Possibility of a Better World'. *Mediaeval Studies* 38:291–312.

Mews, C. J. 1984. 'A Neglected Gloss on the 'Isagoge' by Peter Abelard'. *Freiburger Zeitschrift für Philosophie und Theologie* 31:35–55.

———. 1985a. 'The Lists of Heresies Attributed to Peter Abelard'. *Révue bénédictine* 95:73–110.

———. 1985b. 'On Dating the Works of Peter Abelard'. *Archives d'histoire doctrinale et littéraire du Moyen Âge* 52:73–134. Reprinted in Mews 2001.

———. 1985c. 'Peter Abelard's Theologia Christiana and Theologia "Scholarium" Re-examined'. *Recherches de théologie ancienne et médiévale* 52:109–58. Reprinted in Mews 2001.

———. 1986. 'The Sententie of Peter Abelard'. *Recherches de théologie ancienne et médiévale* 53:130–84. Reprinted in Mews 2001.

———. 1988. 'Un lecteur de Jérome au XIIe siècle: Pierre Abélard'. In *Jérôme entre l'Occident et l'Orient: XVIe centenaire du départ de saint Jérôme de Rome et de son installation à Bethléem,* edited by Y.-M. Duval. Paris: Études augustiniennes. Reprinted in Mews 2001.

———. 1995. *Peter Abelard.* Authors of the Middle Ages 2.5. London: Variorum.

———. 2001. *Abelard and His Legacy.* Aldershot: Variorum.

———. 2002. 'The Council of Sens (1141): Abelard, Bernard, and the Fear of Social Upheaval'. *Speculum* 77:342–82.

———. 2005a. *Abelard and Heloise.* New York: Oxford University Press.

———. 2005b. 'Postface: Les *Epistolae duorum amantium* et les débats sur l'amour au XIIe s. sur quelques aperçus récents'. In *La voix d'Héloise: Un dialogue des deux amants,* trans. E. Champs with F. X. Putallaz and S. Piron. Vestigia 31. Fribourg: Academic Press; Paris: Éditions du Cerf.

———. 2006. 'Saint Anselm and the Development of Philosophical Theology in Twelfth-Century Paris'. In Gasper and Kohlenberger 2006, 196–222.

———. 2008. *The Lost Love Letters of Heloise and Abelard: Perceptions of Dialogue in Twelfth-Century France.* 2nd ed. Trans. N. Chiavaroli. New York: Palgrave Macmillan.

———. 2011. 'William of Champeaux, the Foundation of Saint-Victor (Easter, 1111), and the Evolution of Abelard's Early Career'. In Rosier-Catach 2011, 83–104.

Miethke, J. 1973. 'Abaelards Stellung zur Kirchenreform: Eine biographische Studie'. *Francia* 1:158–92.

Miramon, C. de. 2011. 'Quatre notes biographiques sur Guillaume de Champeaux'. In Rosier-Catach 2011, 45–82.

Moonan, L. 1989. 'Abelard's Use of the Timaeus'. *Archives d'histoire doctrinale et littéraire du Moyen Âge* 56:7–90.

Nicolau d'Olwer, L. 1945. 'Sur la date de la *Dialectica* d'Abélard'. *Revue du Moyen Âge latin* 1:375–90.

Noonan, J. T. 1977. 'Who Was Rolandus?' In *Law, Church, and Society: Essays in Honor of Stephan Kuttner*, edited by K. Pennington and R. Somerville, 21–48. Philadelphia: University of Pennsylvania Press.

Normore, C. G. 2004. 'Abelard's Stoicism and Its Consequences'. In *Stoicism: Traditions and Transformations*, edited by S. K. Strange and J. Zupko, 132–47. Cambridge: Cambridge University Press.

———. 2006. 'Who Is Peter Abelard?' In *Autobiography as Philosophy: The Philosophical Uses of Self-Presentation*, edited by T. Mathien and G. D. Wright, 64–75. Abingdon: Routledge.

Nuchelmans, G. 1973. *Theories of the Proposition: Ancient and Medieval Conceptions of the Bearers of Truth and Falsity*. North-Holland Linguistic Series 8. Amsterdam: North Holland.

Oakley, F. 1984. *Omnipotence, Covenant, and Order: An Excursion in the History of Ideas from Abelard to Leibniz*. Ithaca: Cornell University Press.

Ormsby, E. L. 1984. *Theodicy in Islamic Thought: The Dispute over al-Ghazālī's 'Best of All Possible Worlds'*. Princeton: Princeton University Press.

Ott, L. 1937. *Untersuchungen zur theologischer Briefliteratur der Frühscholastik*. BGPMTA 34. Münster: Aschendorff.

Pagani, I. 2004. *Epistolario di Abelardo e Eloisa*. Turin: Unione tipografico-editrice Torinese.

Peppermüller, R. 1972. *Abaelards Auslegung des Römerbriefes*. BGPTMA n. f. 10. Münster: Aschendorf.

Perkams, M. 2001. *Liebe als Zentralbegriff der Ethik nach Peter Abaelard*. BGPTMA 58. Münster: Aschendorff.

———. 2003. 'Divine Omnipotence and Moral Theory in Abelard's Theology'. *Mediaeval Studies* 65:99–116.

———. 2006. '*Rationes necessariae—rationes verisimiles et honestissimae*: Methoden philosophischer Theologie bei Anselm und Abaleard'. In Gasper and Kohlenberger 2006, 133–42.

Peter Abelard. 1836. *Ouvrages inédits d'Abélard pour servir à l'histoire de la philosophie en France*. Edited by V. Cousin. Paris: Imprimerie royale.

———. 1969. *Pietro Abelardo: Scritti di logica*. 2nd ed. Edited by M. Dal Pra. Florence: La Nuouva Italia. www.letterefilosofia.unimi.it/files/_ITA _/Filarete/034.pdf.

Peter of Poitiers. 1943. *Sententiae*. Vol. 1. Edited by P. S. Moore and M. Dulong. Publications in Mediaeval Studies 7. Notre Dame: University of Notre Dame.

Peter the Lombard. 1971. *Sententiarum libri IV*. 3rd ed. Vol. 1. Spicilegium Bonaventurianum 4. Grottaferrata: Editiones Collegii S. Bonaventurae ad Claras Aquas.

Piazzoni, A. M. 1982. 'Ugo di San Vittore "auctor" delle "Sententiae de divinitate". *Studi Medievali* 23:861–955.

Piron, S., ed. and trans. 2005. *Lettres des deux amants attribuées à Héloïse et Abélard*, Paris: Gallimard.

————. 2009. 'Heloise's Literary Self-Fashioning and the *Epistolae duorum amantium*'. In *Strategies of Remembrance: From Pindar to Hölderlin*, edited by L. Doležalová, 103–62. Newcastle-upon-Tyne: Cambridge Scholars Publishing.

————. 2011. 'Héloïse et Abélard: L'éthique amoureuse des *Epistolae duorum amantium*'. In *Histoires de l'amour, fragilités et interdits, du Kâmasûtra à nos jours*, edited by J. Dakhlia, A. Farge, C. Klapisch-Zuber, and A. Stella, 71–94. Paris: Bayard.

Pitra, Joanes Baptista. 1888. *Analecta novissima: Spicilegii solesmensis*. Vol. 2. *Tusculana*. Paris: Typis Tusculanis. Reprint, Farnborough: Gregg, 1967.

Plato. 1975. *Timaeus a Calcidio translatus commentarioque instructus*. Ed. J. H. Waszink. 2nd ed. Plato Latinus 4. London: Warburg Institute; Leiden: Brill.

Poirel, D. 2002. *Livre de la nature et débat trinitaire au XIIè siècle: Le 'De tribus diebus' de Hugues de Saint-Victor*. Bibliotheca Victorina 14. Turnhout: Brepols.

Porphyry. 1966. *Isagoge (translatio Boethii) et anonymi fragmentum vulgo vocatum 'Liber sex principiorum'*. Edited by L. Minio-Paluello. AL 1.6–7. Bruges: Desclée de Brouwer.

Putnam, H. 1975. 'The Meaning of "Meaning"'. In *Mind, Language and Reality: Philosophical Papers I*, vol. 2, 215–71. Cambridge: Cambridge University Press.

————. 1988. *Representation and Reality*. Cambridge, Mass.: MIT Press.

Rateau, P. 2008. *La question du mal chez Leibniz: Fondements et élaboration de la théodicée*. Travaux de philosophie 15. Paris: Champion.

Recktenwald, E. 1998. *Die Ethische Struktur des Denkens von Anselm von Canterbury*. Heidelberg: Winter.

Reiners, J. P. 1910. *Der Nominalismus in der Frühscholastik: Ein Beitrag zur Geschichte der Universalienfrag im Mittelalter*. BGPTMA 8.5. Münster: Aschendorff.

Rivière, J. 1936. 'D'un singulier emprunt à saint Anselme chez Raoul de Laon'. *Revue des sciences religieuses* 16:344–46.

Robson, M. 1996. 'The Impact of *Cur Deus Homo* on the Early Franciscan School'. In *Anselm, Aosta, Bec and Canterbury*, edited by D. E. Luscombe and G. R. Evans, 334–47. Sheffield: Sheffield Academic Press.

Rogers, K. 2008. *Anselm on Freedom*. Oxford: Oxford University Press.

Roland. 1891. *Die Sentenzen Rolands nachmals Papstes Alexander III*. Edited by A. M. Gietl. Freiburg: Herder. Photographic reprint, Amsterdam: Rodopi, 1969.

Rosier-Catach, I. 1999. 'La notion de translatio, le principe de compositionalité, et l'analyse de la prédication accidentelle chez Abélard'. In Biard 1999, 125–64.

————. 2003a. 'Abélard et les grammairiens: Sur la définition du verbe et la notion d'inhérence'. In *La tradition vive: Mélanges d'histoire des textes en l'honneur de Louis Holtz*, ed. P. Lardet, 143-59. Turnhout: Brepols.

————. 2003b. 'Abélard et les grammairiens: Sur le verbe substantif et la prédication'. *Vivarium* 41:175–248.

————. 2004. 'Les discussions sur le signifié des propositions chez Abélard et ses contemporains'. In Maierù and Valente 2004, 1–34.

————. 2007. 'Priscian on Divine Ideas and Mental Conceptions: The Discussions in the *Glosulae in Priscianum*, the *Notae Dunelmenses*, William of Champeaux and Abelard'. *Vivarium* 45:219–37.

————, ed. 2011. *Arts du langage et théologie aux confins des XIe-XIIe siècles: Textes, maîtres, débats*. Studia artistarum 26. Turnhout: Brepols.

————. 2012. '"Vox" and "Oratio" in Early Twelfth Century Grammar and Dialectic'. *Archives d'histoire doctrinale et littéraire du Moyen Âge* 78:47–129.

Searle, J. R. 1983. *Intentionality: An Essay in the Philosophy of Mind*. Cambridge: Cambridge University Press.

Sharpe, R. 2009. 'Anselm as Author: Publishing in the Late Eleventh Century'. *Journal of Medieval Latin* 19:1–87.

Spade, P. V. 1980. Review of *Abailard on Universals*, by M. M. Tweedale. *Nous* 14:479–83.

Stalnaker, R. 1997. 'Reference and Necessity'. In *A Companion to the Philosophy of Language*, edited by B. Hale and C. Wright, 534–54. Oxford: Blackwell.

Thomas Aquinas. 1929. *Scriptum super libros Sententiarum magistri Petri Lombardi episcopi Parisiensis*. Vol. 1. Edited by P. Mandonnet. Paris: Lethielleux.

————. 1965. *Quaestiones disputatae de potentia*. Edited by P. M. Pession. Turin: Marietti.

Thomas Netter. 1532. *Doctrinale fidei antiquae Liber primus*. [Paris]: Badius Ascensius.

————. 1557. *Doctrinale fidei antiquae Liber secundus—De sacramentis*. Salamanca: Iohannes Maria da Terra noua and Iacobus Archarius.

Trego, K. 2010. *L'essence de la liberté: la refondation de l'éthique dans l'œuvre de saint Anselme de Cantorbéry*. Études de philosophie médiévale 95. Paris: Vrin.

Tweedale, M. M. 1976. *Abailard on Universals*. Amsterdam: North Holland.

Van den Eynde, D. 1960. *Essai sur la succession et la date des écrits de Hugues de Saint-Victor*. Spicilegium Pontificii Athenaei Antoniani 13. Rome: Pontificum Athenaeum Antonianum.

Vanni Rovighi, S. 1965. 'Notes sur l'influence de saint Anselme au XIIe siècle: Suite et fin'. *Cahiers de civilisation médiévale* 8:43–58.

Von Moos, P. 2003. 'Die *Epistolae duorum amantium* und die säkulare Religion der Liebe. Methodenkritische Vorüberlegungen zu einem einmaligen Werk mittellateinischer Briefliteratur'. *Studi medievali* 44:1–116.

————. 2005. *Abaelard und Heloise*. Vol. 1 of *Gesammelte Studien zum Mittelalter*. Edited by G. Melville. Geschichte: Forschung und Wissenschaft 14. Münster: Lit Verlag.

Weingart, R. E. 1970. *The Logic of Divine Love: A Critical Analysis of the Soteriology of Peter Abailard*. Oxford: Oxford University Press.

Wiggins, D. 1994. 'Putnam's Doctrine of Natural Kind Words and Frege's Doctrines of Sense, Reference, and Extension: Can They Cohere?' In *Reading Putnam*, edited by P. Clark and B. Hale, 201–15. Oxford: Blackwell, 1994.

Wilks, I. 1998. 'Peter Abelard and the Metaphysics of Essential Predication'. *Journal of the History of Philosophy* 36:365–85.

————. 2012. 'Moral Intention'. In *The Oxford Handbook of Medieval Philosophy*, edited by J. Marenbon, 588–604. New York: Oxford University Press.

William of Auxerre. 1980. *Summa aurea*. Vol. 1. Edited by J. Ribaillier. Spicilegium Bonaventurianum 16. Paris: CNRS and Collegium S. Bonaventurae.

William of Lucca. 1975. *Summa dialetice artis, dal Codice 614, sec. 12, della Biblioteca Feliniana di Lucca*. Ed. L. Pozzi. Università di Parma, Istituto di Filosofia, Collana di testi e saggi 7. Padua: Liviana.

William of Ockham. 1974. *Summa logicae*. Edited by P. Boehner, G. Gál, and S. Brown. Guillelmi de Ockham opera philosophica 1. St. Bonaventure, N.Y.: Franciscan Institute.

————. 1979. *Scriptum in librum primum Sententiarum, Ordinatio, d. XIX–XLVIII*. Edited by G. I. Etzkorn and F. E. Kelley. Guillelmi de Ockham opera theologica 4. St. Bonaventure, N.Y.: Franciscan Institute.

Williams, D. C. 1953. 'On the Elements of Being'. *Review of Metaphysics* 7:3–18.

The Index of Passages in Abelard gives the pages on which each passage of texts by Abelard (including those reporting on his work, or of doubtful authenticity) is cited.

GENERAL INDEX

All authors who died before 1500 are indexed under their Christian names (e.g., Aquinas is indexed under Thomas Aquinas).

possibility and necessity (*cont.*)
36, 217; what makes modal
sentences modal?, 67. *See also*
alternative choices; life stories,
alternative possible
power, 111; contrasted with lack of
power (*impotentia*), 98; potency
understood relative to the sort of
thing concerned, 99. *See also*
God, power of; possibility and
necessity, possibility as potentiality; possibility and necessity,
possibility as potentiality for a
species
presentism, 171
principle of sufficient reason, 47, 58,
63–65, 85, 104, 120, 125, 127,
135–37
Priscian, *Institutiones grammaticae,*
Glossulae on, 213
properties, 153, 159, 162–64, 174, 181,
195, 198; essential, 160, 164–65,
170; of persons of the Trinity, 193
proprium, 34, 159–60
providence, 158. *See also* God, providence of
Putnam, Hilary, 2, 149, 154, 164–66,
241

quaestio form, 119
quantity, 190; composite, 171
Quincey, 19
Quoniam de generali, 214. *See also*
Walter of Mortagne

Ralph of Laon, 94
rationality, Rationality Passage,
179–81, 185; used to mean human
soul?, 186–87
Ravaisson, Félix, 33
realism, material essence theory,
217

reason, 48, 153; compelling and
permissive reasons, 58, 62, 64,
75–76; God as highest, 224;
necessary reasons, 100–102, 107;
worthy reasons, 102, 107. *See also*
cause, reasonable; principle of
sufficient reason
redemption (of humankind), 101–8;
devils' rights theory of, 100;
explanation of, 22; satisfaction
theory of, 101
reductionism, 167, 197
reference, 149–50, 153–54; causal
theory of, 150–52, 156, 158, 162,
164; description theory of, 150–51,
157; direct reference, 149–50, 155,
201; rigidity in, 165. *See also*
sense, sense-reference distinction
relations, 174, 181, 190, 192–98
relatives, and quasi-relatives, 216
representations, mental, 165–66
rightness, universal criteria for, 94
Robert of Melun, *Sententiae,* 234
Robert Pullen, *Sententiae,* 234
Robson, M., 229
Rogers, Katherin, 103
Rolandus, *Sententiae,* 119–23, 125, 127,
235
Rolandus Bandinelli (Pope Alexander
III), 234
Roscelin of Compiègne, 16, 21, 35–36,
95, 210, 217; letter to Abelard, 95,
101, 105, 107, 210, 229
Rosier-Catach, Irène, 146, 153, 213,
240–41

Saint Denis, monastery of, 18, 47;
library of, 42
salvation. *See* NAG argument, the
damnandus objection to
sameness. *See* difference and sameness

Schmitt, F. S., 94–95
scope distinctions, 67
semantics, 29, 149–66, 200–201, 203;
    Aristotelian-Boethian tradition
    of, 152–55; emphasized in ana-
    lytical philosophy, 147; of human
    language not explained by God's
    Ideas, 163; intensional rather
    than extensional approach to,
    201; of propositions, 43 (see also
    dictum)
Sens, Council of (1141), 19–20, 23, 75
sense, sense-reference distinction,
    154–55, 158
sententia, 158–64, 242
Sententie divine pagine, 94
shape, 182
Sharpe, Richard, 95
signification, 154, 156–57; usual
    understanding of in Middle
    Ages, 157
similarity, 190–92
sin, 86, 100, 112, 212; Original, 85
Soissons, Council of (1121), 18, 20–21
soul, 183–84; and body, 186, 190;
    creation of, 120, 122; is it a form?,
    186–87; passions of the, 153;
    Plato's world-soul, 42
species, is the phoenix a species?, 38.
    See also universals
speech, does not exist as a whole, 97
states of affairs. *See* possibility and
    necessity, synchronous possible
    states of affairs
status, 157–58
St Ayoul of Provins, 18
St Gildas de Rhuys, monastery of, 19,
    24
St Medard, monastery of, 18
stoicism, 87, 201, 229
Stout, Geoffrey, 174
Strub, Christian, 40–41, 219

subject, in a, 168–70, 174, 176–77, 179,
    190, 251; said of a, 168–70
substance, 169–77, 181–82, 184, 186,
    193, 195, 201, 246, 248; bare, 172;
    bodily, 250; substantial essence,
    175. *See also* form, substantial
substantive verb 'to be', 43
Suger, Abbot of St Denis, 19
Summa fratris Alexandri, 130–31
Summa sententiarum, 76, 227, 234
Summa sophisticorum elenchorum, 29
supervenience, 182–86, 191
syllogisms, modal, 132

Tarlazzi, Caterina, 217, 248
teaching, in relation to written
    records, 27
textual connections, with past phi-
    losophers studied by historians
    of philosophy, 91
theology, and philosophy, 2–3;
    negative theology, 137; the word
    '*theologia*', 2
things, bare, 197–98; thing-aspects,
    196–98, 252; things said with
    and without combination, 168
Thomas Aquinas, 202; commentary
    on *Sentences*, 134–35; *Questions on
    Power*, 135–37, 239; *Summa theolo-
    giae*, 136–37
Thomas Netter, *Doctrinale antiquae
    fidei*, 138–41
Thomas of Morigny, 118
time, everything has its own temporal
    accidents, 43. *See also* God, and
    time
topical reasoning, 43
Tours, 16
*Tractatus de dissimilitudine argumen-
    torum*, 30
Trinity, 37, 96, 193; generation of the
    Son, 122, 138; the persons of the

JOHN MARENBON

is senior research fellow at Trinity College, Cambridge, and honorary
professor of medieval philosophy in the University of Cambridge.
He is the author of *The Philosophy of Peter Abelard*.